Paris, 1200

Paris, 1200

John W. Baldwin

STANFORD UNIVERSITY PRESS
STANFORD, CALIFORNIA

Stanford University Press
Stanford, California

Paris, 1200 was originally published in French ©2006 Éditions Flammarion, department Aubier.

Library of Congress Cataloging-in-Publication Data

Baldwin, John W.
  Paris, 1200 / John W. Baldwin. -- American ed.
     p. cm.
  Includes bibliographical references and index.
  ISBN 978-0-8047-6271-7 (cloth : alk. paper) -- ISBN 978-0-8047-7207-5 (pbk. : alk. paper)
  1. Paris (France)--History--To 1515. 2. France--History--Philip II Augustus, 1180-1223.
I. Title.
  DC725.B35 2010
  944'.361023--dc22

                        2009048525

Typeset by Bruce Lundquist in 10.5/14 Adobe Garamond

For Ian

Contents

Preface to the American Edition

Paris, 1200 was originally written and published for a French audience. Its immediate reception by the media and eventual sales suggest that it had hit its intended mark. Its success was certainly facilitated by the skill of Béatrice Bonne, who has become my faithful translator and friend. I am now grateful to the Stanford University Press for making it available to an Anglophone audience.

The book was obviously inspired by the millennial celebrations surrounding the year 2000. Amidst a world awash in historical memories, I realized that the Paris I knew best was celebrating an anniversary that would be the closest one to a millennium I would ever experience. For a half-century I had lived in Paris off and on and had immersed myself in the period of French history revolving around the year 1200.

The history of medieval Paris, however, has been written many times and by each generation. The prime obstacle to the enterprise has been the lack of sources for the period preceding 1250. The favored solution to this dilemma has been to select two to three centuries and to fill in the gaps in the early stage from the abundance of sources from the later years. The history of medieval Paris, therefore, has become, invariably, that of the late Middle Ages generally overshadowed by the gloom and miseries in which the medieval period ended, thus confirming the stereotypic conception of a dark Middle Ages. My innovation in this volume is to pick the year 1200 and try not to stray more than ten years before and after the date. This austere optic has the advantages of precision, immediacy and authenticity in exchange for comprehensive and voluminous coverage. Judging by its reception, this strategy has apparently worked for a French audience.

The history of Paris during the reign of King Philip Augustus (1179–1223) retains acknowledged significance to the French today. The year 1200 witnessed the great interdict on Paris (playing out a clash between an assertive monarchy and an encroaching papacy), an important peace treaty between Philip Augustus and King John of England (which positioned the French monarchy to break out of encircling English domination) and the threat of a master-student strike (that signaled the emergence of the celebrated University of Paris). Although these three events are of interest in themselves and important for French history, they involve broader concerns for an Anglophone audience as well. Here we can also detect the intersection of religious and secular values in medieval culture, the emergence of the centralized, bureaucratic administration that became the modern French state, and the appearance of the University of Paris, which, along with its sister at Bologna in Italy, became the mother of the modern university system as well as the creator of the scholastic method that dominated medieval thinking. Additionally, Paris saw the virtual birth of polyphonic music at Notre-Dame, one of the turning points of musical history, and the creation of the great cathedral itself, which is preeminent among the monuments of Gothic architecture and remains the number one attraction for tourists today. The year 1200 is therefore an occasion to view an important moment in medieval society in which multiple aspects of society come together in concrete, vivid and fascinating detail. Writing *Paris, 1200* for my French friends gave me great pleasure. It is my hope that my native audience will experience some of that pleasure for themselves.

Paris, 15 November 2008

Paris, 1200

Paris in the Year 1200

For the inhabitants of Paris, the calendar year 1200 began on Easter, 9 April, and ended on Holy Saturday, 24 March 1201, following the custom of the king's chancery. (To avoid confusion, however, I shall remain with the system of dating employed today.) The reigning monarch was Philip, the second of his name in the Capetian dynasty. The royal historiographer Rigord bestowed the sobriquet "Augustus" on him because the king had *aug*mented the royal domain with the addition of Vermandois and because he was born in the month of August.

Born in Paris on 12 August 1165, Philip Augustus was thirty-five in 1200, and he had already benefited from two decades of political experience, having been crowned on 1 November 1179 at the tender age of fourteen. The year 1200 was, however, a moment of political transition in Western Europe. At Rome the aged Pope Celestine III had expired two years earlier, and the cardinals replaced him with Innocent III, a youthful successor. The leadership of the Empire to the east was contested by two candidates, Otto of Brunswick and Philip of Swabia, each crowned king of the Romans in 1198. To the west, King John had just succeeded his brother Richard the Lionheart, who died unexpectedly in 1199. He was not only king of England now but also duke of Normandy, count of Anjou and duke of Aquitaine. Eudes de Sully, a first cousin of the king, had just replaced Maurice de Sully, whose long service as bishop of Paris ended in 1196. The royal administration of the city was confided to two prévôt-baillis (royal agents), Robert de Meulan and Pierre du Thillay, after the disgrace of a certain Thomas.

As with newspapers today, medieval chroniclers reported the memorable events of their day and arranged them in chronological order, year by year. Among the events that most affected the city of Paris in 1200, three were broadcast with banner headlines by both the French and English chroniclers. The first was a papal interdict on royal lands to discipline King Philip Augustus for his unlawful marriage; the second, a peace at Le Goulet negotiated between King Philip and the English King John over the latter's fiefs in France; and the third, a general strike by the students of Paris to protest infringements against their rights.

ALL THE LAND OF THE FRENCH KING
IS PLACED UNDER AN INTERDICT.
—Rigord de Saint-Denis.[1]

On 13 January, Pope Innocent III closed the churches in Philip Augustus's lands to force the king to dismiss his concubine, Agnès de Méran (Andechs-Meranien), and to restore Queen Ingeborg of Denmark as his legitimate wife. Philip's first wife, Isabelle de Hainaut, died in 1190 on the eve of the Third Crusade, leaving Prince Louis as his only son—and sickly at that. Thus, on his return from the crusade in 1191, the king's urgent business was to remarry and reinforce the royal lineage.

Philip's second marriage, to the Danish princess Ingeborg, lasted only the wedding night of 14–15 August 1193. What happened on that fateful night may remain forever an enigma, but what is known is that the next morning Philip announced his intention to separate from her and refused her admittance to his bed. After obtaining an annulment from a church council composed entirely of his familiars and headed by his uncle Guillaume, archbishop of Reims, he married Agnès de Méran to leave no doubt about his intentions to make the separation permanent. Agnès pleased the king well because she delivered him a daughter, Marie, in 1198 and a son, Philippe, in 1200.

Ingeborg, however, refused to return to Denmark, as she was bidden, and instead appealed her case to the papacy. Pope Celestine III was slow to respond, but the energetic Innocent III, who succeeded him in 1198, made the king's marital irregularity an urgent item of business. After encountering nothing but recalcitrance, Innocent finally levied the interdict that closed the churches to the faithful on the king's lands.

The French chroniclers detailed the people's sufferings when they were refused the sacraments, and churchmen endured the king's displeasure as well. Among the bishops of the kingdom under royal control, thirteen remained loyal to the king and refused to obey the papal command. These included the king's uncle, Guillaume, archbishop of Reims, as well as the abbots of Saint-Denis and Saint-Germain-des-Prés at Paris. At least six observed the interdict, though, most notably the bishops of Paris and nearby Senlis. Philip's agents ruthlessly despoiled the lands of these prelates, especially Eudes de Sully, bishop of Paris, who was punished more severely because he was a royal cousin.

The rigors of the interdict, however, did prompt the king to reopen negotiations. Philip argued that he had acted in good faith, believing that his marriage to Ingeborg had been annulled by the previous council. When the archbishop of Reims admitted that the oath declaring the annulment had been fraudulent, Philip made him the scapegoat for the aborted affair and upbraided him: "You were a fool for having pronounced such a judgment."

By September Philip agreed to a temporary reconciliation with Queen Ingeborg and to submit his plea for annulment to the judgment of the papal court. At these concessions, the pope lifted the interdict, but Philip swept Ingeborg off to his castle in Etampes to the south of Paris and sequestered her there. When Agnès died in 1201, thus removing the stigma of bigamy, the pope was further persuaded to legitimize the births of Marie and Philippe.

Despite the tribulations, Philip had finally attained his immediate goal, that of producing a second legitimate heir to the throne, but the scandal of his marriage had been broadcast by the interdict that closed down the churches in Paris, and it was publicized by the chroniclers. His erratic behavior jeopardized royal authority at a crucial moment when it was contested by two parties, the kings of England under John and the students of Paris.

PEACE IS ESTABLISHED BETWEEN THE FRENCH KING PHILIP AND KING JOHN OF ENGLAND.
— Rigord de Saint-Denis.[2]

The greatest threat to the French king's authority arose from the dynastic inheritance of Henry II, the Angevin king of England. From his mother,

Henry had received Normandy, with overlordship over Brittany; from his father, Anjou, Maine and Touraine in the Loire valley; and from his wife, the vast duchy of Aquitaine to the southwest. Thus most of western France, encircling Paris and the royal domain on three sides, had passed intact to Henry's son, Richard the Lionheart.

Richard and Philip Augustus were persuaded to depart together on the Third Crusade in 1190, but their return the following year opened a decade of warfare during which Philip attacked and Richard defended his French lands. The more spectacular victories of the 1190s went to Richard. At Fréteval, for example, Philip lost his baggage train in an ambush, and at Courcelles-lès-Gisors a bridge collapsed under the weight of heavily armored troops. Twenty French knights were drowned, and Philip himself was fished out of the waters. Richard's determination to resist French aggression is made evident by the massive fortress he erected at Château-Gaillard on the Norman frontier between Rouen and Paris. Even the count of Flanders, the king's brother-in-law, allied himself with Richard. Intermittent truces and treaties had little effect in breaking the Angevin's stranglehold on Paris and the royal domain.

Then, on 6 April 1199, a totally unexpected event changed Philip's fortunes. Richard, the renowned warrior, was killed while besieging a castle in the southern province of the Limousin. At the age of forty-one and at the height of his powers, he had paid little attention to his own succession and thereby left the English-Angevin throne open to dispute. What followed was classic in such dynastic contests. There were two contenders. One was a younger brother, John, count of Mortain; the other was a nephew, Arthur, count of Brittany, the son of an older brother, Geoffrey. Who had precedence was not yet established in English law.

Philip's strategy was to support the claims of Arthur, the weaker of the two, just as he had previously supported John against Richard. A year after Richard's death, Philip found himself in position to strike a bargain with John. In return for recognizing John's disputed claim to the throne and for compelling Arthur to submit to his uncle as overlord, Philip was able to extract important concessions.

Already in January 1200, Philip had conceded lands to the count of Flanders in the treaty of Péronne, from which John benefited.[3] Now John granted Philip the Norman county of Evreux, the contested parts of the Vexin, the borderland between Normandy and the Île-de-France, the considerable sum of 20,000 marks of silver and, most important, formal recognition that John held all of his continental lands as vassal of the king of

France. These terms were recorded in a "peace" sealed at Le Goulet in the Vexin on 22 May 1200.[4]

As was customary, this important agreement was confirmed by a marriage between the two families. In this case, it was between Louis, age nearly thirteen, eldest son and heir of Philip; and Blanche, age twelve, daughter of Alphonese VIII, king of Castille, and niece of John through his sister, Eleanor. On 23 May 1200 the nuptials were concluded in the Norman part of the Vexin at the village of Port-Mort, not, as might be expected, in Paris, because the bishop had closed the churches of the diocese of Paris during the interdict. John was given an open invitation, nonetheless, to visit the royal capital after the ban was lifted, and he took advantage of it, arriving the following Spring in Paris, where Philip entertained him regally at his palace.

SERIOUS DISCORD BETWEEN THE SCHOLARS AND BOURGEOISIE AT PARIS.
—Roger de Hoveden.[5]

Whatever hindrance the papal interdict posed to Philip Augustus in his maneuvers with King John and the count of Flanders, it must have severely restricted him in a police action in 1200 that involved the students of Paris.

Throughout the twelfth century, masters and students had flocked to the schools of the royal city, swelling the population on the Île-de-la-Cité and the Left Bank. Whether mature masters or youthful students, these men were *clerici*, thereby claiming clerical status that placed them under the exclusive jurisdiction of the ecclesiastical authorities. Signified by the tonsure, the shaving of the crown of the head, this status endowed clerics with two important privileges. The first, the *privilegium canonis*, protected their persons as sacrosanct. Any physical violence against their bodies would result in automatic excommunication for the perpetrator, a consequence that could be relieved only by severe penance. One did not treat a cleric roughly without serious consequences. The second was the *privilegium fori,* which placed them solely under the jurisdiction of the ecclesiastical courts.

Guaranteeing immunity against the police and secular courts, these privileges were not clearly defined and did little to inhibit the unruly behavior of clerics. Philip Augustus was quoted as marveling at the bravery of clerics who entered mêlées brandishing swords but without armor or helmets. Little should he marvel, however, when the clean-shaved pate offered more protection than a helmet.

An incident occurred at Paris in February 1200 that was not unexpected in the pre-Lenten season and became a routine throughout the thirteenth century. Kindled by the abundance of wine, a riot broke out in a tavern. Fighting between a group of German students and the proprietors of the establishment left one of the latter close to death. The owners enlisted the royal prévôt, Thomas, and his agents to riposte against the students' hostel, provoking a mêlée in which five students were killed.

Outraged, the masters sought justice from the king, and he, fearing that the masters and students would depart from the city en masse, responded in July with a solemn charter that dealt with two major issues.[6] The immediate one was punishment of the prévôt and his accomplices. The masters requested that the royal officer be whipped like a school boy, but the king had more severe measures in mind. The prévôt was kept in jail until he agreed to submit to an ordeal. If he lost, he was to be executed; if he was cleared, he must abjure all royal functions and renounce Paris. An inquest was ordered to ferret out and punish his accomplices.

With justice to the malefactors satisfied, Philip turned to the larger issue of police jurisdiction over masters and students who enjoyed clerical status. In careful detail, the two basic privileges of personal immunity and exclusive jurisdiction of the church courts were defined, reinforced and implemented. In effect, Philip's charter granted to the Parisian scholars the clerical liberties for which the martyred Thomas Becket, the English archbishop of Canterbury, had given his life, and in turn it refused the compromise that King Henry II had proposed in the Constitutions of Clarendon of 1164. We shall return to these issues later but simply note here that Philip's charter of 1200 was a clear victory at Paris for Becket's principle. The document concluded that on the first or second Sunday after a new prévôt took office, he and the Parisian townsmen were to swear in a church in the scholars' presence to observe the charter.

Philip's quick capitulation to Thomas Becket's unusual interpretation of the issue of criminous clerics was doubtlessly induced by his vulnerability under the interdict, but it was also reinforced by the masters' and students' threat to leave town, as the chronicler Roger de Hoveden asserted. With clerical masters and students constituting a significant proportion of the Parisian population, however, it compromised maintenance of law and order in the royal city. We shall see that, in effect, every cleric was allowed one major crime, free from corporal punishment. Once the king was in a stronger position in 1205, however, he renegotiated the terms of the question and induced the clergy to accept the basic compromise of Henry II. By then Philip was no longer under threat of interdict, but the menace of a university strike and migration became a permanent condition in the royal capital of the thirteenth century.

. . .

On 3 September 1200 the Latin poet Gilles de Paris presented a book, titled the *Karolinus*, to Prince Louis just two days before his thirteenth birthday.[7] (Miniatures in the manuscripts illustrate the poet presenting the work to the seated prince.) A canon of the church Saint-Marcel to the south of Paris, Gilles belonged to a small circle of court poets that included Guillaume le Breton, the royal historiographer, all of whom were inspired by the Vergilian verse of Gautier de Châtillon.

Gilles had been working on his book for two years, one in writing and the other in correcting the work. Just as Vergil had created the hero Aeneas to instruct the emperor Augustus, so Gilles aspired to promote the emperor Charlemagne as an exemplar for the young prince. One book each was devoted to the Frankish emperor's cultivation of the four cardinal virtues, and a fifth applied these teachings for Louis's benefit (*utilitas*). In a lengthy work (2,232 verses by Gilles's count), the elaborated style of the *Karolinus* might have been hard going for the young man, but it incorporated an educational program that included a thorough training in the liberal arts, a program that Philip Augustus undoubtedly desired for his son.

Since the *Karolinus* was written for an occasion, it was revised up to the last minute; a concluding section (the *captatio benevolencie*) was added after it was presented. A work of circumstance, it also acknowledged the three major events of the year that had attracted the chroniclers' attention. In various separate passages, Gilles returned to the scandal of the king's marriage. Although the interdict had been lifted by the time the captatio was composed, Gilles could not refrain from recalling the clergy's and the people's sufferings; the chants of the office were suspended, the prelates and clergy were expelled, and the land groaned under exploitation and taxation. The king, Gilles wrote, should renounce his concubine and return to his legitimate marital bed. In September, the young prince Louis had been married for little more than three months, thus recalling the treaty of Le Goulet with King John. Despite the turbulent times and the king's failings, Gilles nonetheless reaffirmed that France fared better under Philip's yoke than other lands fared with their kings. The king had defended the realm and extended his power abroad, even to Acre in the Holy Land. Strong castles protected the borders against Normandy, where the church and people suffered under Richard the Lionheart, an impious king, rightfully slain. Now, the text concluded, the brother John seeks to make peace and to cede land, sealed by a marriage between his niece Blanche and the royal youth. (This portion of the text evidently had not yet been fully brought up to date.) Despite the father's marital scandals, Louis was nonetheless of pure royal blood, the heir of a chaste mother, Isabelle de Hainaut, and a good father—good fruit from a good tree. To illustrate the prince's dynastic heritage, Gilles appended to his poem a diagram of a genealogical tree in which Louis's major forebears were underscored in red.

No direct allusion was made to the great student strike of 1200, but the atmosphere of the Parisian schools thoroughly informed Gilles's captatio. Against the calumny of those who claimed that the city of Paris contained no learned men, he invoked the names of some sixteen celebrated scholars, including, of course, that of Guillaume le Breton, his former student and now a great teacher. "Let no one obscure the city's renown in so many teachers," he concluded. "Lutetia [that is, Paris] remains the fertile mother of so many poets." On completion of his verses for the young prince, however, Gilles announced his own intention to abandon the arts for the doctrines of faith and good works, the domain of theology, certainly the preeminent subject taught in the Parisian schools.

We shall return to these three events of 1200, but it is sufficient now to recognize that they signify important transitions. The events themselves were fortuitous: the consequences of a traumatic wedding night, an unforeseen death and a banal tavern brawl, all brilliantly illuminated by brief flashes of lightning. Nonetheless, they reveal that the royal power of the Capetians was expanding, that urbanization required better policing and that the schools were playing an increased role in the city's life. Equally important, Philip's matrimonial behavior suggests that, despite the inexorable momentum of institutions, there is always space for caprice, the unforeseeable and the inexplicable. The king's personal comportment defies any assessment of his character before and after the event. History that does not acknowledge the intervention of fortuity is not worthy of the name.

In the accounts of the contemporary French and English chroniclers, the decade preceding 1200 was a period of disappointment and setbacks for the ruler of Paris. It opened with an unglamorous crusade (in contrast to Richard's) and was punctuated by military reverses, Philip's messy marital life, bad weather, famine and destruction. These gloomy events have conspired to conceal fundamental transformations that were also taking place. The royal domain was expanding, royal administration was improving, vast construction projects were undertaken, urbanization was progressing and the schools were transformed into the university—changes that altered the face of the city. The year 1200 itself was a brief moment of peace, when the clouds of war rolled back before they gathered again for the invasion of the Norman-Angevin lands. It was a fortuitous moment of sunlight, and it gives us a better view of the Capetian capital.

An obstacle that plagues historians of medieval Paris is the penury of sources. Often, enough material survives to raise one's expectations, but rarely is it enough to give satisfaction. I shall simply offer what is available and attempt to resist (not always successfully) the litany of what is missing and what I cannot know. The scarcity of sources and my efforts to avoid anachronism also preclude the genre of history that is generally called "the history of everyday life"—that is, how ordinary people lived, ate, clothed and housed themselves. Unfortunately, information for this kind of inquiry is rare before the late thirteenth and fourteenth centuries.

The normal procedure for writing the history of Paris during the Middle Ages, therefore, is to select an extended period of two to three centuries, allowing one to benefit from the relative abundance of documentation that accumulates at the close of the period. This approach has been undertaken by Jacques Boussard (1976) and Raymond Cazelle (1994) in their authoritative volumes in the *Histoire générale de Paris* and recently and successfully by Simone Roux in her *Paris au moyen âge* (2003). Often, however, it succumbs to the temptation to read backwards from the late evidence to fill in the lacunae of the early period, thus committing the historical sin of anachronism. Historians of medieval Paris have long benefited from the riches found in the well-known *Livre des métiers* of Étienne Boileau (1268), the *Livre de taille* of 1297, the *Cris de Paris*, *Mesnagier de Paris* and the *Journal d'un bourgeois* (thirteenth to fifteenth centuries). Although continuity cannot be disregarded, these late texts have too often served to characterize the earlier period as well. Whenever we hear the phrase "In the Middle Ages one did such and such at Paris . . . ," we may suspect that the late medieval period is again being privileged.

Rather than proposing a history of Paris over several centuries, my approach is completely different. I shall concentrate as much as possible on the year 1200 to sharpen and capture the significance of the historical moment.

The meager sources encompassed in one year, of course, offer a minimum of data. The date 1200 is therefore emblematic—indeed a code word. I have allowed myself a decade in either direction, occasionally succumbing to the need to include a little more, but my constant effort has been to tighten my inquiry as much as possible around the single year.

My project has been made possible by the appearance of new collections of sources that originated around the year 1200 in Paris and were in fact generated by the institutions in which I am interested. The Capetian monarchy, for example, began to record its financial accounts in 1190 (first extant copy 1202–1203), to establish archives at the royal palace in 1194 and to compile chancery registers in 1204. At the same time, Bishop Eudes de Sully began collecting the synodical statutes (1208) and drawing up a list (*pouillé*) in 1204 of all the churches in his diocese. The masters of theology began enlisting their students as *reportatores* to write down the lectures and disputations of their classrooms to be circulated in multiple copies. Thanks to these new collections, we are offered a sustained look at Paris for the first time in the city's history. To be sure, I have also made use of those sources that have traditionally served the historians of Paris: the chronicles written for the king and the churches, the mass of charters preserved in ecclesiastical cartularies, the notices in the obituaries and the corpus of royal documentation that has constituted the common patrimony for historians.[8]

My particular contribution, however, is to add to this traditional heritage another company of witnesses who have not been exploited for their testimony on the city. Drawing on my study *Masters, Princes and Merchants: The Social Views of Peter the Chanter and his Circle* (1970), I offer the testimony of the theologians who formed a circle around the figure of Pierre, chanter of Notre-Dame (d. 1197) one of the celebrated scholars of his time. An extended portrait will be offered of the Chanter in Chapter Two, but since the others of his circle are not as well known in a Parisian context I shall offer brief introductions here. They were (1) Stephen Langton (d. 1228), an Englishman, who was perhaps the Chanter's student, but certainly his colleague since the 1180s. He was prolific in commenting on the scriptures, in arguing disputations and preaching. In 1207, Pope Innocent III elevated him to the rank of cardinal and appointed him archbishop of Canterbury, which drew him into English politics. (2) Robert of Courson (d. 1219) was likewise English and the Chanter's chief student before he became canon of Noyon and Paris. His writings include a collection (*Summa*) of *questiones* that reorganized and completed the Chanter's own collection. Pope Innocent made him a cardinal in 1212 and commissioned him as papal legate for France to prepare for the Lateran council of 1215. (3) Thomas of Chobham (d. 1233–1236) was a third Englishman who evidently studied with the Chanter at Paris before he returned to Salisbury as subdean. His *Summa confessorum*, a guide to confessors, adapted the discussions of the Chanter's school at Paris to be applied in England. (4) Pierre de Roissy (d. ca. 1213) first appears in 1198 in the company of the charismatic preacher and student of the Chanter, Foulques de Neuilly. Having spent years at Paris, he became chancellor of Chartres by 1208 and wrote a *Manuale de mysteriis ecclesie* that bears the imprint of the Chanter's and the Parisian influence.[9] These masters were keenly interested in the sacrament of penance as it was applied in the confessional. Absorbed with identifying and curing sin, they sharpened their sensitivities to their surroundings and recorded, without inhibition, what they saw. Their lectures on the Bible, their classroom disputations, their sermons and moral treatises cast a penetrating light on the Paris of 1200 that they inhabited.[10]

The members of the Chanter's circle of theologians were not only perceptive observers; they were also convinced reformers who were sharply critical of their society. Conditioned by Pierre's French temperament, they could not resist the temptation to *faire la leçon* to their contemporaries. Although the history of medieval Paris is often treated as triumphal progress, this vision can be corrected by the criticism and doubt their perspective provides. Benefiting from this perspective, I shall not treat Paris in the year 1200 as the poet Dante viewed paradise, that is, as a heavenly choir of angels all singing in harmony. Rather, I shall consider the contentious issues that were raised at the time. For example, should money be expended on sumptuous architecture, such as Notre-Dame, when the poor are still going hungry? Is it reasonable to enforce celibacy on the lower and younger clergy when it promotes fornication and pederasty? Are ordeals the best way to arrive at judicial verdicts when they often produce false judgments? Is the death penalty appropriate—even for convicted heretics—when innocent victims may suffer? Is hereditary succession the best way to select kings, when it often produces immature and unsuitable candidates and when election by the people offers a viable alternative? Thanks to the sensitive conscience of these theological masters, important issues such as these will be raised as we consider Paris around the year 1200.

To approach the world of the laity, who were illiterate in Latin and understood only the vernacular, I have also explored the literature that was composed in French for their enjoyment. I have chosen the contemporary romances of Jean Renart, who wrote between 1200 and 1209, but because his writings were devoted to the concerns of the aristocracy who lived outside of Paris I have enlisted them only occasionally.[11] For my purposes, therefore, the contemporary chroniclers, the ecclesiastical charters, the royal documentation and the treatises of the theologians serve as four powerful searchlights that sweep simultaneously across the terrain of the city and help illuminate its features during the night of history.

To capture Paris in the year 1200 aspires to the optimism of Jules Michelet, who fashioned history as "resurrection"—that is, to bring a historical moment back to life. Although all historical epochs are equal in the sight of God, as Leopold von Ranke famously maintained, some epochs have not commanded the same attention as others. In the twelfth century, for example, historians have been so seduced by the self-fashioning of an Abélard, a Suger, a Pierre the Venerable or a Bernard de Clairvaux that they close down the century by 1153 at Bernard's death; in the thirteenth, the remarkable piety of St. Louis, the monumental ratiocinations of Thomas Aquinas and the traumas of Philip the Fair have likewise monopolized historians' attention. Although Paris in 1200 has no stellar heroes to entrance the imagination, important forces were nonetheless at work. Like the half-completed construction of Notre-Dame or the walls surrounding the city, Paris was in transition. The full realization of its potential was yet to come, but enough can be perceived for us to anticipate the power of the future monarchy, the renown of the university and the influence of the church—including its architectural and musical triumphs—all to prepare for Paris's eventual domination not only of the kingdom of France but of Western Europe as well.

To attempt this resurrection I shall first introduce the city itself and the majority of its inhabitants, the bourgeoisie, before I uncover the faces of its two leading figures in their respective spheres, Pierre the Chanter and Philip Augustus. Since they are both male, I shall also seek to discern the visages of women that remain stubbornly hidden behind the sources. I shall then turn to the major concerns of the city—the royal government, the church and the schools—and shall conclude with its contemporary delights and pleasures, balanced by its approaching fears and sorrows, before assessing its final achievements.

The recent millennial celebrations naturally prompted me to write *Paris, 1200*, but I have mentally inhabited the city of Pierre the Chanter and Philip Augustus for a half-century; it is from this familiarity that the idea grew. When I first arrived as a student in 1953, I encountered the formidable figure of the Chanter in the manuscript folios of his *questiones* at the Bibliothèque Nationale Richelieu. When my wife and I returned to take up residence in the city in 1997, we found ourselves drawn to an apartment on rue Charlemagne, which is protected by the largest surviving segment of Philip's wall. Between these two dates I have been happily occupied with numerous projects, all centered on the year 1200 and all focused in one way or another on the city of Paris. It would not be too much to say that the temptation to write *Paris, 1200* has been irresistible, arising, indeed, from the core of my being.

During the four years of writing this book, Caroline Bourlet has graciously included me in her Groupe de travail sur Paris au Moyen Âge at the Institut de Recherche et d'Histoire des Textes, where I have profited from the experience of colleagues in the later Middle Ages. Boris Bove, in particular, shared with me his research on the bourgeoisie before he published his important thesis. Good friends and colleagues have always responded to my questions, however importunate. Among those helpful on this project were Nicole Bériou, Françoise Bercé, Dany Sandron, Patricia Stirnemann and Michel Zink. Craig Wright lent me his indispensable book on Notre-Dame when the Johns Hopkins Library was so inconsiderate as to have lost its copy. And, as during the past half century, Jenny Jochens has been my first and last reader and my most dependable critic. To all I wish to record my gratitude.

On 13 November 2000 the Department of History at Johns Hopkins University, as is its custom, invited me to deliver a valedictory lecture on the occasion of my retirement from teaching—after forty years. In the spirit of the moment, I chose for my talk the title that has become the subject of this book, and I was overwhelmed by the number who attended. If I needed it, this response was final confirmation of how much I owe to my friends, colleagues and the great university that have encouraged and supported me over the past four decades. I trust that this book testifies to my heartfelt thanks.

Map. 1. Paris in 1200.

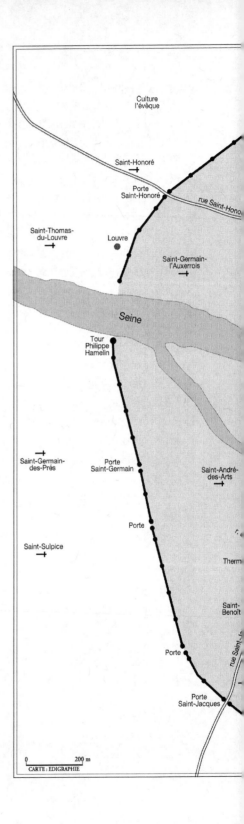

Hôpital de la Trinité =
    Hospital of the Trinity
Nord = North
Palais royale = Royal Palace
Palais Episcopal = Bishop's Palace
Tour Philippe Hamelin =
    Tower of Philippe Hamelin
Vielle enceinte = Old Wall
Cloître = Cloister
Thermes = Baths
Porte = Gate

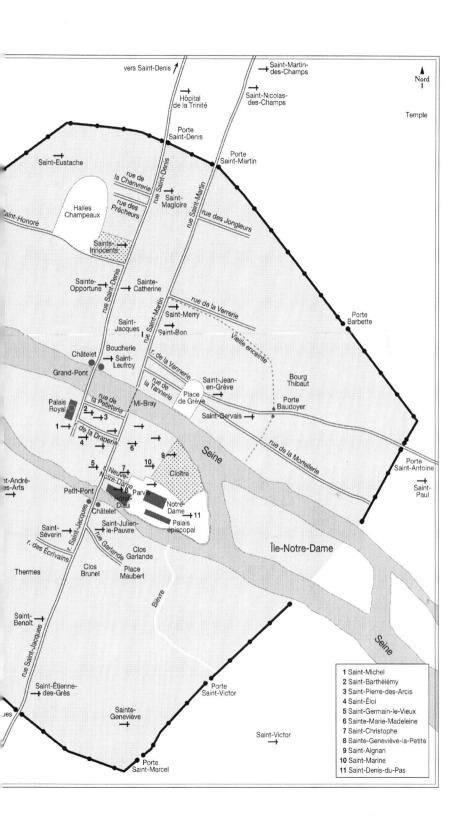

CHAPTER ONE

The City and Its Bourgeoisie

Paris, a Construction Site

In the year 1200 Paris was a vast construction site encompassing two major projects, the new gothic cathedral of Notre-Dame on the Île-de-la-Cité and the complete encirclement of the town with walls on the Right and Left Banks. Before turning to these enterprises, we shall consider the location of the city that had been long established by history and geography.[1] From time immemorial the Gaulois had occupied the firm sand on the Right Bank of the Seine at the Place de Grève, protected by the marshes of the Marais to the north, which were evidence of the former meandering of the river. The Romans preferred to build their administrative palace on the western end of the Île and to protect the island with a wall. They erected their amenities, the monumental thermes and arena, on the Left Bank. The Merovingians followed by making the imperial palace the center of their expanding kingdom. The Gallo-Roman Christians who succeeded in converting the Franks to their faith shared the island by placing the bishop's cathedral at the eastern end. Although the Carolingians largely ignored Paris, the succeeding Robertian-Capétians found the town central to ruling their lands to the north and the south. Philip Augustus's father and grandfather had dated a third to a quarter of their charters at Paris.

The geographical advantages of the site prompted and confirmed these historical choices.[2] Located on the Seine where the river could be easily forded (thanks to a cluster of islands) and situated between the confluence of the Marne and the Oise, Paris was connected to northern and central France through the vast network of fluvial tributaries. Of equal importance, it controlled access to the sea that was exceeded only by Rouen further downstream. Astride the Seine on the Île-de-la-Cité and the two banks, the city nonetheless rode a mighty and fickle steed. As recently as 1197 a destructive flood evicted the king to the higher ground of Sainte-Geneviève and the bishop to the shelter of Saint-Victor, on the Left Bank, but the raging crest returned within a decade. The Petit-Pont was destroyed and the waters rose to the level of the second floor.[3] Paris also took advantage of the north-south roads across France that followed the *route des seuils* by skirting the geological shelf formed by the eastern hills. A decade or two earlier Guy de Bazoches had eulogized the city as lying in the lap of a luscious valley that provided it with the pleasures of Ceres and Bacchus.[4] To the north lay the fertile *plaine de France*, whose abundant grain supplied the city's bread basket. Throughout the region vineyards ascended the slopes, producing highly reputed wines from the days of the Emperor Julian, who remembered them as fondly as he did the mild winters. And beneath the rich soil lay the apparently inexhaustible layers of limestone that supplied the present construction needs.

Many of the city's prominent architectural features were already in place before the period of the great constructions. The Île-de-la-Cité had long been shared by the bishop and the king. Since Merovingian times the former had dominated the eastern end with an impressive late-antique basilica dedicated to Saint Stephen and later to the Virgin Mary. In the eleventh century the Capetian Robert II had enlarged the Roman palace on the western end with a spacious hall for holding audiences.[5] By the time of Philip's father the palace contained two chapels dedicated to Saint Nicholas and Saint Michel. His grandfather contributed the Grosse Tour that measured nearly 12 meters at the base and probably approached 30 meters in height. Guy de Bazoches was indeed impressed by the royal presence, because he described the king's palace and its appurtenances as rising head and shoulders above the city.[6] The middle of the island that separated the king from the bishop contained the most densely inhabited quarter of the city.

Two stone bridges connected the Île-de-la-Cité with its surrounding banks, each fitted with a châtelet (flanking castle) to guard its approaches. To the north the Grand-Pont (so named because the Seine was wide here) linked the royal palace with the rue Saint-Denis that leads north to the abbey of that name.[7] As the principal north-south artery, this street had supplanted the rue Saint-Martin that lay not far to the east, because since the twelfth century the energetic Abbot Suger had closely identified the royal abbey of Saint-Denis with the emerging fortunes of the monarchy. The Right Bank, now known as "beyond the Grand-Pont" (*ultra magnam pontem*), was the commercial quarter of Paris and thickly inhabited. The merchants' activities clustered around two centers: the old market (*vetus forum*) located at the quays of the Place de Grève on the Seine and the new market (*novum forum*) situated to the northwest in the fields of Champeaux. Further to the west was the church of Saint-Germain-l'Auxerrois, whose vast parish occupied nearly half of the Right Bank. Since the eleventh century the old market had been protected by walls that also included the parish churches of Saint-Gervais, Saint-Merry, and Saint-Jacques. To the north were the fortifications of the Knights Templars, known as the Temple, the Cluniac priory, Saint-Martin-des-Champs (from which the other north-south street was named), and further north the influential Benedictine abbey of Saint-Denis, located on the second bend of the meandering Seine.

The bishop's side of the Île-de-la-Cité was connected with the Left Bank by a stone bridge called the Petit-Pont, because the river was narrow there. Designated the quarter "beyond the Petit-Pont" (*ultra parvem pontem*), it was appropriately connected with the bishop because, apart from the Roman monuments now in ruins, it was dominated by the three major religious houses, the Benedictines at Saint-Germain-des-Prés to the west (whose stone tower can still be recognized in the present church), the regular canons at Sainte-Geneviève to the south (whose cloister has been preserved in the present lycée Henri IV), and the regular canons of Saint-Victor to the east (on the grounds of the present Université de Paris at Jussieu). Sparsely settled, the intervening territory consisted mainly of gardens and vineyards and a major street, the rue Saint-Jacques, leading south from the Petit-Pont, presumably to the pilgrimage goal of Santiago de Compostela in Spain, although it did not proceed much beyond Paris.

When the youthful Philip Augustus acceded to the throne in 1179, he immediately began to stamp his own mark on the city. According to the often-remembered story circulated by the royal historiographer Rigord, in

1185 the king went to the window of his palace to enjoy a view over the Seine but was so nauseated from the stench of the mud churned up by horses below that he resolved to pave the major squares and streets of the city: for example, the rues Saint-Denis, Saint-Antoine, Saint-Honoré, and Saint-Jacques.[8] Aided by the bourgeoisie, the resulting transformation was impressive. The rue Saint-Denis was enlarged to 10 meters, whose surviving paving stones measure 35 to 40 centimeters in thickness.[9] Earlier in 1181 he had bought out the rights to the fair of the lepers of Saint-Lazare and moved this fair to his new market in the field of Champeaux.[10] There in 1183 he built the Halles, or permanent sheds, to protect the stalls of merchandise from the weather and enclosed them with walls so that the goods could be left unattended over night. Business was so brisk in this new market that the neighboring cemetery of the Holy Innocents also had to be protected by walls in 1186 to keep the crowds and livestock from desecrating the graves.[11] The fiscal accounts of 1202–1203 reveal Philip adding stables, repairing the roof, and generally making improvements to the royal palace on the island, as well as shoring up the vaults under the Grand Châtelet.[12] Except for the stone tower of Saint-Germain-des-Prés, nearly all of these architectural features of Paris have since disappeared under the relentless urbanization and transformations of the French capital. Only the great projects of Notre-Dame and the city walls undertaken by the bishop and the king at the turn of the century have left a lasting (or near-lasting) imprint on Paris today.

Notre-Dame

In the year 1200 the cathedral of Notre-Dame on the eastern end of the Île-de-la-Cité had been under construction for nearly a half-century and the process would continue into the second half of the new century.[13] If the initiating architect himself was anonymous, as were most architects of the day, his patron and animator was undoubtedly Maurice de Sully, bishop of Paris, from 1160 to his recent death in 1196. There is no doubt that Notre-Dame was his personal creation. Although of modest social station, he possessed inordinate ambition as a builder—indeed a second Abbot Suger of Saint-Denis. When he came to the episcopal throne, he had inherited the Merovingian basilica that, despite recent remodeling and adornment, had remained a relatively old-fashioned and modest structure (measuring 75 by 35 meters). In the intense architectural activity surrounding Paris in the second half of the century, many of the neighboring prelates were already experimenting with larger edifices in a new mode, known then as the "French style" (*opus francigenum*), and now called Gothic. Not only had Abbot Suger pioneered in this style close by at Saint-Denis, but the abbot of Saint-Germain-des-Prés and the prior of Saint-Martin-des-Champs were adding Gothic elements to their churches as well. His fellow bishops at Senlis, Noyon, and Laon, not to speak of his archbishop at Sens, were likewise experimenting in this architectural idiom. Not to be outdone, Maurice was determined to surpass them in length, height, and modernity.

Figure 1. Christ builds the Holy Church, *Bible moralisée*, fol. 50rb, Austrian National Library, Vienna, Picture Archiv+Signature.

At least by 1163 the first architect had established the initial design for the choir (the eastern end of the church) after which the rest of the church was patterned. Since the old Merovingian church and dense housing on the island presented barriers to the west, the choir was placed well beyond the old Roman wall to the east to allow a lengthy church. This set the foundations in marshland where up to 9 meters had to be excavated to reach solid ground. To the west a street 6 to 7 meters in width, named the rue Neuve-Notre-Dame, was cut through the crowded tenement quarter to enable transport of materials. A workshop for the construction was established in the marshes to the east. Two crews of masons worked simultaneously, which permitted sharing cranes and scaffolding. Because the work proceeded with astounding rapidity and continuous overlapping, only minor modifications were added to the basic plan. The project benefited from ample wood from the bishop's lands for masonry forms and scaffolding, abundant limestone from quarries on the Left Bank that could be transported down the Bièvre to the Seine and a large labor workforce supplied by the Parisian population and its environs. Work continued at a rapid pace even through the slow season of winter. The chronicler Robert de Torigny noted that the head (*caput*) of the choir was finished in 1177 except for the roof, which must have been added by 1182 when the papal legate Henry de Château-Marcay consecrated the main altar. These solemnities, officiated by a cardinal of the Roman church surrounded by a hundred clerics, signified that the choir was

Figure 2. Notre-Dame from the southeast, photo. C. Rose, © CMN, Paris.

ready for service. Measuring 38 meters long and 32.5 meters high, the stone vaults of the choir now challenged the king's Grosse Tour at the opposite end of the island.

Before the choir was completed, a second architect joined the project to start work on the nave. During the decades between 1180 and 1200 the two sides were raised in conjunction, beginning with the south but terminating with the north. The elevation consisted of an arcade, a tribune and a rose window surmounted by clerestory windows. (The original elevation, which was altered in the thirteenth century, may be seen in the northeastern- and southeastern-most bays of the nave at the crossing of the transept, as restored in the nineteenth century by Viollet-le-Duc.) By 1196 the nave lacked only a roof, to which Bishop Maurice contributed 100 *livres parisis* in his testament. The construction workshop was now moved to the west. With the second architect disappearing by 1200, a third turned his attention to the west fa-çade before the nave was completed. Pillars were laid for the west works, and space was cleared for the Parvis in front that required dismantling of the Merovingian church. Sculpture that was designed for the latter was transported and inserted into the southern portal of the west front. In the first decade of the thirteenth century work continued on the two remaining portals of the west façade, reaching the gallery of kings in the 1210s.[14]

Although the nave still lacked a roof, in the year 1200 the inhabitants of Paris were nonetheless able to appreciate the potential achievement of Maurice de Sully and his architects. Enough of Notre-Dame could be seen to demonstrate that it was the largest and most technically perfect edifice of its day. Consisting of five bays in the choir, a transept, and eight bays in nave, its length attained 122.5 meters; in comparison the cathedral of Sens, its archepiscopal superior and major competitor, measured 113 meters. The central vessel was 12.5 meters wide with an additional 5.9 meters on either side for the aisles. Most spectacularly, the vaults of the nave reached a record 33.1 meters while Sens achieved 24.4 meters, Noyon 21.7 meters, and Laon 26 meters. It would take another generation of cathedrals at Chartres and Bourges to reach 37 meters. A half-century later the competition ended with 48 meters at Beauvais, the structural limit of limestone. But these towering vaults were supported by thin walls open largely to glass and in need of lateral buttressing. Architectural historians continue to debate to what extent flying buttresses were included in Maurice de Sully's church, but the placement of flying buttresses on both the original choir and the nave remains the most reasonable solution.[15]

Notre-Dame mastered techniques and characteristics that came to be known as the high Gothic style: volume, verticality and light. Rising from arcades, to tribunes, to clerestory windows, the interior was unencumbered, since all supporting structure was placed outside in the flying buttresses. Yet the floor plan admits no exterior protrusions; all is contained within an encompassing envelope. If we subtract the later features of the western rose, the arcade and towers, the elaborated facades of the south and north transepts with their rose windows, and the lateral chapels that

Figure 3. Flying buttresses around 1200, *Bible moralisée*, fol. 50va, Austrian National Library, Vienna, Picture Archiv+Signature.

were inserted between the buttresses, we can still envisage today the Notre-Dame of 1200. The present flying buttresses are the work of Viollet-le-Duc in the nineteenth century, but they rest on foundations that supported similar structures in Maurice de Sully's church.

Although the most ambitious, Notre-Dame was not alone among Bishop Maurice's buildings. At the same time, he undertook construction of a new episcopal palace and a Hôtel-Dieu, both to the south of the cathedral in the marshes outside the Roman walls. In contrast to the former palace to the east, the new palace was sumptuous, consisting of a vaulted first floor and an upper hall to the west, a chapel of two floors to the east, a gallery linking the palace with the third bay of the cathedral choir and finally an imposing square tower between the palace and the church. The Hôtel-Dieu, a hospital, extended beyond the cathedral on the south side of the Parvis. And considerable rebuilding was required to accommodate the rue Neuve-Notre-Dame entering the Parvis from the west whose breadth (6 to 7 meters) enabled those who approached the church to have a clear view of the rising west façade.

Chanter of Notre-Dame by 1183, Pierre, who was known to posterity by this office, died in 1197, one year after Bishop Maurice. As second-ranking dignitary after the dean, one of his duties was to attend meetings of the cathedral chapter, where decisions concerning the building and its financing were endlessly discussed. Taking the first seat on the epistle side to the south opposite the dean on the north, the Chanter's jurisdiction extended over the choir of the cathedral, where he supervised the offices and liturgy, the conduct of the choir boys, and the correction of the song books. Since Pierre was preoccupied with the teaching of theology, he most likely delegated these responsibilities to the subchanter. In these transitional decades between the old and new cathedrals, it is not certain where the services were held. The new choir was operational since 1182, but the Merovingian basilica was not torn down until the late 1190s. (Most likely both edifices were in use simultaneously.) Whatever the confusion, the daily performance of divine services in the choir was most certainly incommoded by the dust of the stone masons and the noise of construction. For this reason those who attended his Biblical lectures and read his *Verbum abbreviatum* may have taken notice of a theme repeated on their pages: "Against superfluous builders" (*contra superfluos edificatores*). The protest against extravagant building was not new, since it appeared as early as the classical authors and was renewed in monastic writings of the twelfth century, particularly those of the

Cistercian Bernard of Clairvaux against the Cluniacs. Much of Pierre's argument reechoes this traditional disapproval, but given his position, his target is unmistakable. Referring to the great churches (*maiores ecclesie*) of the secular clergy, he wrote that "just as Christ who as the head [*caput*] of the body of the church was humble and lowly, so the choirs [*capita*] of our churches should be lower than the edifices." Imagining a conversation between a holy prelate and a building prelate, he has the former chide the latter: "Why do you want your houses so tall? Of what use are your towers and ramparts? Do you believe that the devil cannot scale them? Nay, I say that you thereby become the neighbor and companion of demons, the spirits of the air."[16] These criticisms were seconded by his student Pierre de Roissy, later chancellor of Chartres.[17] Bishop Maurice would certainly have felt the sting of the charges. Yet in 1190 the bishop faced a further worry. About to depart on the crusade, King Philip, professing his great love for Notre-Dame, confided construction of the new cathedral to the hands of Hervé, dean of the chapter, and Pierre, its chanter, should the bishop die and the see of Paris fall vacant during the king's absence.[18] Pierre was doubtlessly chosen because of his rank, but Maurice would have been relieved that he himself was still alive when the king returned to Paris in 1191.

The Walls of Philip Augustus

Although not as long in the making, the other great construction project was also at midpoint in the year 1200.[19] On the eve of his departure for the Holy Land in 1190, the king, in the words of Rigord, "commanded the bourgeois to enclose the city of Paris, which he dearly loved, with a superb wall suitably fitted with turrets and gates. All this was completed in a short time."[20] The surviving traces of this wall indicate that it proceeded around the Right Bank for 2,600 meters in straight segments, containing thirty-nine turrets and five gates. Circumscribing a greater scope than its eleventh-century predecessor, the wall enclosed not only the older commercial nucleus at the Place de Grève but also the more recent markets at the Halles as well as the large parish of Saint-Germain-l'Auxerrois to the west. It excluded the Temple and Saint-Martin-des-Champs to the north. The gates accommodated the major roads exiting the city: rue Saint-Honoré to the west, the parallel rue Saint-Denis and rue Saint-Martin to the north, and rue Saint-Antoine to the east. Since most scholars assume, with little discussion, that the construction proceeded from east to west, the turrets are numbered and the wall is usually described in that direction. It is equally likely, however, that construction started at the Seine near the porte de Saint-Honoré and Louvre and advanced north and eastward to terminate upstream near the porte de Saint-Antoine. Priority may have been assigned to the western flank of the city, which faced the Anglo-Norman-Angevin menace no more than 60 kilometers distant at Gisors. As Rigord suggests, this half of the wall was rapidly completed, most probably within a decade.

The threat from the west doubtlessly induced the construction of the castle of the Louvre in that direction on the banks of the Seine just outside the walls. Following the Capetian policy of building cylindrical towers, as we have seen exemplified in the Grosse Tour of the royal palace, work most likely began with a similar tower surrounded by a dry moat.[21] It measures 18 meters at the base, tapering to a diameter of 15 meters, and attained a height of 30 meters to compete with the tower of the royal palace and the vaults of Notre-Dame. Eventually this cylindrical tower was enclosed in a nearly square wall (72 by 78 meters) with turrets on each corner, two gates flanked by two turrets towards the city walls (to the east) and the river (to the south) and two additional turrets on the opposite sides. The ten turrets were regularly spaced at 25 meters apart. The outside walls were further encompassed by a moat filled with water. Drawbridges gave access to the gate facing the city and over the dry moat to the central tower. The central tower probably neared completion in 1204, when a royal charter identified land "where our tower of the Louvre is located," and the surrounding walls were probably under way by 1210, when another royal charter mentioned land "which is now within the circuit of the new walls around our new tower."[22]

With the walls on the Right Bank and the Louvre well under way, work began on the Left Bank around 1200. Since it was financed by the king (as opposed to the bourgeoisie for the Right Bank), a building estimate (*devis*) survives in the royal registers that includes a description: "The piece-work of the walls of Paris surrounding the city on the side of the Petit-Pont has 1260 *toise* [a furlong] (at the rate of 5 livres for each toise with turrets) and at the width of the old walls on the side of the Grand-Pont and with three feet of height of the old walls, and above shields and crenelation, and six gates (each gate should cost 120 livres)."[23] From archeological remains this wall measures 2,500 meters, is fitted with 38 towers and like the Right Bank proceeds in straight segments. Its circumference included the abbey of Sainte-Geneviève to the south, which was apparently without protection, but omitted Saint-German-des-Prés to the west and Saint-Victor to the east. The

monks of Saint-Germain had long been sheltered behind important fortifications around their *bourg* to which the surviving Porte papale testifies.[24] In
1209–1210 Philip Augustus confided to the abbot the upkeep of the gate in
his walls facing west.[25] Only the factor of distance may explain why the abbey of Saint-Victor was not also protected. The river Bièvre, however, flowing from the south, had been deflected by the canons into their lands. The
king took advantage of this canal to introduce water into his walls through a
postern in the east. Unlike the Right Bank most of the territory enclosed on
the Left consisted of open space given over to gardens and vineyards. The six
gates opened to roads from Saint-Germain-des-Prés, from Saint-Marcel and
the rue Saint-Jacques both from the south, and from Saint-Victor. As scholars commonly agree, work began at the Tour de Philippe Hamelin (later
the Tour de Nesle) across from the Louvre on the Left Bank and proceeded
south and east rejoining the river upstream before the abbey of Saint-Victor.
According to the testimony of the royal historian Guillaume le Breton,
the fortifications were completed by 1211–1212.[26] The growing threat of the
Anglo-Flemish-imperial coalition, which was not allayed until the decisive
battle of Bouvines of 1214, doubtlessly made the king anxious to complete
fortifications of his capital city. As the builders descended the slope of the
hill from Sainte-Geneviève on the final eastern flank, they showed signs of
haste. Instead of laying the stones with a plumb line, they began to set them
according to the contours of the terrain, an ill-advised practice they had
previously avoided.

Construction of the walls on both banks was characterized by rapidity and uniformity. Philip Augustus's engineers took their model from the
Gallo-Roman fortifications that had survived at the towns of Senlis and
Bourges and consisted of standardized *courtines*, regularly spaced turrets,
and fortified gates flanked with two towers. The walls stood 6 to 8 meters
high and measured 2.6 meters at the base and 2.3 meters at the summit. The
interior side was vertical, leaving a slight slope on the outside. The surfaces
were faced with regular blocks of limestone measuring 0.26–0.32 meters in
height and 0.35–0.40 meters in length, procured from the quarries readily
accessible from the Bièvre, as at Notre-Dame. The space between the surfaces was filled with rough stone and pebbles mixed with mortar and topped
with a road protected by crenelations. No exterior moat was envisaged for
the original wall. The 77 turrets were spaced at 60 meters, thus covering the
wall within the range of crossbow fire. Each turret was 7 meters in diameter
with walls 2 meters thick and consisting of three floors with the first usually

vaulted. Like the Gallo-Roman models each of the eleven gates was flanked with towers. The repetition of the gates, the regular spacing of the turrets and the uniformity of the dimensions right down to the limestone blocks suggests a project that approached industrial techniques like those Philip's military engineers had applied to construction of cylindrical towers.[27]

Paris was only one example of Philip Augustus's policy to fortify the towns of his domain.[28] As early as 1184 the count of Flanders had threatened to plant his banner on the Petit-Pont, but since the 1190s the greatest danger came from the Anglo-Norman-Angevins down the Seine in Normandy. As befalls most large projects, Philip's engineers took advantage of the terrain in some areas but were forced to expose the walls to danger in others. The full summit of Mont-Sainte-Geneviève was probably not enclosed either because of the expense or the time involved as the threat of the Anglo-Flemish-imperial coalition approached. In fact, however, Philip's wall was never tested militarily before it was superseded on the Right Bank by the expanded fortifications of Charles V in the fourteenth century. But the function of the wall was not simply defensive. We shall see that its circumscription also served to aid policing, delimit jurisdiction and define identity. Not only did it become the source of disputes between authorities but, more important, it encouraged settlement and increased the pace of further building. When Guillaume le Breton took notice of the walls on the Left Bank in 1211–1212, he averred that the walls "forced the owners of fields and vineyards to rent their lands to residents for the construction of new houses—or they even built new houses themselves—so that the whole city was filled with habitations up to the walls."[29] Signs of the future could be seen as early as 1202, when the Clos Bruneau and the Clos Garlande-Mauvoisin were ceded to the abbot of Sainte-Geneviève to be divided into lots for construction.[30]

Since the devis in the king's registers provides unit costs (5 livres per toise of wall and turret and 120 livres per gate), the total expense for the Left Bank amounted to 7,020 livres parisis. At these rates the cost of the Right Bank can likewise be estimated at 7,165 livres, although it was most likely assumed by the bourgeoisie; 14,185 livres paid over two decades amounted to 12 percent of the king's ordinary revenues (115,000 livres) in the fiscal year of 1202–1203. The financial burden of the fortifications was therefore not unreasonable. Tearing down habitations in the straight path of city walls, however, can be crippling to the residents through whose lands they pass. Pierre the Chanter was aware of such problems confronting the urban dweller. In discussing cases where individuals suffer for the welfare of the whole community, Pierre cited examples of houses razed to contain the blaze of conflagration in a crowded city and of houses torn down to make room for a wall required by public necessity. After considering conflicting arguments, the Chanter concluded that divine law demands that those who benefit from the sacrifice of others should indemnify the latter. In commenting on the constructions of the Left Bank the chronicler Guillaume le Breton marveled at the king's example. Although Roman law permits building on others' lands for the public utility, Philip, preferring equity to strict law, compensated those damaged from his own treasury. A surviving ecclesiastical charter shows him indemnifying the bishop of Paris for losses in construction of the new walls of the Louvre.[31]

Figure 4. Excavation of the tower of Philip Augustus in the Louvre, photo. A. Longchampt, © CMN, Paris.

Unlike Notre-Dame, which remains the focal point of Paris today, Philip Augustus's walls have succumbed to the expansion and modernization of the city, beginning in the fourteenth century with the larger walls of Charles V on the Right Bank and culminating with the urbanization of Baron Haussmann in the nineteenth. But enough survives today to permit glimpses of Philip's original achievement. A large section remains on the Right Bank when houses were demolished next to the Lycée Charlemagne, and a comparable section was uncovered on the Left Bank with the excavation of a parking garage on rue Mazarine. A cross section of the wall revealing both the surface and the filling is available on rue Clovis, and the haste of the masons as they descended the hill of Sainte-Geneviève is evident at the fire station of rue Cardinal Lemoine. The postern allowing water to enter from the canal of Bièvre is found in the basement of the nearby post office at the corner of rue des Écoles. But most spectacularly the foundations of Philip's cylindrical tower and surrounding wall of the Louvre buried under the Cour Carée of the present palace are now on impressive display near the visitors center on the underground floor of the museum (Figure 4). Both Notre-Dame and the walls of Philip Augustus may serve as emblems for our historical quest of the Paris of 1200. Although half-finished, enough remains to enable us to appreciate both the outline and the texture of the city at the time.

The Population of Paris

No statistical evidence has survived that might allow calculation of the population of Paris within the walls in 1200. When rolls of tax assessments did appear a century later, demographers arrived at figures as disparate as 80,000 and 210,000 inhabitants, of which the higher estimate is in favor today.[32] To say that the walls contained as many as 50,000 to 60,000 inhabitants in 1200 can therefore be only speculation. What is certain is that the walls, measuring 5,100 meters in circumference, enclosed 250 hectares of land (roughly a square mile) and made Paris the largest walled city in the kingdom, exceeding by far its nearest competitors Poitiers (180 hectares), Toulouse (154 hectares), Bourges (110 hectares), and Troyes (80 hectares). But Paris was not as large as Ghent (644 hectares) in Flanders or Cologne (401 hectares) in the Rhineland.[33] Since the density of habitation varied between the Île-de-la-Cité (highest), the Right Bank (high) and Left Bank (low), coefficients of people to square meter are of little use.

Equally incontrovertible are the signs of rapid growth. In a statute regulating the wine trade in 1192 the king justified his intervention because of the "increase of the *ville* [Right Bank] of Paris and of his bourgeoisie." We have already noticed that in 1211–1212 Guillaume le Breton testified that the lands of the Left Bank were filling up to the walls with houses.[34] We shall see that this growth was translated into the redistribution of parishes within the city that followed population trends. The tiny Île-de-la-Cité, for example, contained thirteen; the enormous parish of Saint-Germain-l'Auxerrois and the sizable Saint-Gervais were divided up on the Right Bank, and the influx of students undoubtedly altered the demography of the Left Bank, just as it presented problems for the police.[35] At the end of the century Henri de Suso, archbishop of Embrun, remembered that the parish of Saint-Germain-l'Auxerrois contained 40,000 souls, more than his present archbishopric. His reminiscence is worthy of note because he was an archdeacon in Paris during the period of redistricting.[36] The appearance of new cemeteries represents still another sign. Paris's original cemetery was located at Champeaux, next to the church of the Saints-Innocents. Philip protected it with walls because, as Rigord reports, "the citizens of Paris were accustomed to bury so many there, that it contained thousands."[37] Outside the city's walls to the north the parish church of Saint-Martin-des-Champs could no longer accommodate the demand; a new cemetery was inaugurated at the neighboring Saint-Nicholas-des-Champs in 1221 "because of the great increase of people."[38] We shall see that the king's installation of an accounting bureau and courts of justice at his capital likewise promoted a seasonal influx of royal officers. Three times a year forty prévôts and twelve baillis and their entourages arrived to do business at the Temple and the royal palace. The bailli of Caen, Pierre du Thillay, owned a house on the rue des Prêcheurs near the Halles; Count Thibaut de Blois, the seneschal at the king's court, rented a house from the bourgeois Thibaut le Riche. The abbots of Saint-Denis had long held a house outside the walls on the road to their monastery, and the archbishop of Reims shared a residence with the bishop of Beauvais near the Louvre.

The Working Poor

It is equally impossible to estimate how much of the population residing within the walls was poor, that is to say, without property, and therefore leaving no trace in the documentation. The last decade of the twelfth century must have been hard times for the poor of Paris. King Philip's return from the crusade not only rekindled intense warfare with the Anglo-Norman-Angevins that was destructive to the economy but was accompanied by deteriorating weather conditions as well. Between 1194 and 1197 Rigord recorded heavy rains and hailstorms that destroyed crops, vineyards and livestock and induced severe conditions of famine. The price of wheat and barley doubled and quadrupled, prompting the king to urge his bishops and abbots to increase their alms to the poor.[39] Undoubtedly these adverse conditions affected the urban poor of Paris, whose numbers we can only speculate. From evidence from the late Middle Ages, the involuntary poor, that is, those who begged, numbered more than 10 percent of the population, and the working poor (but without property) may have constituted at least a half.

The Hôtel-Dieu, the hospital to the south of Notre-Dame, had doubtlessly served both poor men and women from antiquity, and the established abbeys of the region likewise provided aid to the needy in keeping with their monastic obligations. On the Right Bank the parish of Saint-Gervais itself possessed a hospital, the nearby Sainte-Catherine (formerly Sainte-Opportune) a refuge for young women since 1186, and the bourgeoisie established the Hospital of the Holy Trinity for pilgrims to Compostela on the rue Saint-Denis since 1202. Outside the walls to the north, lepers had long been received at Saint-Lazare and later by another house Le Roulle.[40] By targeting specific segments of the population according to gender and profession, other endowed charitable institutions extended aid to the working poor. In 1180 a rich London merchant arranged that a room in the Hôtel-Dieu be set aside to house and feed eighteen poor scholars who attended the schools. It subsequently was known as the Collège-des-Dix-huit. By 1186 a similar institution was established on the Right Bank by the king's uncle; it eventually acquired the name of the Collège de Saint-Thomas-du-Louvre, and still a third consisting of thirteen beds not far away at the Bons-Enfants de Saint-Honoré was endowed by two bourgeois couples between 1204 and 1209.[41] If these foundations were restricted to young men, the king made similar provisions for aging males, his retired sergeants. In 1208 a house, chapel and cemetery were established in the vicinity of Sainte-Geneviève on the Left Bank for these lowest officers of royal administration to which the king later bequeathed 2,000 livres in his testament.[42] Most surprising of these recent foundations, however, was Saint-Antoine, devoted to a distinct segment of the poor, working females, that is, to prostitutes.

Working Prostitutes

Accommodating courts, schools, and immense construction projects, Paris attracted throngs of men to the largest urban concentration in the kingdom, thereby fostering an environment conducive to this female profession. In a rhetorical passage that is often quoted, Jacques de Vitry, a preacher and former student of Pierre the Chanter, illustrated how these women were integrated into the urban landscape: "Public harlots were everywhere throughout the squares and streets of the city, often dragging away passing clerics to their lairs. . . ." In the crowded Île-de-la-Cité "the same house contained a school on the upper floors and a brothel on the ground. While the masters lectured above, the women exercised their shameful profession below. While clerics conducted disputations, the whores argued with their pimps."[43]

Since canonists, theologians and other clerical writers were celibate males, they were rarely able to curb their fascination for this profession, and the masters in particular as residents of Paris were justified in taking up the issue. Pierre the Chanter, Robert de Courson and most especially Thomas of Chobham devoted long pages to it in their treatises and manuals.[44] Because there was no question of legitimizing sexual activity outside of matrimony, their condemnation of the profession was, of course, assumed. Thomas catalogued the various definitions, ranging from different forms of promiscuity to "those who sell themselves openly to the lusts of many." Adopting the Roman law dictum that a prostitute is "a woman who publicly earns money with her body," the theologians took particular note of the issue of money and turned to the attendant question of whether the prostitute was required to do restitution of her earnings in order to be absolved from sin. Roman law had offered remedies for recovery of money realized in immoral acts, but it further stipulated that if both the giver and the receiver act immorally, no restitution is required. Roman law further clarified that "a prostitute acts immorally for what she does, but she does not receive money immorally because she is a prostitute." The conclusion was therefore unanimous that prostitutes, unlike usurers, were not bound to do restitution of their money in a court of law. (Whatever the personal disappointment, their clients were poorly placed to contest the decision.) Thomas specified that since the woman works with her body, she is entitled to the gains of her labor. The only qualification was that of fraud. If, for example, a woman anoints her eyes, rouges her face with cosmetics, or declares herself to be of noble birth, she should, according to the Chanter, refund the money to her client to the extent of her deception.

Since there was no doubt that prostitutes were wage earners whose profits were legitimate, they can be numbered among the working population. Although some became rich and others may have performed their profession chiefly for pleasure, Thomas (again supported by Roman law) likewise took notice of those who were motivated more by poverty than by lust. These women were part of the working poor who, like young school boys and aged sergeants, deserved help. This observation served to shape the reform proposed by the Parisian masters. Fresh from the theological school of Pierre the Chanter, Foulques, a rustic but charismatic priest from Neuilly, began in 1195 to preach at the church of Saint-Sevérin on the Left Bank and in the market place of Champeaux on the Right and then proceeded into the Île-de-France and to Flanders. Possessing talents both as a healer and as an orator, he was particularly successful in converting prostitutes and usurers. To shelter the former from relapsing and to provide for their sustenance, he founded in 1198 the monastery of Saint-Antoine outside the walls to the east. A quarter-century later it was followed by another, the Filles-Dieu, to the north on the rue Saint-Denis.[45] (By 1204, however, Bishop Eudes de Sully had transformed Saint-Antoine into a house of Cistercian nuns that subsequently served a richer and more respectable clientele.[46]) To those women who lacked the courage or desire to remain continent and preferred to marry, Foulques raised a fund to supply their dowries. The scholars of Paris were said to have donated 250 livres and the bourgeoisie 1,000 livres to the cause. In the same year as the founding of Saint-Antoine, Pope Innocent III, likewise a graduate of the Chanter's school, issued a decretal (decree) assuring remission of sin to all men who married such women and thereby rescued them from brothels.[47] Poverty in general and specifically the lack of dowries were therefore judged by the Parisian theologians to be the root cause of prostitution.

Less merciful measures were also on hand, stemming from the prostitute's juridical status as an excommunicate. Robert of Courson urged that all public women identified by legal confession or convicted by witnesses or notoriety of fact should be evicted from the city as excommunicates if they remained incorrigible. Later in 1212 as papal legate, he decreed in the council of Paris that such women be expelled from the city, segregated outside the walls and treated according to the custom of lepers.[48] Unlike earlier days in which the women mingled freely with the population, this measure announced a future policy where prostitution was confined to regulated areas, a policy that prevailed throughout Europe within the century.

How firmly established these charitable institutions for the poor were may be seen in one of the earliest surviving bourgeois testaments. In 1227 Jehan de Fontenay-sur-Bois (near Vincennes) and his wife Bauteut provided legacies both for their native village and for Paris, where they resided, most likely in the parish of Saint-Jacques. These included not only major institutions such as the cathedral of Notre-Dame and the Hôtel-Dieu but also the poor clerics of Saint-Thomas, Saint-Honoré, the hospitals of Sainte-Opportune and Saint-Gervais and the Cistercians nuns at Saint-Antoine. The lepers of Sainte-Marie-Madeleine in their home village of Fontenay were particularly well endowed, but the needs of poor women were not forgotten. The Filles-Dieu were remembered and small alms were donated to provide for the dowries of poor girls in the parish of Saint-Jacques, to be administered by the local priest and *preudomes* (respected men).[49]

The Bourgeoisie

The bourgeoisie or those who possessed property within the walls can be more readily identified, because they left traces in the documentation. Concentrated on the Île-de-la-Cité and the Right Bank, their focal point was the Grand-Pont that connected the king's end of the island with the commercial centers at the Champeaux and Halles and the Place de Grève on the other side. Adopting the terminology of his grandfather, Philip Augustus called them "our bourgeoisie (or citizens) of Paris" (*nostri burgenses/ cives Parisienses*) with few exceptions throughout the reign.[50] They were designated *our* because they belonged to the king and collaborated with him on the important projects of paving the streets, building the walls and supervising royal finances during his absence; they were Parisian to distinguish them from the bourgeoisie of other cities in the royal domain. In 1200 the completed walls on the Right Bank doubtlessly contributed to their sense of self-identity and helped to distinguish them from the clerical and Jewish segments of the population, but they nonetheless continued to belong to the king.[51]

Scores of names of bourgeois families appear in the hundreds of documents attesting property transaction found in the cartularies of the Parisian churches, but few contemporary efforts were undertaken to designate the most important. An early attempt occurred in 1190 when the king, about to leave the realm on the crusade, confided his government to regents, Queen Adèle (his mother) and Archbishop Guillaume of Reims (his uncle). At Paris they were aided by six bourgeois with the particular task of supervising the accounts of the prévôts and baillis three times a year at the Temple. Only the initials of the six individuals (T, A, E, R, B, N) were offered in the ordinance-testament, but the first four are easily recognized as Thibaut le Riche, Athon de la Grève, Ebroin le Changeur, and Robert de Chartres. (The last two names may have been Baudouin Bruneau and Nicolas Bocel.)[52] During the next year these bourgeois surface in the royal charters working together in groups of four to six persons.[53] Thibaut may have originated from the family of knights that provided royal prévôts for Paris since the early twelfth century, but by 1200 he was bourgeois and a notorious usurer. The commercial involvements of Athon and Ebroin are suggested by the Place de Grève and the profession of money changer embedded in their names.

Another attempt to distinguish the prominent bourgeoisie came in the foundation of the Grand Confraternity of Notre-Dame sometime prior to 1203. Established for the mutual aid of clerics and bourgeois—the former offered their prayers, the latter their money—it was originally composed of seventy-two (but later increased to a hundred) members, equally divided between the two groups in memory of the early disciples of Christ. At first housed at cathedral cloister, the group later moved to the church of Sainte-Marie-Madeleine on the Cité. Since the origins of this confraternity are murky, the discussions of Pierre the Chanter and Robert of Courson help to illuminate its early function. In one *questio* the Chanter cited the case of the bishop of Paris authorizing seven clerics to establish a spiritual fraternity at the church of Sainte-Marie-Madeleine, which originally was a Jewish synagogue. He inquired if the clerics who endowed the fraternity with prebends (a salary attached to an ecclesiastical position) drawn from other churches were committing simony by purchasing spiritual benefits with material income. In another questio he made it explicit that entry into the confraternity was dependent on a fixed price and an annual fee. Was this simony? Courson carried the discussion further by comparing this situation with the laity who established confraternities on the advice of acquisitive priests by admitting no one without a fixed fee. Thus the spiritual prayers and masses for the dead were not provided free of charge and were thereby simoniacal (the sin of simony was the sale of church services or positions). These were precisely the services rendered by the Grand Fraternity of Notre-Dame, and association with the church of the Madeleine strengthens the connection.[54] Unfortunately no membership roll has survived from the Grand Confraternity in the thirteenth century, but the officers consisted of a clerical abbot and dean and a lay prévôt who served as treasurer. In 1203 the prévôt was Nicolas le Boucher, succeeded by Étienne Pavo in 1217–1218.[55]

Since the names yielded by the king's testament and the Grand Confraternity are meager, a final approach would be to identify those families appearing around 1200 whose descendants were later honored as "prévôts of merchants" and "aldermen" (*échevins*) during the reign of Louis IX, Philip's grandson. Such a selection produces the prominent surnames of Arrode, Augier, Barbette, Bourdon, Hescelin, La Pie, Le Flamant, Pisdoë, Popin, Sarrazin and Tremblay. As a matter of fact, the great majority of the échevinal families that dominated Paris in the second half of the thirteenth century could trace their ancestors back at least to the time of Philip Augustus. The epoch around 1200 therefore saw the birth of the bourgeois elite of the royal capital. Unlike the aristocracy who adopted place names, these bourgeois families made patronymics their hereditary surnames, thereby asserting pride in their lineage. For that reason they could trace their families back to the twelfth century. Like the aristocracy, however, each family adopted a limited stock of baptismal names. The Arrodes, for example, favored Nicolas, Jean and Eudes; the Bourdons, Renier.[56]

The elite bourgeoisie also expressed pride in family lineage through their choice of churches in which they established chapels for burial and endowed masses after their death. In 1230, for example, the Arrodes constructed a chapel at Saint-Martin-des-Champs to which they transferred the graves of five of their ancestors, including Nicolas Arrode, who had died in 1195. The Popins selected Saint-Germain-l'Auxerrois, and the Barbettes and Sarazins Saint-Victor. In fact, Saint-Martin-des-Champs was the favorite church of the bourgeoisie attracting the greatest number of obituaries; Saint-Germain-l'Auxerrois came in a close second, but Saint-Victor on the Left Bank had only half as many. Somewhat surprisingly, Notre-Dame on the Cité was even less popular. Evidently the bourgeoisie patronized the parishes on the Right Bank where they lived.[57]

The most important measure of their standing can be derived from the real estate they held at Paris. Although topographical nomenclature was imprecise, the surviving charters make an effort to locate the properties either by the name of a street or by proximity to a church. Thibaut le Riche lived up to his name by leaving a record of some nine properties, at least six of which were houses and mills within the city, extending from the Petit-Pont, through the Cité, over to the Right Bank, where a whole quarter was eventually named le bourg Thibaut.[58] As would be anticipated, Ebroin le Changeur and his son Jean held a house and a stall on the Grand-Pont, the center of foreign exchange of the city, a house on the rue Neuve-Notre-Dame on the Cité and houses on the Right bank from the parish of Saint-Germain-l'Auxerrois to the Porte Baudoyer.[59] Nicolas le Boucher, whose name appears in the necrologies of both the Grand Confraternity of Notre-Dame and Saint-Germain-l'Auxerrois, held a vault under the Grand Châtelet near the butcheries as well as a mill.[60] Among the properties of Philippe Hamelin were houses near Saint-Pierre des Arsis on the Cité and near Porte Baudoyer on the Right Bank. The tower anchoring the walls on the Left Bank across from the Louvre was named for him during his lifetime.[61] The Arrodes held a house near the Petit-Pont and fisheries on the Seine near the two bridges and at Mi-Bray.[62] On the Right Bank a gate in the walls and gardens outside evoked the name of the Barbette family.[63] By and large, however, the elite of the bourgeoisie concentrated their residences in areas where they worked, that is, at the foot of the Grand-Pont on the Cité and around the Halles and the Place de Grève on the Right Bank.[64] According to the customs of the city of Paris (*consuetudines civitatis Parisiensis*) all of this property was held subject to the payment of a ground rent (*cens*) that was not large but constituted proof of tenancy. The bourgeoisie held property outside Paris as well but with the greatest concentration within a short radius of 10 kilometers.[65]

None of their houses have survived into modern times, for the chief reason that no bourgeois attempted to erect a grand palace in stone. Doubtless their residences were more modest, with a shop on the ground floor occupying around 20 square meters and one or two floors above for living quarters. When a bourgeois wished to expand his quarters he merely annexed structures adjacent to his own.[66] Nor can we be sure of the amenities that the house provided, but when Pierre the Chanter moralized from an ancient proverb he was assuming a modicum of domesticity. The proverb ran: "Three things will expel a man from his house: a nagging wife, a smoking chimney and a leaking roof."[67]

The intermingling of property was matched by intermarriage. Ebroin le Changeur married the sister of Thibaut le Riche and the latter's descendants formed alliances with the Arrodes, who in turn married into the Popins, the Le Flamants and the Pisdoës.[68] Nor could the bourgeoisie withstand encroachment from the royal court. Gautier the Father, the royal chamberlain, for example, whose family was established at the king's court and in the prelacy, was a prominent tenant in Paris with properties on the Petit-Pont, Cité, Grand-Pont, Châtelet, Place de Grève, Saint-Merry and at least three mills. Long associated with Thibaut le Riche, he married the latter's sister, and when Thibaut's children predeceased him Gautier became the latter's heir. A year before he died in 1204 he made a donation to the Grand Confraternity of Notre-Dame.[69] Another contemporary royal chamberlain, Christophe Malocio, was a member of the Grand Confraternity as well. In his testament of 1205 he disposed of his house on the Petit-Pont and made numerous legacies not only to the bourgeois confraternity but also to charitable institutions, such as Saint-Victor, Sainte-Geneviève, Hôtel-Dieu and the Temple, as well as to the parishes of Sainte-Marie-Madeleine and Saint-Jacques.[70] As in 1190, the king likewise had need of his bourgeoisie to assist him in administering the city. If from 1200 to 1202 he relied on two knights, Robert de Meulan and Pierre du Thillay, from the neighboring countryside, by 1205 he drew from the bourgeoisie of the capital. Eudes Popin and Eudes Arrode in 1205, Philippe Hamelin in 1207, and Nicolas Arrode and Philippe Hamelin again in 1217–1219 were among the prévôt-baillis.[71] Since the annual farm (a fixed amount of taxes demanded annually) of the city was large (3,700 livres in 1202–1203), the prévôts preferred to share the responsibility with a colleague.

Provisioning the City

To provision the city was the earliest and most basic function of the bourgeoisie, but it rarely appeared in the royal charters and the contemporary ecclesiastical cartularies. In the 1260s, however, Philip Augustus's grandson, Louis IX, commissioned his prévôt-bailli Étienne Boileau to investigate and record the statutes of the trades of Paris in the *Livre des métiers*. Since the king was interested in reform, Étienne was encouraged to look for precedents from the reign of the grandfather, and thus the Livre throws light retrospectively on Paris in 1200.[72] Both ancient and customary, the regime governing the economy was fundamentally seigneurial. This meant that the king, in competition with the bishop and abbots as lords in the city, had the right to license and regulate the economy. Under such a seigneurial regime, whenever a lord enjoyed a right he could profit from it by exacting payments. Because those revenues belonged to him personally, he could also give, sell or enfeoff them to others. We shall see that this mentality complicated operation of the economy.

Figure 5. Bakers, lancet window at the cathedral of Chartres, bay 0, © Centre Andre Chastel, Paris.

The diet of Parisians in 1200 consisted of three staples—bread, meat (including fish) and wine—that, as staples, were subject to the lord's regulation. The diurnal petition of the Lord's prayer, "Give us this day our daily bread," had profound meaning for Parisians to whom the plaine de France just north of the walls was fabulously fertile in producing grain. The equipment needed, of course, were mills to grind grain into flour, turning under the arches of the Grand-Pont and Petit-Pont and elsewhere on the Seine; and ovens to bake the flour, numbering in the hundreds to feed the thousands of Parisians—many times more ovens than appear in the scattered notices of the contemporary sources. By the end of the reign Philip negotiated an agreement that prevented his prévôts from destroying private ovens and allowed the bakers and bourgeoisie to bake bread at home without paying the customary taxes,[73] but the normal regime was to grant licensed bakers a monopoly over the bread they baked in their ovens within the city. Sale by bakers from outside the walls was limited to Saturdays, and on Sundays Parisian bakers could sell their spoiled wares (hard, rat-infested, burned, etc.) before the cemetery of the Saints-Innocents or on the Cité between the Parvis of Notre-Dame and the church of Saint-Christophe. For the privilege of this monopoly each Wednesday the bakers paid a toll on the bread that they sold at their windows or ovens to a knight Thibaut le Maréchal. The latter was most likely supervised by Barthélemy de Roie, the king's royal chamberlain and trusted familiar who began his career as chief pantler (literally, supervisor of bread) of the royal court. This last office would have had accorded him jurisdiction over the bakers. In all events Thibaut sold the right to a Jew, Dieudonné de Bray in 1209, who in turn sold it to the monks of Joyenval at the request of Barthélemy, who was patron of the abbey.[74]

If bread was baked in ovens throughout the city, preparation of meat required concentrated quarters. The herds of steers, pigs and sheep required pasturage while waiting, sheds for slaughter and shops for distribution. Whereas the herds may have been penned in the field of Champeaux in previous reigns, after 1200 the butchers possessed pastures at Chelles outside Paris on the Marne.[75] The slaughterhouses were concentrated at the Grande Boucherie at the foot of the Grand-Pont on the Right Bank, where they profited from proximity to the Seine to evacuate their malodorous wastes through open ditches. The streets of the neighborhood retained names of

Figure 6. Butchers, lancet window at the cathedral of Chartres, bay 38, © Centre Andre Chastel, Paris.

the trade: *aux Bœufs* (beef), *aux Veaux* (calves), *l'Ecorcherie* (skinners), and *Tuerie* (slaughter houses). Finally, the meat was offered for sale at the house formerly belonging to Guerri the Changer, which provided twenty-three butchers' stalls at an unidentified site, most likely on the Right Bank near the Grande Boucherie,[76] but undoubtedly there were other undocumented markets as well. Headed by a "master of butchers" since 1146, the butchers' trade was precociously organized and often petitioned the king for their affairs. Early in the reign of Philip Augustus (1182), however, they claimed that the customs granted by the king's father and grandfather had not been written down and once again asked for confirmation.[77] Philip granted the butchers the right to buy, sell and handle living and dead animals in the city and the suburbs without paying tolls. They enjoyed an exclusive right to admit to membership in their trade. Three times a year they owed payment to whoever held supervision of the butchers in fief, and those butchers who cut beef or pork on Sundays paid a fee for their stalls to the prévôt.

The butchers also enjoyed the same exemption from tolls for buying and selling saltwater and freshwater fish. Fishing rights on the Seine were divided among (moving upstream) the abbot of Saint-Germain-des-Prés, the bishop and the king. The king's waters began with the Île-Notre-Dame and continued upstream to the confluence of the Marne, and then up the Marne to Saint-Maur-des-Fossés. Jurisdiction over fishing belonged to the family of Guérin du Bois, who had the right to sell licenses. At times the king granted fishing rights himself, such as under the Petit-Pont, Grand-Pont and Mi-Bray.[78]

Throughout the thirteenth century the Île-de-France was known for its fine wine; Saint-Denis, for example, possessed reputable vineyards at nearby Pierrefitte, Deuil and Groslay. Even within the walls, the vineyards of the Left Bank produced wine for local consumption. Simon de Poissy's wine-press at the ancient Roman palace of Thermes was only one among many.[79] Since local production could not match the demand of a populous city, most wine was imported through the major trade artery of the Seine. Noting the rapid increase of the bourgeoisie in 1192, as has been seen, the king granted the monopoly of the wine trade to residents of Paris, certified by neighbors of good repute. This commerce included sale from ships, wholesale or retail in taverns. No one else could transport wine by boat and unload in the city except those who were middlemen, involved in affairs in transit (that is, they bought wine from a boat and exported it by wagon without unloading at Paris).[80] By and large the retail market was confided to local taverns that were served by *crieries* (hawkers), men who circulated through the streets crying out the prices and quality of wines offered by the taverns. Their supervision was confided to Simon de Poissy, from a family of knights long favored by the Capetian kings. For this right Simon, of course, collected a fee.[81]

Beyond the staples, other local markets likewise supplied Parisian consumption. For example, at the Porte Baudoyer fish, meat and especially vegetables from the Marais were on sale, and near the Grand Châtelet a market known as the "Porte de Paris" supplied bread and freshwater fish.[82] From the beginning of the reign, the fair that had been established at Champeaux and protected by the construction of the Halles also served to provision the city.

Consumers of provisions at the capital included the king as well, when his court was in town. As lord, he enjoyed a traditional seigneurial right of the *droit de prise*. A royal "estimator" was authorized to name the price for goods purchased on the market, which could be set to the king's advantage or even gratuitously. Taking notice of the duties of this appraiser (*appreciator*), Pierre the Chanter concluded that if the official offered two sous for goods that were selling on the market for three, he was cheating the merchants and sinning in the performance of his duties. Few instances of this seigneurial right appear in the royal documentation—perhaps reduced by ecclesiastical hostility. The Chanter advised the appraiser to resign his position if he were expected to deviate from the market price—a policy that, of course, would render his function pointless.[83]

Crafts and Industry

Production of books is one industry that deserves to be treated first because it was the specialty of Paris and one in which its craftsmen excelled.[84] The assemblage of great numbers of ecclesiastics, masters and students as well as the royal court and rich bourgeoisie made the city a voracious consumer of books, which would in turn create conditions conducive to production. In the twelfth century manuscript codices were made by religious houses such as Saint-Victor not only for their own consumption but also for wealthy patrons. Production of a manuscript codex required multiple steps: a parchmenter to prepare the smooth parchment membranes; a scribe to copy the text with a careful hand; another scribe to fill in the rubrics and running heads in different colors. Then, if the manuscript was to be sold as a luxury item, a painter was hired to add the miniature illuminations and embellishments to the text, a binder to assemble the quires and enclose them in bindings and finally a merchant to market the finished book. At the outset there was confusion among the names of the agents (*scriptor*, *notarius* and *librarius*), as Pierre the Chanter remarked, but eventually librarius became the name of the entrepreneur for the whole production.[85]

Although no documentation has surfaced for the enterprise before 1240, numerous extant manuscripts demonstrate that full-scale production had begun by 1200. Three groups of manuscripts exhibit telltale signs of a virtual industry. A group of Bibles contain not only distinct uniformities but also penciled instructions to illuminators in the margins. Another group shows one particular illuminator imposing his characteristic stamp on a variety of manuscripts including Bibles, canon law texts, a copy of Ptolemy's *Almagest* (dated 1213) and a copy of Gilles de Paris's *Karolinus* composed for Prince Louis, as we have seen, in 1200. A third group of manuscripts can be attributed to an artisan who identified himself with the signature "Master Alexander made me." At the same time a massive project was under way at Paris to produce the *Bibles moralisées* for the royal court. From ca. 1215 to ca. 1225 scores of parchmenters, scribes and artists were hired to complete the first two volumes (Vienna, Austrian National Library mss. 2254 and 1179), containing in their present state 380 folios and nearly three thousand medallions of miniatures, to constitute the most ambitious illustrated manuscript project of its time. By their common traits, regularity and homogeneity these extant manuscripts embody division of labor and serial production indicative of a commercial industry.

Looking back over the enterprise from the midthirteenth century, the Franciscan scholar Roger Bacon appropriately called these artisans *illiterati* and *uxorati* ("unlettered and married men"). In Roger's view these terms were by no means to be taken as compliments, but they were code words for laymen, although many in the trade may have been clerics in minor orders. It is clear that they concentrated their operations on the rue Neuve-Notre-Dame, which Bishop Maurice de Sully had opened up to bring building materials to the cathedral, and on the rue des Écrivans in the parish of Saint-Sévérin on the Left Bank. In 1224 a certain Robert, identifying himself as "an illuminator and seller of books," and his wife set up shop (*operatorium*) on the rue Neuve. By the 1230s a wealthy bookseller, Emery d'Orléans, was also working there next to a certain Richard the Scribe. In 1231 an Alexander the Parchmenter died on that street where he had labored with his wife for many years. The documents that identify these parchmenters, scribes, illuminators and sellers are late, but because they indicate that this community was long established, doubtless it reached back to 1200. They also suggest a fluid interchange of functions among the various tradesmen. Because of the rarity of the name, Alexander the Parchmenter could have also been Alexander the Illuminator.

The best evidence for the industry was certainly its product. In the twelfth century Bibles were produced in multiple volumes, of large format, on heavy parchment and with large rounded script. Clearly intended for religious houses, their size prevented them from traveling far. In the first decade of the thirteenth century, a radically new Bible, known as the "Paris Bible," made its appearance on the market. It was in one volume, in very small format, on tissue-thin parchment, written in a small "gothic hand" (that is, with angular compressed letters and massive abbreviations) and rubricated with useful titles and running heads. Obviously this Bible was designed to be carried about, but its market is not entirely clear. It was not necessarily for the schools alone but for all customers who could afford them. For example, the Italian Cardinal Guala Bicchieri, who had studied at Paris at the end of the twelfth century and returned to France as papal legate in the first decade of the thirteenth, left a record of the books in his library when he died in 1227. Of the twenty-five Bibles in his collection he carefully took note of the script in which they were copied. Sixteen were Parisian, including "a most precious small Bible in Parisian script with gold letters and purple ornamentation."[86] Hundreds if not thousands of bibles have survived from the thirteenth century—more than any other commodity except for coins. To be sure, the Paris Bible was valuable and durable, thus ensuring its survival, but the scale of production remains impressive.

It was manufacture of woolen cloth, however, that was the primary industry of the central Middle Ages. Parisian cloth was exported to Genoa as early as the midtwelfth century. Because of the demands of the royal court, the prelates and the rich bourgeoisie, Paris offered an expanding market for fine cloth and luxury clothing.[87] The first merchants to appear at the market of the Champeaux were the merciers. When the king constructed the roofs and walls of the Halles, his intention was to protect fragile wares, especially those of the drapiers. His expulsion of the Jews in 1181 gave him an opportunity to bestow on these craftsmen some twenty-four houses in a section of the Île-de-la-Cité that was henceforth named after them. (The furriers likewise received other confiscated houses.) Centuries later the confraternity of the pelletiers dated their foundation not long after, in 1188.[88]

In need of copious supplies of water, fullers and dyers installed themselves along the banks of the Seine south of Saint-Gervais. Étienne Boileau noted the flourishing of the related crafts of tapestry makers and goldsmiths during Philip's reign, remarking that the latter were frequently employed by the church and nobility.[89] Among the professions the contemporary theologians evaluated for their moral failings, Robert of Courson included tailors of luxurious garments and makers of cosmetics, and Thomas of Chobham, makers of floral wreathes. Both treated manufacturers of dice and other games as well.[90] That the theologians found these trades worthy of treatment, seconded by their inclusion in Boileau's *Livre des métiers* two generations later, suggests that the luxury industry in Paris was flourishing around the year 1200.[91] Medieval clothing was made to last, thus serving often as payment of wages or objects of gift giving. For these reasons, as well as the obvious demands of poverty, there was an active market in used clothing. Boileau noted that in the time of King Philip the second-hand garment dealers (*fripiers*) could conduct their trade so long as they could prove that they had acquired their wares openly at the fairs of Saint-Germain-des-Prés, Saint-Lazare, Lendit and Saint-Denis and that the wares were not originally ecclesiastical garments.[92]

The names of streets appearing in the contemporary records indicate the activities of other trades. The nomenclature attests to exercise of these trades, but it is not entirely reliable for their location, because a street could retain a name long after the trade had moved away.[93] Along the Right Bank of the Seine, for example, we find the *Mortelleria* (mortar makers), the *Poteria* (potters) and the *Verrerie* (glassmakers) at Saint-Merri near the Place de Grève; and near the Grande Boucherie, other trades suggestive of leather, for example *Tanneria* (tanners) and *Courroirie* (belt makers). Around the Halles to the west of the rue Saint-Denis appeared the *Chanvrerie* (hemp dressers), the *Tonnellerie* (cooperage), the *Ferronnerie* (iron smiths) and the *Charronnerie* (cartwrights). This last neighborhood was laid out in perpendicular and parallel lines, indicating that the area was planned from the beginning unlike the undulating streets of earlier quarters.

These commercial and manufacturing trades owed the king a yearly payment, called the *hauban*, or a license to exercise a profession. In 1201 Philip set the fee at six sous (or a fraction thereof) to be paid each year on 1 November by his Parisian bourgeoisie. Étienne Boileau explained that the money commuted the traditional payment of one *muid* of wine to the royal cupbearer at the time of harvest, exacted from the bakers and butchers.[94]

In the case of the bakers Boileau noted that tradesmen outside the city were prohibited from selling within the walls because they did not pay the customary *tailles* (arbitrary taxes) and hauban (professional tax) due to the king. Moreover they did not owe duty on the nightwatch (*guet*).[95] Except for pregnant women and men over the age of sixty, this obligation fell on most trades. Boileau was careful to detail who served and who was exempt, noting in particular that from the time of King Philip the bakers, cutlers and tapestry makers did serve, but the goldsmiths were exempt because of their noble clients.[96] A police system of citizens, the nightwatch was entrusted with the security of the inhabitants within the walls every night after curfew.

Long-Distance Trade

Philip Augustus was the preponderant, if not the sole, lord of Paris, but as the crowned king he was also responsible for the peace of the whole realm of France. At his coronation at Reims he took an oath to preserve peace for the church of God and all Christian people. In ecclesiastical terms such peace involved providing protection for the unarmed (*inermes*), which in turn included traveling merchants. As Philip's royal domain expanded, he extended his responsibility. Long-distance trade was, of course, vital to his capital city.

As early as 1185 he offered safe conduct to the merchants of Flanders, Ponthieu and Vermandois when they journeyed to the Lenten fairs at Compiègne in the royal domain in times of war as well as in peace. When he acquired Artois in 1193, he promised the merchants of Ypres protection and safe conduct in his lands in return for payment of tolls, adding that if they were arrested for debt he would treat them as his bourgeoisie of Paris. After the great fiefs of Champagne came under his wardship in 1201, he extended royal protection to the countess's major asset, her flourishing international fairs at Troyes, Provins, Lagny and Bar-sur-Aube. In 1209 merchants from Italy and other lands were accorded safe conduct coming and going to the fairs, again on payment of their customary tolls, as if they were merchants of the king's lands. If they made themselves unwelcome, they nonetheless had three months to return home.[97] As the romancier Jean Renart phrased it, the merchants of the realm felt as safe as being in church.[98] Philip's letters lauded his defense of merchants, but he could be equally a predator, as the Parisian theologians were not afraid to point out. During the conflict between the English and French kings in which merchants were unjustly seized, for example, the Chanter discussed the moral responsibility of a Parisian bourgeois to whom Philip assigned disposal of confiscated goods for the king's profit.[99]

Protection, however, was rarely accorded without a price in the form of tolls or customs (*pedagia* and *consuetudines*). In addition to these cases, Philip confirmed the tolls of the merchants trading on the Somme from Corbie to the sea in 1198 and later regulated the tolls paid by merchants of Corbeil and Melun on the Seine. If they brought goods destined for Paris, however, they owed no tolls at Corbeil unless they proceeded further downstream. The ubiquity of these commercial taxes attracted the attention of Robert of Courson. He observed that tolls (*pedagium*), sales tax (*tonleatio*) and wagon tax (*roagium*) were originally justified when France was heavily wooded and castellans and princes provided protection from robbers and highwaymen to merchants traveling to fairs through their lands. The fees reimbursed the local lords for hiring armed sergeants to accompany the merchants. But now that, in 1200 the roads are no longer dangerous, the castellans should no longer exact these charges. To illustrate how local lords themselves continued to commit highway robbery, Robert cited a lord's decree that if a wagoner set down a cask of wine because of a broken wheel, he was nonetheless obliged to pay a toll as if he had unloaded it for sale.[100]

Along the waterways of the Seine, Marne, Oise and their tributaries, the long-distance merchants who received the king's greatest attention were naturally those of Paris. As early as 1121 Louis VI protected a group of boatmen dealing in wine. By 1170 they were called "water merchants" (*mercatores per aquam*) when Louis VII recorded their ancient privileges, which consisted chiefly of a monopoly over the trade on the Seine downstream between the bridges of Paris and Mantes. All others had to go into partnership with a Paris merchant to participate in this commerce. Merchants from Rouen without partners could proceed with empty boats only as far as the stream of Le Piq at Saint-Germain-en-Laye.[101] When Philip Augustus confirmed the monopoly over the wine trade to the residents of Paris in 1192, he envisaged the water merchants. Apparent competition from the Burgundian wine merchants resulted in an agreement in 1204–1205 over the extent of this Parisian monopoly. On the approaches from Burgundy the boundaries were set on the Yerre at Villeneuve-Saint-Georges, and on the Marne at Gournay. Downstream on the Seine Le Piq was retained and Argenteuil and Cormeilles were added. Within this enlarged region all other merchants must seek the participation of a merchant resident, one who was established, that is, "hansed" (*hansato*) at Paris.[102] Throughout his reign Philip intervened in behalf of these water merchants. Settling disputes between them and Gathon de Poissy in 1187 over the commerce of wine and salt at Maisons-Alfort (located between the fork of the Marne and the Seine), the king established a standard measure in stone for salt at the chapel of Saint-Leufroy near the Grand Châtelet that could serve in future negotiations.[103] In 1214 he set the rate for tolls of such standard commodities unloaded at Paris as wine, salt, herring, lumber, hay and grain. In exchange the water merchants agreed to improve the facilities of the Port de Paris between the Châtelet and the Place de Grève. A year later he authorized an agreement between the water merchants and the abbot of Saint-Denis over assignment of stalls at the fair of Lendit.[104] This fair, long held by the monks of Saint-Denis, constituted, with that at Champeaux instituted by the king, the two major fairs for traveling merchants of the Parisian region.

Finally at the end of the reign (1220) Philip granted to his water merchants hansed at Paris the crieries (wine hawkers) formerly assigned to Simon de Poissy, general supervision of measures, jurisdiction over minor crimes involving clubs and stones (reserving to himself high justice over robbers) and various sale taxes according to the customs of Paris. All of this came at the cost of an annual fee of 320 livres.[105] In effect the king conceded considerable powers over the commerce and justice of Paris to a group of merchants who had not yet become a municipal authority with recognizable organization and officers. The future prévôt of merchants had not yet appeared in the documentation, nor any fixed location for a municipality. In 1212, however, the king did acquire a house on the eastern side of the Place de Grève, called the "Maison aux Piliers," that became the seat of the Parisian municipality two centuries later.[106] It was not until the reign of Philip's grandson, however, that the disparate institutions, associations and personnel began to congeal. In 1263, for example, the confraternity of the merchants of Paris agreed to an "epitaph" with the Grand Confraternity of Notre-Dame over the payment of cens on various properties. Representing the former were échevins bearing the family names of Evroin, prévôt of the merchants of Paris, Barbette, Le Flamant and Bourdon. The lay prévôt of the Grand Confraternity of Notre-Dame was Pierre Thibaut.[107]

Around 1200 the walls of Philip Augustus sheltered a population of unprecedented size whose basic needs of shelter, food and clothing were supplied by the bourgeoisie, but it also contained wealthy churches and a royal court whose demand for luxury goods was satisfied by an elite bourgeoisie of merchants. The king not only regulated the conditions of the former but also encouraged the latter by providing protection and privileges for their trade. To the latter he began to assign authoritative functions over the city that reinforced the status of the bourgeois elite.

The Merchant and the Theologians

Installed at the cloister of Notre-Dame to the north of the cathedral, theologians enjoyed a front seat on the commercial life of Paris. They observed the numerous ships plying the Seine and unloading their wares at the Port de Paris, the buying and selling of goods on the Place de Grève directly across the river, and the activities of the money changers on the Grand-Pont downstream. As churchmen they were keenly aware of the great distrust that the mercantile world inherited from Biblical and ancient classical texts, distrust that was encapsulated by formulae in canon law as "it is difficult to transact commercial affairs without committing sin," "buying cheap to sell dear was shameful gain" and "no merchant can please God."[108] Contemporary Roman lawyers, however, offered a precise analysis of the functions of the merchant that would serve to absolve them from these reproaches. Both the canon lawyers and the theologians of the Chanter's circle began to adopt these distinctions of the Roman lawyers, thus producing a growing literature that was summarized by Thomas of Chobham. A preliminary task was to differentiate the merchant from the craftsman. The craftsman bought raw materials, transformed them into products through additional expenses and labor and sold them for a profit justified by his contribution of the expenses and labor. The merchant, in contrast, made few material changes to the product but bought the goods cheaply in areas of abundance and sold them more dearly in areas of scarcity. The resulting profit was justified by labor and the expenses of transportation and distribution.[109] As with all the commercial professions, two besetting sins plagued the merchants. In addition to a strong proclivity toward greed, merchants were unusually tempted to commit fraud to realize profit. But deceptions involved in defective goods, fraudulent measures and other chicaneries implicated butchers, bakers and other tradesmen as well.

The Roman lawyers, followed by the canonists, divided commercial activity according to well-defined contracts such as sale (*emptio-venditio*), barter (*permutatio*), lease-hire (*locatio-conductio*) and lending (*mutuum*), of which the first pertained primarily to merchants.[110] According to the Roman lawyers a contract of sale came into being when a price (*pretium*) was freely agreed on by a buyer and seller. If this price was without fraud, it became the just price and could not be rescinded under normal circumstances. (The only exception to this agreed or market price was that set by the decree of constituted authority, thus creating an official price.) The chief legal remedy to the market price open to buyers and sellers was that of *laesio enormis*, that is, the contract of sale could be rescinded when the agreed price differed by more than double or less than half the just (market) price. The canonists accepted the Roman-law theory of laesio enormis, but the theologians hesitated. Thomas of Chobham recognized the Roman-law remedy (*leges humanas*) but asserted that any deviation from the just price—even a penny—should be restituted according to divine law.[111] Although the theologians declined the remedy of laesio enormis, they nonetheless accepted the Roman-canon law definition of the just price. Since prices differed according to time and place, they could be determined only in specific cases. Accepting the regime of free bargaining, the lawyers agreed that "a thing was valued at that price for which it could be commonly sold." In other words, the just price was the going or current price of the market, which included both free, competitive prices and regulated prices. Because Pierre the Chanter accepted this regime, he was able to advise the princely appraiser to respect the market price as he discharged the droit de prise. Although the theologians accepted the legal definition of the just price, they made little effort to reconcile the rationale of the free market with the observation that a merchant's profits depended on his expenses and labor. Robert of Courson approached this problem when he advised a merchant to observe the fluctuations of the markets. If he valued his wares at ten sous and estimated his labor at an additional sous, he could wait until he found a market offering eleven sous for his sale.[112] Implicit was the principle that the current price will remunerate expenses and labor; otherwise the market will not be supplied.

Credit

Credit is indispensable to any economy, no matter how primitive. Peasants require seed and tools at planting to be reimbursed later at harvest; nobles, cash before departing on a crusade; and ecclesiastics, advanced funds for building churches. But townsmen engaged in industry and trade had the greatest need for credit, for example, to purchase raw materials before production and sale of finished goods and to buy and sell simultaneously before final sale at the fairs. Such needs were rarely noted in the royal and ecclesiastical documentation generated at Paris, but the theologians were acutely sensitive to all aspects of credit because of the general ecclesiastical prohibition of usury. According to Roman law, any profit derived from a loan (mutuum) was defined as usury (usura). (Technically speaking, the economic concept of "interest" had not yet been formulated.) Inspired by the Old Testament strictures against usury and reinforced by the New Testament command "to lend freely hoping for nothing in return" (date mutuum, nichil sperans), the theologians were adamant that anything exceeding the principal of a loan was usurious (quodcumque sorti accedit). Definition and application of the usury prohibition generated enormous discussion among the canonists. Among the theologians at Paris, Pierre de Poitiers, chancellor of Notre-Dame, preferred to leave it there,[113] but Pierre the Chanter's casuistic approach encouraged his fellow theologians to engage fully in the discussion. From their writings we have the clearest picture of credit at Paris in 1200. Their chief arguments against usury were threefold: it constituted gain unearned without labor, it amounted to unwarranted sale of time that belonged exclusively to God and, as shall be seen, it guaranteed a profit that was free of risk. But the theologians were less interested in discussing the rationale against lending for profit than investigating current commercial practice to uncover disguises for the forbidden profit. Although temptation to commit usury permeated all levels of society, we shall limit ourselves to the theologians' discussion of mercantile practices relevant to the bourgeois economy of Paris.

A prominent example was the credit sale, which combined sale with a loan. If the contract price of the sale was set higher than the present current price for a delay in payment, it could be a disguise for usury. The Chanter cited the case of a buyer short on cash who agreed to a price higher than the present price in exchange for a delay of payment until the next fair. Such practices were current in the cloth trade. Courson exclaimed that hardly a merchant could be found who did not sell an ell of cloth worth ten sous for twenty-five because of the payment delay.[114] Following the decretal of Pope Alexander III, the theologians decided that although the formal features of the contract were legitimate, if the seller was certain to gain from the delay of time then the transaction was unlawful. If, however, there was reasonable doubt about the future price, the factor of risk excused the contract.

The bearing of risk therefore justified the profit. At a more practical level, Thomas of Chobham advised that a "good man" experienced in fluctuations of the market could, after considering the time and circumstances, decide whether reasonable risk was present.[115]

If uncertainty in the future price exonerated a credit sale, Robert of Courson, continued, then the risk of committing one's capital to fortune should also be considered. The problem with usury is that it involves a loan (mutuum) that transfers ownership. Employing pseudo-etymology, the theologians derived mutuum from *meum-tuum* (what is mine is yours). When one loans money, ownership is transferred and therefore risk is assumed, because the lender is obligated to return the full sum no matter the circumstances. The immunity from risk in a mutuum makes it usurious to profit from the transaction. But the mercantile profession is beset with innumerable risks: of shipwreck, piracy, instability of prices and all the uncertainties of the commercial market. If risk is the chief problem in credit, the solution is not a loan but partnership.

We remember that all foreign merchants wishing to trade in wine and other goods within the Paris region were obliged to form partnerships (*societates*) with a Parisian water merchant. After Normandy was annexed to the royal domain, King Philip confirmed an agreement between the bourgeoisie of Paris and Rouen over the commercial partnership (*societatem mercature*). The issue at stake was how the oath between the partners was to be administered.[116] Although the features of the Parisian partnerships were not revealed, the Italian merchants of the twelfth century devised a series of partnerships called *commenda, collegantia* and *societas maris*. These involved various combinations of two or more merchants who contracted to combine their money and skills in a venture and shared their profits or losses according to an original contract. What distinguished these partnerships from loans was the factor of risk. The canonists paid little attention to these contracts, but at Paris Pierre the Chanter, Robert of Courson and Thomas of Chobham were the first to treat the features of the partnership. They condemned a safe form of the partnership whereby a partner was guaranteed return on his investment despite the outcome of the venture, as practiced by the notorious Flemish usurer William Cade a generation earlier. If, however, all partners shared in the losses as well as the gains, the theologians agreed that the factor of risk legitimated the profits.[117] Partnerships thereby afforded a socially beneficial function of risk bearing.

Currency and Exchange

Since France was divided into multiple lordships, different currencies were minted by local lords throughout the realm. In 1200 at Paris silver coins circulated from England, Anjou, Flanders and Touraine, including even a gold coin from Byzantium (the bezant). The principal currency, however, was that of the king of France minted at Paris, Montreuil-sur-Mer, Bourges, Sens and numerous other places in the royal domain. It consisted of two silver coins, the denier and the obol (half-denier); both carried the inscription "Philip king of the French" on one side and a central cross and the inscription "City of Paris" on the other. Later the denier tournois, minted at Saint-Martin-de-Tours was accepted along with Paris money at the rate of five to four. The silver coin was the only one minted; the sous (equal to twelve deniers) and the livre (twenty sous) were solely fictitious monies of account.[118]

This multiplicity of coinage created a widespread need for foreign exchange not only in local markets at the Place de Grève but especially for the long-distance merchants traveling to the fairs of Lendit and Champagne. At Paris exchange was concentrated on the Grand-Pont (later known as Pont-aux-Changeurs) where Ebroin le Changeur had a house and stall. Even the chapter of Notre-Dame acquired an exchange table on the bridge in 1204.[119] Manual exchange—that is, exchanging one currency directly for another—practiced on the bridge drew a comment from Stephen Langton. If a money changer gave 39 sous for a mark of silver worth 40, the difference could be justified as his commission, provided it was moderate and according to the regulations of the trade.[120] Equally important was the exchange that took place at the fairs. Lasting over days, these occasions often required merchants to buy before they sold and settle their accounts at the end, and in different currencies. Robert of Flamborough, who composed a penitential at Saint-Victor, examined these problems and concluded that merchants who demanded more for a delay of final payment were not committing usury but were merely providing a convenience at the fair.[121]

Finally, the sophisticated techniques of the Italian merchants in contemporary fairs created an instrument of exchange by letter, later known as a letter of credit. Long-distance merchants could thereby transfer funds deposited in one currency to be paid out later in another. Because of the passing of time between the two transactions the letter involved credit as well as exchange. Furthermore, the letter of credit could also involve a "dry exchange"; that is, one had the option of finally paying in the original currency but at a sum that was higher than what was deposited. This contract was presumably usurious because money was lent over time at a fixed and certain rate. At Paris both Robert of Courson and Thomas of Chobham were aware of the features of the letter of credit and vaguely of dry exchange, but they doubted their legitimacy despite the fact that the pope often confirmed such contracts with his seal when prelates transferred money to Rome.[122] The testimony of these theologians demonstrates that the latest techniques of foreign exchange, with their potential for extending credit, were known to Parisians.

The Fight Against Usury

Following a long tradition, the papacy renewed sanctions against the practice of usury throughout the twelfth century. The Lateran Council of 1139 deprived usurers of the sacraments of the Church; the subsequent Lateran Council of 1179 extended the penalties to manifest (public) usurers who were further denied Christian burial. As cardinal legate, Robert of Courson repeated the sanctions in the local councils he held at Paris (1213), Rouen (1214) and Montpellier (1214). Foulques de Neuilly's preaching missions from 1195 to 1200, which were so effective in converting prostitutes, were directed equally toward usurers. Imitating his success, Courson, Stephen Langton and Pierre de Roissy joined forces in preaching against usurers in the northern region of Arras and Saint-Omer. The royal historiographer Rigord was impressed with Foulque's ability to convince repentant usurers to do restitution for their ill-gotten gains.[123] According to canon law, usurers, unlike prostitutes, were required to make full restitution of their profits. Since prostitutes earned their money through their labor, they were not obligated to do restitution to their victims, but usurers were not so absolved because of the absence of labor. Owing to the complexities of commercial life, restitution of usury was an extraordinarily complicated process that generated a massive literature among the canonists and the Parisian theologians prone to casuistry. One question, however, was of particular relevance to Paris in 1200 because of the building boom, particularly at Notre-Dame. Could usurers make contributions from their ill-gotten gains to the building of churches in expiation of their sins? This question applied to prostitutes as well. Pierre the Chanter noted that certain women actively engaged in the trade wished to donate chalices and stained-glass windows to the church. Elaborating on the incident, Thomas of Chobham specified that the women proposed a splendid window to Notre-Dame. After considerable discussion, the theologians agreed it could be accepted if it were done discreetly, but Thomas reported that the bishop finally refused the money since it would appear to have given approval to the women's conduct.[124]

Amidst voluminous discussion, the Parisian theologians, following the canonists, agreed that usurers, unlike prostitutes, could not contribute to pious projects until they had restored their usurious profits to their victims. The canonist Huguccio explained that usury was like theft and did not transfer ownership of gains to the wrongdoer; therefore, the usurer could not donate them in alms. The Chanter was involved in two cases that pertained directly to Paris. A certain layman by the name of Reginald was authorized by the papacy to preach publicly in churches, homes and squares throughout the city and received contributions for the Hôtel-Dieu, among which were those from acknowledged usurers. Pierre wrestled with arguments pro and con for keeping the donations but came to no resolution in the extant version of his *Summa*. A second case was reported by Caesar of Heisterbach, however, that clarified the Chanter's hesitation. A certain exceedingly rich usurer named Thibaut became repentant for his sins and sought advice from Bishop Maurice de Sully on how he might atone for them. Preoccupied with building his new cathedral, the bishop succumbed to temptation and suggested that Thibaut might make donations to the construction. The usurer Thibaut was rightfully suspicious of the advice and turned to the Chanter for a second opinion. Because of Pierre's aversion to grandiose buildings, his advice was predictable and conformed to current canonist opinion: Thibaut should restore first to all whom he had defrauded before he could make his contribution. The usurer sent a crier throughout the city announcing that he was prepared to make restitution. A balance remained after this exercise, so he was able to give with a clear conscience.[125] Because Bishop Maurice and the bourgeois Thibaut le Riche were prominent contemporaries, the public could not miss the identification.

Both Robert of Courson and Stephen Langton addressed the precise question posed by Thibaut to Maurice. Rehearsing arguments pro and con, again they had difficulty in coming to an unambiguous conclusion, but at the council of Paris (1213) Robert decreed that any priest or other religious person who knowingly received alms from usurers without sufficient restitution was excommunicated and suspended from office. But what about all of the churches, hermitages, Hôtels-Dieu and leprosaria already constructed with usurious money? Should they be destroyed? Robert devised two replies. The first and more consistent was to call for a general council of bishops under the presidency of the pope, who would decree that all men should work physically and spiritually for their bread. Under this regime brigands, usurers and the indolent would be removed from society, and churches could receive alms from those honest people who remained. Recognizing the highly utopian character of this proposal, Robert turned to a second solution that distinguished whether the church in question was consecrated. If so, the prelate should seek to redeem the proportion that was due to usury by restoring to the victims. If unconsecrated, it should either be redeemed or destroyed and the proceeds given to the defrauded. In fact, Robert approved of dismantling several prominent leprosaria and Hôtels-Dieu to dissuade construction of new ones. No one can live in a state of salvation who knowingly and willfully lives off the proceeds of usury.[126] The draconian character of Robert's opinions and conciliar measures produced an immediate reaction. Philip Augustus wrote Pope Innocent III protesting that the legate's measures against usurers were too severe and lacking papal authorization. When the legate convoked a new council at Bourges in 1215, the prelates refused to attend, again protesting, according to one chronicler, the severity of his measures.[127]

This lively theological discussion about usurers contributing to the construction of churches was immediately pertinent to contemporary Parisians, who observed the rising vaults of Notre-Dame, but the cartularies and archives of the cathedral are remarkably mute on where the bishops of Paris, Maurice and Eudes, found the funds for their extraordinary project. Only the obituary of the chapter noted that King Louis VII bequeathed 200 livres to the building in 1179 and Bishop Maurice 100 livres for the new roof in 1196, both derisory sums in comparison to the full cost.[128] The discussions of the Chanter's circle suggest two contradictory explanations. It is possible that the vigorous campaign of churchmen against accepting usurious donations effectively discouraged the wealthy bourgeoisie from contributing to the enterprise, in which case the construction was financed largely from other sources, most notably the chapter's income from its vast properties.[129] By contrast, the theological campaign effectively drove the contributions of Thibaut le Riche and other bourgeoisie underground so that they were not reported in the church's documentation. In that case, the construction of Notre-Dame did, in fact, benefit from the vigorous commercial life at Paris around 1200.[130]

Manifest Usurers: The Exceptional Status of the Jews

If the Parisian bourgeoisie found it difficult to extricate themselves from the opprobrium attached to usury, one trade did qualify unequivocally and without controversy for condemnation. This was the pawnbroker, who was also known as a manifest usurer because the shop where he lent money at usury and secured by pledges was open, known and accessible to all. Some Christians practiced the trade, but it was largely in the hands of the Jews, who benefited from special status. As non-Christians they were both immune to the restrictions of the Church and under the special protection of the king as well. In the year 1200 the scope of their money-lending business was enormous. We shall see that a contemporary inquest into the money owed them reached the figure of 250,000 livres parisis, more than twice the estimated annual royal income for the fiscal year 1202–1203.

The reign of Philip Augustus's father, Louis VII, may be considered the golden age of Jewry in the kingdom of France. Not only was there a flourishing community at Troyes that boasted the leading school of rabbinical studies at the time, but at Paris the Jews were even more numerous. Densely settled on the Île-de-la-Cité, they left their name on the rue de la Juiverie long after their departure. The royal chronicler Rigord complained that they owned nearly half the city where they grew rich on lending money with impunity. Moreover, they owed their prosperity to the benign protection and support of their lords, the count of Troyes and the French king.[131] Rigord may have exaggerated their success at Paris, but his comments echoed current opinion.

Then suddenly, with little warning, a violent storm burst upon the Jewish community of Paris.[132] Beginning in February 1180—even before Louis VII was dead—and lasting for two years, the young Philip hurled three successive thunderbolts at his father's Jews. He first captured them in their synagogues on the Sabbath, seized their gold, silver and clothing, and then, on the advice of his ecclesiastical advisor, Brother Bernard de Vincennes, canceled all Christian debts, keeping a fifth for himself. Finally he expelled all the Jews from the royal domain and confiscated their property, allowing them to sell only their movables. Rigord attributes pious motivation to these brutal measures, but the profit incentive cannot be concealed. An English chronicler reported that the Jews paid 15,000 marks (31,500 livres parisis) to ransom the initial confiscation that contributed to Philip's war chest against his enemies during the first decade of his reign.[133] Royal charters attest that the confiscations on the Île-de-la-Cité also benefited Christian neighbors. The synagogue was converted into the parish church of Sainte-Marie-Madeleine, and the densely settled houses of the Juiverie were given to the drapiers and the pelletiers.[134]

The policy of expulsion and confiscation, however, deprived Philip of whatever revenue his father could have expected from the Jews. For their part, the Parisian Jews had joined their co-religionists elsewhere, but principally in the lands of the count of Troyes. In 1198, the king had second thoughts and readmitted his Jews to Paris, "much against common opinion and his own decree," Rigord complained.[135] Returning to his father's policies, Philip signed a treaty with the count of Troyes that made it possible for his Jews to return, and the two lords respected the separate jurisdictions over the Jews in their lands. By 1202–1203 Jean Cherchelarron was named keeper of the king's Jews and reported from them an annual income of 1,250 livres, barely 1 percent of the royal income.[136] Evidently the reestablishment was too recent to produce much revenue. Since their property on the island was in Christian hands, the returning Jews settled on the Right Bank near the church of Saint-Bon and on the Left Bank, where they established a cemetery between rue de la Harpe and rue Garlande. At least a half-dozen tombstones have been recovered from the cemetery that display with large, clear inscriptions the names of the deceased.[137]

In the year 1200, therefore, the newly returned Jews once again began to prosper under a regime that had been perfected by King Henry II in England and Normandy and was adopted by Philip's father as well. Its chief features were outlined in an ordinance (*stabilimentum*) of 1206, an agreement with the countess of Troyes that reestablished the traditional regime of royal protection and regulation of "our Jews" (*nostri judei*), as Philip called them, not unlike the epitaph "our bourgeoisie" for Parisian townsmen.[138] Prévôts of the Jews were appointed throughout the royal domain to help them collect their debts, later aided by two sworn men who possessed a seal for certifying their loan contracts (the Parisian Jews had their own seal) and a scribe for writing them down. Because business increased, the seals were later limited to contracts in excess of 60 sous, but duplicate copies were kept of the transactions. By offering the services of protection, supervision, certification and record keeping the king assisted the Jews in managing their lending business, for which he naturally demanded a fee in the form of tailles or arbitrary taxes. In 1217 the Jews returned him 7,550 livres and in 1221 8,600 livres, on the order of a sevenfold increase over 1202–1203.

Before 1212, and probably around 1210, two documents were transcribed into the royal Register that illuminate the economic position of the Jews in Paris around 1200. One was a list of 26 Jews from the Île-de-France and 14 from Normandy who "will remain in the châtelet of the Petit-Pont"; the other was an inquest into the debts owed to the Jews. It is not clear whether the first records an imprisonment in another effort to despoil them; if so, it was short-lived and the financial benefit to the king has left no trace. If the context is murky, the two texts are a remarkable revelation of the economic and social position of the Jews.[139] As has been noted, the inquest discovered that the debts owed to Jews in the royal domain totaled 251,900 livres parisis, more than twice the annual royal income. Four of the individuals detained in the Petit-Châtelet also figure in the inquest. Moses of Sens had the greatest business with 60,000 livres, followed by two brothers from Paris, Dieudonné and Heliot, with 30,000 livres between them. The remaining Jews from Paris accounted for an additional 12,500 livres. Consequently this small group of individuals administered loans amounting to nearly as much as the king realized in ordinary annual revenues a decade before. Thanks to the record keeping required by royal supervision, estimates of the credit business were possible. Although no other global figures survive except for the royalty, it is hard to imagine other contemporary trades in a position to compete with Jewish lending. The ubiquity of Jewish lending appears throughout the royal inquests and charters. Pierre, count of Nevers, for example, owed Moses 800 livres and Henri de Sully, from the same family as Eudes, the bishop of Paris, owed him 300. The king bought property from knights so that the owners could pay off their Jewish debts; Dieudonné de Braye, we remember, held the tolls of bread from Paris, before he sold them to the abbey of Joyenval; and the wife of Moses of Sens, later married to Samuel de Bray, held extensive properties at Gonesse to the north of Paris.[140] Wherever local charters cast light, the Jewish lender appears.

Since the king and the Jews were clearly complicit in the lending business, it is difficult to judge who profited most. Recognizing the situation, Pierre the Chanter was wont to designate all usurers as the "king's Jews"—not only laymen but also clerics who were known as "our clerical Jews and our clerical usurers." They became the king's leeches, sucking funds from their victims and disgorging them into the royal coffers. (We should keep in mind, however, that the metaphor of the leech referred to the common medical procedure of bloodletting, which was considered therapeutic and not necessarily harmful.) Aware of English royal practices, Robert of Courson and Thomas of Chobham warned that kings could not appropriate Jewish property or earnings without first restoring what was due to the victims who were forced to pay usury.[141] This advice would have prevented Philip from profiting from his earlier despoliations as well. The problem of conscience nonetheless remained troublesome. How could the king encourage Jews to perform what was immoral for Christians?

As manifest usurers, Jews diversified their practices, which extended from demanding security for loans in the form of gold or silver vessels, rich clothing and other precious objects as did pawnbrokers, to demanding security in the form of land or other sources of income for larger loans, to demanding pledges or cautions of third parties who guaranteed the loans. For all these loans they required compensation at a high rate. Their operations covered the credit market from consumer to investment loans.

Ecclesiastical and moral considerations nonetheless prompted Philip Augustus to introduce reforms into Jewish lending practices. The ordinance of 1206 set the rate of usury at two deniers per week (or 43 percent annually if not compounded) and forbade compounding during the first year. (This figure has been the rate endemic to pawnbrokers throughout the history of the profession.) In addition, restrictions were placed on securities, forbidding, for example, use of ecclesiastical ornaments and goods suspected of being stolen. A second general ordinance in 1219 repeated many of the earlier provisions but added a clause that protected those who were without land or other sustaining movables and were forced to work with their hands. They were allowed three years to pay off their debts. Furthermore, canons and monks were forbidden to borrow from Jews without the expressed consent of their prelates.[142] However, in November 1223, four months after Philip's death, Louis VIII began to remove royal participation from Jewish usury in a third major ordinance. The king's officials, for example, were no longer allowed to seal Jewish contracts and keep records of loans over five years old.[143] To Philip's godly grandson, Louis IX, fell the complicated and painful task of extricating the king from the Jewish credit market. The churchmen and moralists of the Chanter's generation had finally won their argument that left the Jews on their own and without royal protection. The result was to make way for the Lombards and other Christian usurers to compete with the Jews in the credit market.

Lords of Paris

As the principal city of the royal domain, Paris likewise became the capital of the king's government, as shall be seen. Philip ruled Paris from his towers at the royal palace on the western end of the Cité, the Louvre just outside the walls and the two châtelets guarding the Grand- and Petit-Pont on the Right and Left Banks. His chief agents were the prévôts, who became prévôt-baillis in 1219. But like most medieval cities, the king had competitors to his lordship even in his own capital. Although he had responsibility for keeping the peace of the Left Bank, as seen in the student disturbances of 1200, he divided his jurisdiction principally with the abbots of Sainte-Geneviève and Saint-Germain-des-Prés in unspecified ways. His chief competitor, however, was the bishop facing him from his palace and cathedral on the eastern end of the Cité, who not only divided jurisdiction with the king on the island but held claims to the Clos-Bruneau on the Left Bank. On the Right Bank the bishop's jurisdiction extended beyond the western walls to the Marais in areas called Bourg-l'Evêque and Culture-l'Evêque as well as along two major highways called the "Royal and Public Roads." Within the walls he claimed every third week, known as the "Bishop's week," to collect tolls in the markets of the Champeaux. No friction has surfaced, in reading the sources, between the bishop and king until the end of the reign, when Philip ordered two inquests into the bishop's jurisdiction. In 1222 the king and bishop came to an agreement called a *forma pacis* that regulated and confirmed the items under contention.[144] Except for the aforementioned items, Philip's rights to jurisdiction over the Right Bank, including the major pleas of justice and night watch, were confirmed. The major exceptions were those the king had granted to the water merchants over hawkers, measures, sales taxes and petty justice, but since this group had not yet achieved a discernable organization they impinged little on royal jurisdiction at Paris. Despite its vigorous economy, its celebrated church and its flourishing schools, the largest city north of the Alps was allowed little semblance of self-government. A commune that might contest the king's power was never countenanced. This was the price Parisians paid for residing at the capital of Capetian power.

CHAPTER TWO

The Faces of Pierre the Chanter and Philip Augustus and the Hidden Visages of Women

Of the 50,000-some inhabitants of the royal city, not one composed an autobiography that has survived and would reveal his or her personality. The days of the self-revelations of Abélard and Heloise, Guibert de Nogent, Suger of Saint-Denis or Pierre the Venerable of the early twelfth century had disappeared. The sole exception from the years surrounding 1200 was composed by a Norman-Welshman Gerald and entitled "Concerning the deeds done by himself" (*De rebus a se gestis*). This archdeacon from south Wales and courtier at the royal court of England recounted his thwarted ambition to obtain the bishopric of Saint-David. The garrulous narrative of his travels and activities included two residences in Paris, one in 1165 when as a young student of arts he witnessed the rejoicings at the birth of the future King Philip, the other in the late 1170s when he recounted a lecture he delivered before the masters of canon law. Although these random events highlighted two noteworthy concerns at Paris—dynastic politics and the schools—Gerald of Wales, the disappointed habitué of the English court, could scarcely be numbered among Parisians.[1]

From the thousands of individuals who lived within the walls, the bourgeoisie are known only through their names, occupations and property

recorded in the contemporary documentation. Traces of the clerical population of the churches and schools were likewise limited to the same sparse
information except when they were promoted to the prelacy of cathedrals
or abbeys. Among the bishops, a few anecdotes were recounted about Maurice de Sully that might suggest his personal traits, as shall be seen, but
most information is limited to his official duties.[2] Étienne, abbot of Sainte-
Geneviève, for his part left a collection of letters that reports the condition
of the schools before he left Paris to become the bishop of Tournai in 1192
but reveals less about himself.[3] Again, the abbots of the other monasteries
and the deans of the collegiate churches survive only as names. If we seek to
uncover the individualized faces of Parisians within this obscurity, our best
candidates are two figures: a cleric, Pierre the Chanter, and a king, Philip
Augustus. Naturally, no single individual can adequately stand for a diversified population, but these two exceptional personalities did reside at Paris,
played significant roles in the lives of their contemporaries and are accessible to us. As chanter of Notre-Dame and a distinguished theologian, Pierre
attracted the notice of contemporary chroniclers and left his imprint on
the ecclesiastical records, but most important he revealed his forceful personality in classroom lectures, disputes and especially a treatise, the *Verbum
abbreviatum*. On the other hand, Philip left no written testimony that was
not redacted by the clerics of his chancery; nonetheless, as king of France,
he was of central interest to the royal historiographers and also fascinated
the English chroniclers who warily observed his maneuvers against their
own sovereign. Although the real Philip may remain an enigma behind the
formulas of chancery texts and the adulation of royal history, we nonetheless observe him as his court wished him to be seen. Despite these severe
limitations, Pierre and Philip present the two most distinctive faces available
in Paris around 1200. As king of the realm and master of the schools, they
likewise personify the city's dual importance at that time.

Pierre the Chanter

The Chanter's career can be sketched from extant church documentation
and chronicles.[4] Born to a family of knights at Hodenc-en-Bray in the
Beauvasis, Pierre had a brother Gautier, lord of Hodenc, and two nephews,
Pierre and Raoul. (The last-named may well have been the Raoul de Hodenc
who wrote Arthurian romances and moral treatises in vernacular verse, but
the connection with the Chanter is not yet clear.)[5] Pierre likewise possessed

a house in nearby Gerberoy, the seat of a family of *vîdames* who supported the bishops of Beauvais in the turbulent politics of this border territory situated between Beauvais, Gournay and Gisors. Troubled for a century, Gerberoy was last besieged by the Anglo-Normans in 1197, this time by Count John, brother of King Richard. Pierre received his early schooling at Reims under Master Robert *de Camera* before the latter became bishop of Amiens in 1165. When the young scholar left Reims for Paris he was already enjoying financial support from a prebend in that chapter. His arrival at the royal capital as a master must have occurred before 1170 because he was reported to have participated in a public debate over Thomas Becket, archbishop of Canterbury, which, we shall see, would have lost its controversy after Becket's martyrdom in that year. In all events he was chosen chanter of Notre-Dame in 1183 and thereafter was commonly identified by the title "chanter of Paris" (*cantor Parisiensis*). Although he never advanced within ecclesiastical orders beyond the rank of deacon, he was responsible for supervision of the choir of Notre-Dame, but not of the liturgy, which he appears to have delegated to a subchanter.

As the second-ranking dignity of the chapter of Paris, Pierre was active in the public affairs of the church.[6] Most of these concerned the business of the chapter in and around Paris, but he was also called on to serve as judge and arbitrator in cases involving other churches. The popes appointed Pierre as judge-delegate in at least fourteen cases that required traveling to places as distant as Cambrai, Châlons-sur-Marne and Troyes. In at least ten of these missions he collaborated with his Parisian colleague, Master Étienne, abbot of Sainte-Geneviève. The best known and riskiest occurred in 1196 when Pope Celestine III assigned him to a panel to judge the king's attempt to separate from Queen Ingeborg of Denmark. It is possible that Pierre's journeys took him to Rome in 1179 to attend the Third Lateran Council called by Pope Alexander III (he presents vivid vignettes of its sessions). A brief reference in a letter of Innocent III reveals that Pierre returned to Rome at the end of his life (1196–1197), but the nature of the business is not revealed.

These activities and responsibilities naturally singled him out as an apt candidate to the prelacy. The first opportunity came in 1190 when the chapter of Tournai elected him as their bishop. Apparently a procedural irregularity beclouded the election because his colleague and friend Étienne, abbot of Sainte-Geneviève, was recruited to write a strong letter in his support.[7] When the outcome was finally revealed, however, it was not Pierre but Étienne himself who received the post. Whatever the Chanter's disappointment, a more rewarding opportunity presented itself in 1196 when, according to the English chronicler Ralph of Coggeshall, the chapter of Paris with the consent of the king chose him to succeed to Bishop Maurice de Sully at Paris, but this time it was Pierre who declined the honor, citing its heavy burdens.[8] Still his merits could not be ignored. The following year Guillaume, archbishop of Reims, urged him to accept the chapter's invitation to return as dean to the city of his former schooling and where he still possessed a prebend. He could not resist this appeal to his loyalties. Pierre took the road to Reims, but intimations of mortality intervened. Approaching Soissons, he broke his journey at the nearby Cistercian abbey of Longpont. Taking pleasure in some books that he had brought along, he drew up his testament, donned the habit of a Cistercian, commended himself to the prayers of the brothers and expired on 25 September 1197. Dying "in the odor of sanctity," his memory was cherished at the abbey of Longchamps until the two world wars destroyed what was left of his grave.

Pierre the Chanter's enduring fame did not result from a public career, but from teaching theology at the cloister of Notre-Dame.[9] For the year 1194 the chronicler Otto of Saint-Blaise noted three prominent theologians active at Paris: Pierre, chanter of Paris; Alain de Lille, a versatile author; and Prévotin, chancellor of Notre-Dame.[10] In terms of number of manuscript pages and subsequent theological influence, the Chanter's professional production far outweighed the other two. By adopting Pierre's own classification of theological practice, one can sort his surviving works into three major categories: lecturing, disputing and preaching. His lectures consisted of commentaries to the books of the Bible according to the literal, allegorical (doctrinal) and tropological (moral) interpretations. Whereas former theologians limited themselves largely to the Psalms and the epistles of Paul, Pierre was the first theologian to present commentaries to all of the books of the Old and New Testaments. His disputations or questiones were collected in the *Summa de sacramentis et anime consiliis*. The modern edition (which is not entirely complete) runs to four substantial volumes of questions organized according to the scheme of the seven sacraments, with penance and the attendant practice of confession taking the largest part. A specialized treatise, the *De tropis loquendi*, used logical tools to resolve Biblical contradictions. Both the lectures and the disputations were recorded and assembled from his classroom through the cooperation of the master and unidentified students who served as reportatores and wrote down the proceedings on wax tablets later to be recopied on parchment. Although Pierre enjoyed a reputation as a famous preacher in the thirteenth century, none of his sermons have survived. Their place is taken by his most popular work, the *Verbum abbreviatum*, surviving in at least three versions and more than ninety manuscripts. It consisted of a florilegium of scripture, patristic opinion, classical quotations and pertinent *exempla*, short and edifying stories on various moral themes that were drawn from his classroom lectures and debates. Apparently it sought to render his ideas accessible to other preachers for their sermons. Accompanying it was the *Distinctiones Abel*, which gave preachers an alphabetical list of key Biblical terms and their allegorical and tropological interpretations. In terms of manuscript pages the Chanter's theological output exceeded all of his contemporaries with the exception of Stephen Langton, his former student and colleague. Attracting a coterie of disciples that included, in addition to Langton, Robert of Courson, Pope Innocent III, Thomas of Chobham, Pierre de Roissy and the penitentialists at Saint-Victor, Pierre the Chanter was without doubt the most influential theologian of his day in Paris.

When Étienne of Sainte-Geneviève wrote the archbishop of Reims in support of the Chanter, his rhetorically charged letter characterized his friend as "a man whose fame was diffused throughout all the churches," but he struck the Chanter's true personality when he equated him with the Greek church father Origen, "who taught to live and lived as he taught."[11] This equation between life and knowledge, to be sure, was a commonplace of the school of Saint-Victor and was adopted by Pierre Comestor at Notre-Dame. The Chanter himself was accustomed to repeating that equation because Jesus first acted before he taught (Acts I, 1); a holy life therefore precedes knowledge. Theology was the science of things, not of words. *Res non verba* was the controlling maxim of Pierre's life and teaching. As a result, he ignored the *Sprachlogik* or grammatical logic that Abélard and Gilbert de la Porrée applied to theology; he rejected the Aristotelian proposition that knowledge was valued for its own sake, and he was not tempted by the classical privileging of rhetoric. Pierre the Chanter's treatises were not overtly autobiographical, but because he ranked life above teaching he was incapable of concealing his own personality in his writings.

Preoccupied with the problems attached to application of penance, Pierre sought to sharpen the confessor's eyes and ears, and this in turn bore two consequences for his writing. In the first place he was acutely sensitive to the world around him. We have already seen that as a cleric at Paris he reacted to the two great construction projects of his day—unfavorably to the expenditures at Notre-Dame and with approval of the royal policy to compensate damages incurred in the building of walls. He was ever vigilant against funding church construction with money derived from usury. Closer at home, he responded to the breakdown of discipline in the chancel of Notre-Dame and protested vociferously when a canon of the chapter wished to endow his son with a prebend.[12] He found the division of the Île-de-la-Cité into thirteen parishes beyond reason, but as a loyal member of the chapter of Notre-Dame he protested against exemption of the neighboring and powerful Benedictine abbeys from the bishop's authority.[13] As a Biblical scholar, the Chanter concurred with the current opinion of his day that unequivocally opposed all expression of homoerotic activity.[14] A descendant of a family of knights, he was equally sensitive to the conditions of the aristocratic world. He recalled that a cousin was prosecuted for not preventing his brother from assaulting another vassal of his liege lord and noted the difficulty of another member of his family to determine whether consanguinous relations impeded his marriage. He wrestled with the important but thorny question of burying in church cemeteries knights who had died in tournaments, certainly the most popular of all aristocratic sports.[15]

Once detected, however, sinful practices must be corrected before they can be forgiven. Pierre the Chanter's preoccupation with penance reveals a second major feature of his personality that permeated his writing: a compelling impulse for reform. To enumerate just a few items on his agenda, to which I shall return in later chapters: with Philip Augustus he shared an aversion to uninhibited swearing. Since unreasonable decrees of consanguinity placed an impediment on marriage and encouraged divorce, he sought to reduce the system to protect the indissolubility of marriage, a reform that would protect knightly marriages as well as curb the king's abuse of Queen Ingeborg. He argued that clerical temptation to indulge in concubines, prostitutes and homoeroticism would be alleviated if church authority reduced the requirement of celibacy for subdeacons and clerics in lower orders. His greatest energies, however, were directed to eradicating the judicial practice of ordeals, which subjected defendants to the caprice of iron and water. So adamant was his opposition that he declared that as a priest he would sooner disobey the universal church's authority than to bless the elements.

Robert of Courson, his closest student, testified that the Chanter preferred to implement these reforms by convoking a general council of the

church, just as Pope Alexander III
had done in 1179—a dream that
was not realized until 1215 at the
Fourth Lateran Council nearly two
decades after his death. These compulsions are relevant here for their
sense of Pierre's character. Sensitive
to his world and forever the reform-
er, Pierre the Chanter was a scholar *engagé* who was both outspoken
and independent. He was willing
not only to investigate the king's
marriage and question the choice of
episcopal appointments, as shall be
seen, but even to defy ecclesiastical
condoning of ordeals.

If the evocation of Pierre's character in Étienne's letter and his
own writings limits us to his moral
compulsions, how might he have
looked to the eyes of his contem-

Figure 7. Alain of Lille and Pierre the
Chanter, manuscript of the abbey of Otto-
buren (1228–1246), Ms. London, British
Library, addit. 19769. © British Library
Board. All Rights Reserved.

poraries? True portraiture was nonexistent around the year 1200, but in the
second quarter of the following century the monks of Ottoburen in distant
Bavaria commissioned a manuscript containing a version of his *Verbum abbreviatum* along with treatises of Alain de Lille that was prefaced by a color
image of the two authors (Figure 7).[16] To the left is a clean-shaven Alain, depicted here as the author of the secular poems *Anticlaudianus* and *De planctu
naturae*, because he is outfitted in aristocratic garb, consisting of a beret,
a short *bliaut* gathered together by a belt and revealing elegant hose and
pointed shoes and a mantel fastened by a broach. To the right and facing
him is Pierre the Chanter, with a prominent tonsure, beard and long toga
that conceals all except his pointed shoes. Certainly not drawn from the likeness of two individuals long dead, the dual portraits nonetheless represent
how they might have appeared to near contemporaries. Although the local
artist fitted Alain out in the style of the German nobility, Pierre is indisput-
ably a cleric in any setting. Alain's left hand and forefinger are raised and his
right hand is pointed toward his companion as if to admonish or instruct
him. Pierre's arms come together in a circle at his waist as if he is listening to

Alain's words, but his hands point in opposite directions. His head is tilted back slightly and his eyes and mouth bear a quizzical expression suggesting that he is responding to Alain with a "yes, but." This interpretation is doubtlessly influenced by a reading of Pierre's writings, but I suspect that this is the closest that we shall come to uncovering the Chanter's physical face.

Philip Augustus

As king, Philip's public career naturally coincided with the political history of his reign. In the following chapter we shall examine his contributions to the Capetian monarchy through bureaucratic skill, successful generalship and political acumen. Our task here will be to plumb his personality and uncover his private face. The attempt is complicated by an abundance of sources, much of which is unhelpful. Since Philip acceded to the kingship at the age of fourteen and had no time to complete his schooling, he was most likely illiterate in Latin; nonetheless, this deficiency did not preclude a functional literacy to carry out the tasks of government with the assistance of clerics. The hundreds if not thousands of documents that bear his name were all redacted by the royal chancery and are virtually devoid of self-revelation. Since the royal historians, Rigord de Saint-Denis and Guillaume le Breton, were commissioned to record the deeds that brought glory to the French monarchy, ideology impregnated their chronicles. The other contemporary chroniclers were forced to draw on common opinion. Although the English chroniclers were wary of his aggressions against their king and fascinated with his political achievements, they were often blinkered by partisan suspicions. During Philip's lifetime, but increasingly after his death, edifying stories or exempla were retailed about him, but these accounts benefited from hindsight and favored his precocity and exemplarity. To uncover Philip's private persona, therefore, each item must be evaluated individually and with caution.[17]

Because the moment of death is the customary occasion to assess a famous person, it is not surprising that the fullest account occurred at that time. What is unexpected is that it was not furnished by the court historians, but by a canon at Tours. Although it has been cited and glossed by virtually every modern historian of the king, this is no reason to exclude its quotation in full. In rapid strokes, and in a mix of individual traits with the stereotypical, Philip is described as having

> an agreeable appearance, well-formed body, cheerful face, a bald pate, ruddy complexion. [He was] given to drink and food, prone to sexual desire, gener-

ous to his friends, stingy to his foes, skilled in stratagems, orthodox in belief, solicitous of counsel, holding to his word, a scrupulous and expeditious judge, fortunate in victory, fearful of this life, easily moved, easily assuaged, putting down the wicked of the realm by sowing discord among them, killing no one in prison, availing himself of counsel of lesser men, bearing grudges only momentarily, subduing the proud, defending the church, and providing for the poor.[18]

Apparently no individualized representation was made of his likeness during his lifetime. His most widespread image—like those on the coinage of the Hellenistic and Roman emperors—is found on the great seal of majesty that authenticated his diplomas and was distributed throughout the realm (Figure 8). As with preceding Capetian monarchs he is portrayed as crowned, robed with a tunic fastened with a clasp on the right shoulder, seated on a campstool throne and holding a *fleur de lis* in his right hand and a long scepter in his left. Following his Merovingian forebears, he wears his hair long. The physical description of the chronicler of Tours ("agreeable appearance, well-formed body, cheerful face, and ruddy complexion") suggests nothing out of the ordinary. That he was bald in old age is to be expected, but he probably attained this condition by the age of twenty-five. Known for his unruly hair as a young man (*le valet maupeigné*), he lost it all from a sickness called *arnaldia* (French *la suette*) while in the Holy Land.

His birth at Paris on 21 August 1165 was the occasion of exceptional rejoicing for his parents, and for the Parisian population because it brought long years of anxiety to a close. The earliest success of his Capetian forebears was to establish their dynastic right to the French throne. Since 987 they had produced a surviving male heir for six generations and saw each son crowned during the lifetime of the father, thus ensuring their hereditary claim. The blood right of the Capetian family to the French crown was uncontested, but it took Louis VII three decades and as many wives to replicate the results in 1165 because his former wives had yielded only daughters. By 1179 the aging king, in poor health, decided to proceed directly to

Figure 8. Seal of majesty of Philip Augustus, 1198, wax. Source: Bridgeman Art Library.

the coronation of his son at Reims in August to confirm his succession, but a grave incident placed his plans in jeopardy. The fourteen-year-old boy was allowed to go hunting in the woods outside Compiègne, where he was separated from his party and was not found for several days. Severely emaciated and thoroughly frightened, Philip was close to death. The old king roused himself from his sick bed and made a pilgrimage to Canterbury to implore the aid of his old friend Thomas Becket, now a thaumaturgic saint. Apparently the saint's intercessions were effective, because the young man recovered in time to be crowned on All Saints Day, 1 November 1179, although his father returned to his bed mortally stricken by a stroke.

Philip's first duty was to prolong the Capetian lineage; after his father's near failure, the king's sex life was of foremost importance to the kingdom. Throughout fifty-eight years his sexual behavior can be divided into six phases.[19] Six months after his coronation the adolescent king, age fourteen, married the child Isabelle de Hainaut, age ten, in April 1180. (In canon law the minimum age was fourteen for boys and twelve for girls.) Philippe, count of Flanders, who then dominated the royal entourage, imposed the choice of the bride, but the royal duty was to engender a son just as soon as the young couple attained fertility. Four years later, however, the king precipitously threatened his young wife with divorce. The motives were more likely political than physiological because the girl had barely attained puberty. In all events, Isabelle did fulfill her queenly duties by giving birth to a boy, Louis, in September 1187, to the great rejoicing of the kingdom, but she suddenly died in 1190 at age twenty, most likely while giving birth to stillborn twins.

In 1187 Philip defended himself against the powerful English-Angevin family by befriending each of the sons and turning them against the father, King Henry II. While Isabelle was carrying the future Louis, the Capetian turned his attention to Richard, duke of Aquitaine. The English chronicler Roger de Hoveden evoked the friendship between the king and duke in a frequently quoted passage that has been often read as alluding to homosexuality:

> When peace was made, Richard, duke of Aquitaine and son of the English king, lived with Philip, king of France, who honored him so much that they ate each day at the same table from the same plate, and the bed did not separate them. And the French king loved him as his own soul; and they so loved each other that the English king was profoundly surprised by the ardent love between them and wondered what it could mean.[20]

In context, however, the love between Philip and Richard was the friendship/
love formulated by Cicero and celebrated for kings by Latin poets since
Alcuin. It was reserved for aristocratic men (thus excluding the lower classes
and women), public and honorable (and thus virtuous) and in no way
sexual. Totally incompatible with love that was private, ignoble, dishon-
oring and sexual, it rigorously excluded physical sodomy.[21] In addition, it
should be noted that Richard's sexual behavior was at complete variance
with Philip's. Whatever Richard's own sexual proclivities, he had avoided
marriage with his long-suffering fiancée for decades, and after he married
another woman he refused to consort with her, thus eliminating the possibility of an heir of his body to the English throne.

The birth of Louis to Philip, however, was only a temporary solution to
the royal succession because Isabelle's death and the nearly mortal sickness
of the prince during the king's absence on the Third Crusade required urgent
attention. High among the priorities that awaited Philip on his return to
France in 1191 was a new wife and reinforcement of the royal lineage with a
second son; this opened the third, the longest and the most enigmatic phase
of Philip's sexual life. In the first place, it is difficult enough to understand
why the king chose the Danish princess Ingeborg in 1193. The paranoid sug-
gestion of the English chroniclers that he sought Danish aid in order to
invade England can be explained by the vulnerability of Richard, then captive in a German prison, but when Normandy remained steadfastly faithful
to Richard it is hard to understand what help the Danes could have supplied. Philip's only tangible benefits were a bride of royal blood and a dowry
of 10,000 marks of silver. When Ingeborg arrived at Amiens on 14 August
1193, the king married her that very day. The next morning, during the coronation ceremonies, he became extremely agitated and suddenly announced
that he would have the marriage annulled and send her back to her country.
It would be an understatement to say that great trauma had occurred on
the night of 14–15 August between a bridegroom of twenty-eight years and
a bride of eighteen, the one who knew no Danish, the other no French,
and both obliged to communicate in the most rudimentary of Latin.

Whatever the difficulties of explaining the choice of the bride, that of
the marital disaster puzzled contemporaries just as it continues to per-
plex modern historians—with, perhaps, no solution in sight. An English
chronicler offered the expected conjectures—bad breath, a hidden defect
or even lack of virginity—but most contemporary observers defended the
bride's beauty and virtue without qualification. (Besides, most royal and

aristocratic marriages were never a matter of personal choice, and marriage partners were accustomed to make do with what they were given. Philip's minimum obligation was to endure his spouse until he sired a second son.) What is clear is that the king's aversion was profoundly sexual and personal—so overwhelming that he absolutely refused to take her back for two decades, and then only as queen, never as spouse. So deep were his feelings in 1200 that he was willing to risk an interdict on his lands that placed in jeopardy his authority at Paris and his political plans. For her part, Ingeborg refused to return home and appealed her case to the papacy. After the hesitations of the aged Pope Celestine III, the young and vigorous Innocent III decided in 1198 to make the king's behavior a public cause for asserting papal jurisdiction over all cases of marriage (starting at the highest level) and to defend the interests of the Danish princess. The dispute was then turned over to the lawyers.

The king's lawyers argued that because Ingeborg was related to him within the prohibited degrees of affinity, the marriage was thereby impeded. When the genealogies presented by the French were proved to be deficient by the Danes, Philip's clerics shifted the argument to asserting that Ingeborg had rendered Philip temporarily impotent on the marriage night through sorcery, but the Danish princess steadfastly insisted that the marriage had been consummated. With direct contradiction between the sole witnesses, the claims were impossible to establish. We shall avoid pursuing the arguments, counterarguments, motions and appeals that were recorded in the papal registers and that prolonged the case interminably. Suffice it to say that Ingeborg's obstinacy was rewarded with continuous sequestration, indeed virtual imprisonment, as she was shuttled around the royal domain from monastery to castle.

Since Philip found sexual relations impossible with his spouse Ingeborg, he opened a fourth phase of his sexual life to reinforce the royal lineage. Disposed to believe that a council called at Compiègne in 1193, composed of his relatives and familiars, had annulled his marriage on the grounds of affinity, he found a new partner in Agnès, daughter of the duke of Méran (Andechs-Meranien), whom he married in June 1196. Agnès quickly cured the king of whatever impotence Ingeborg had afflicted because she presented him with a daughter, Marie, in 1198 and a son, Philippe, in 1200. Philip found the Bavarian bride beautiful and agreeable in ways that Ingeborg was not, but to the pope she was bigamous, or a concubine (*superintroducta*) at best. When Innocent demanded that Philip separate himself from her and exile her from the kingdom as a condition for lifting the interdict, the king removed her from the royal domain only temporarily, because she was again pregnant. Agnès served Philip well by producing the greatly desired second son and by dying soon thereafter (18–19 July 1201), thus relieving the king of the complication of bigamy. He buried her at the abbey of Saint-Corentin in Mantes with memories of a fecund and happy marriage. Then, three months later, the pope quite unexpectedly responded by legitimizing Marie and Philippe, thus confirming the latter as a second heir to the throne. Most likely Innocent thought that this gesture of goodwill would enlist the king's support for the papal candidate to the imperial throne in Germany (which it did not), but Rigord reported that the decision did not please many at the time—certainly not Ingeborg, who undoubtedly felt betrayed by the rehabilitation of her rival's offspring.

Whatever distress the interdict inflicted on the population of Paris, the year 1200 found the king personally content because a second son had reinforced the royal lineage. The king could now forget Ingeborg and turn to a fifth phase of satisfying his sexual needs wherever convenient. Doubtless many ladies entered the royal bed, but only one was acknowledged: a certain demoiselle from Arras who gave birth in 1208–1209 to a royal bastard, Pierre Charlot, for whom the king furnished a career in the church. (He later rose to become bishop of Noyon.) The king's trysting, however, eventually had to be set aside for a final phase made necessary by political demands. In 1213 King John of England and Otto of Brunswick, emperor of the Germans—roaring lions on either side, as one chronicler called them—joined forces to launch a two-pronged attack against the Capetian. As the decisive hour neared, Philip's chief vulnerability was his treatment of his longsuffering spouse, which placed him at odds not only with the papacy but also with his subjects, as the royal historians averred. Having broken off negotiations with the papacy, he suddenly reversed himself and dramatically announced that he would take Ingeborg back into his good graces. This was the final resolution to his marital problem, and it won him papal blessing for the ensuing conflict and was followed by victories at La Roche-aux-Moines and Bouvines in 1214. Guillaume le Breton testified to the great joy of the people toward a monarch whose only fault was mistreatment of his wife. It is improbable that Ingeborg gained entrance to the royal bed, but Philip, now forty-eight, was satisfied to treat her as queen and with "marital affection," a minimal attitude that the pope had long enjoined. This public display of affection remained mutual until the king's death; thereafter, the queen remained faithful to her husband's memory. Although it ended peacefully, the tortuous relationship between Philip and his second wife became a pronounced anomaly in his character; the canon of Tour's comment that the king was "prone to sexual desire" was hardly an exaggeration.

If Philip Augustus took care of his progeny, he was equally "fearful for his own life," as the same chronicler observed. After his return from the crusade in 1191, he intercepted letters that suggested Richard had hired the "Old Man of the Mountain" (Sheikh al-Jabal, a Syrian) to have him exterminated by one of his Assassins. (Like Muslim extremists today, the Assassins believed that such a deed would earn them immediate salvation.) Extremely agitated, Philip immediately retreated to a castle, kept the keys in his own hand and created a bodyguard. Even after the complicity of the Assassins was disproved, the king indulged his paranoia. In 1205 another assassination plot was uncovered, this one implicating a Norman cleric who was duly executed.[22] The institution of Philip's bodyguard, however, contrasted markedly with the reputation of his father, who, when discovered sleeping without armed protection, replied, "Why not? I fear no one. Here in France we have our bread, wine and complete happiness."[23]

The king's piety, if sincere, was nonetheless conventional, as suggested by the chronicler's stereotype "defending the church and providing for the poor." In 1163 Pope Alexander III revived the epitaph "most Christian [*christianissimus*] king of France" for Louis VII, and Innocent III continued to apply it to Philip. The king's alms were respectable if not as extravagant as Louis IX's, his grandson's. Orthodox in belief, he could be harsh both against the Jews, as has been seen, and against heretics, as will be seen, but always within limits. His attitude toward the Crusades was similar. Having participated once, he could not be persuaded to return again, even against the Albigensians, yet his final testament included enormous sums for future expeditions. When the Seine overflowed its banks in 1196, the king took a conspicuous part in the penitential processions.[24]

Philip followed, nonetheless, certain clerical injunctions with such ardor as to set him apart from the aristocratic classes in general and most notably King Richard. Doubtless remembering his near escape from death in the forest of Compiègne, he was never found hunting again. We shall see that after attending the tournament of Châtillon-sur-Marne immediately after his coronation, he was never recorded as participating in these aristocratic amusements; nor were tournaments permitted near his capital. He was notorious for refusing to distribute robes and gifts to *jongleurs*, actors and other entertainers, preferring to bestow them on the poor. As a consequence, no vernacular author dedicated a romance to his memory (although he did surreptitiously patronize a popular *trouvère*). And, following a Capetian tradition, he abhorred the utterance of ignominious oaths. Unlike the Angevin kings of England, who took malicious delight in swearing on God's body parts, Philip's own swearing consisted of the innocuous utterance "by the lance of Saint James."[25]

His main virtues were political, as befitted a king. The chronicler of Tours emphasized Philip's "mastery of stratagems" and his "ability to sow discord" as especially felt by his Angevin rivals while Philip played son against father and nephew against uncle. His "speed to execute justice" was demonstrated in the numerous cases heard in the royal courts throughout his reign. The prominence of minor figures such as Gautier the Young, Barthélemy de Roie and Brother Guérin at his court demonstrated his "availing himself of the counsel of lesser men." The famous incident of precipitously cutting down the elm tree at Gisors was just one example that he was "easily moved"; his tolerance of the treacheries of Renaud, count of Boulogne, was another of his being "easily assuaged" and "bearing grudges only momentarily." That he "killed no one in prison" may refer pointedly to King John's barbarous murder of his nephew Arthur.

By 1185, when Philip took over the reigns of government from the hands of his father's counselors, he began to exemplify the virtues worthy of royal majesty. He was substantially rich, as the royal accounts documented in 1202–1203 and the great surpluses at the end of his reign confirmed. Although the decade of the 1190s saw embarrassing military disasters against Richard, the Capetian had nonetheless gained the upper hand by 1200, and the triumph at Bouvines would soon add the epitaph "victorious in battle" to his titles. At age thirty-five in the year 1200, Philip had amply demonstrated that he indeed merited Rigord's surname of "Augustus."

Pierre the Chanter meets Philip Augustus

Inhabiting the Île-de-la-Cité, Pierre the Chanter and Philip Augustus were neighbors for the better part of two decades, and their paths doubtlessly crossed frequently. (The former occupied the cloister on the eastern end, the latter the royal residence on the western end, when the king was in town.) In 1190 the king appointed the Chanter to a capitular committee to oversee construction of Notre-Dame during the king's absence, despite

Pierre's scruples about extravagant buildings. In 1196 Celestine III named the Chanter to the sensitive commission investigating the king's separation from the queen and his attempt to marry Agnès. Rigord, however, commented that the king's wrath toward the members of the council, who were subsequently convoked to hear the commission's report, turned them into mute dogs afraid to bark for their skins.[26] Nonetheless, we shall see that the Chanter and the king frequently agreed on such subjects as tournaments, jongleurs and especially blasphemy. (In this last example, Pierre expressly named the king in his *Verbum abbreviatum.*)

Perhaps it was inevitable that the two would be pictured by a contemporary as talking together. A tradition reaching back to antiquity juxtaposed a celebrated philosopher and a king (Aristotle and Alexander, for example) in dialogue for the moral instruction of the reader, a tradition not to be resisted by medieval preachers in the exempla of their sermons. Exactly such a conversation, titled "A Dialogue between the excellent King Philip and the good Chanter of Paris, Master Peter," was inserted into the cartulary of the chapter of Bourges by a canon named Étienne de Gallardon. Étienne was active in the royal chancery until 1220, when he completed the transcription in his own hand of the third and most important of the royal registers. By 1227 he had joined the chapter of Bourges, where he set himself the task of compiling a cartulary for Bourges (Ms. Paris, BnF nouv. acq. lat. 1274) that was modeled on the royal registers. Between two quires (gatherings) he inserted a bifolio (fol. 298–299) containing the conversation. Someone else transcribed the text of the dialogue, but the title was written in Étienne's characteristic book hand. Most likely Étienne was the author of the text as well because the particular vocabulary for addressing the king is likewise found in the register. Insertion of the bifolio into the cartulary can be dated to the 1230s, when the chapter was embroiled in a dispute over the election of a new archbishop, a subject to which the text spoke directly.

> One day Pierre the Chanter of recent memory approached Philip, the most excellent among the kings of this world, who gladly listened to the words of wise and honorable men like the Chanter. When Pierre explained to the king how he should govern himself, his kingdom and his people, Philip, realizing that he was about to be reprimanded covertly, interrupted him, protesting in a gentle and affectionate manner:
> "Lord Chanter, let your ideal king be for the time and accept me as I am, but tell me why ancient bishops like St. Marcel of Paris, St. Euverte of Orléans and St. Sulpice of Bourges were true saints, whereas one would be hard put to find a single modern bishop who is a saint."

To which the Chanter's response was subtle but not entirely making sense:

"Lord King, the wise man does not come to offer his advice unless he is summoned, but the fool arrives without being called."

To which the king, surprised by the answer, replied: "By the lance of St. James, what does that have do with my question?"

"Lord King," the Chanter continued, "I shall demonstrate that my answer is well considered." [The Chanter then proceeds to contrast ancient elections guided by the Holy Spirit with modern elections corrupted by greed and ambition. See below, Chapter Four.]

The Chanter's response was received by the king with good will and entire agreement.[27]

Evocative of the frontispiece of the Ottoburen manuscript, this vivacious dialogue captures an insightful moment when two protagonists reveal their characteristic stances. (In the present dialogue, however, the roles are reversed.) Pierre is caught in the middle of a moralizing sermon in which he censures royal conduct, to which Philip reacts, not with outrage but with a sly counterthrust: "As long as you are talking about bad kings, why not explain to me why there are no more saintly bishops?" In good school fashion, the Chanter counters with an enigma, to which the king's retort is instant— "By the lance of St. James, what is that supposed to mean?"—employing his favorite oath. Then Pierre continues with another edifying sermon on saintly bishops, to which the king yields finally with good nature.

Orderly succession of both the kingdom and the prelacy, the subject they were discussing, was by no means banal, and the stakes were high. As a Capetian, Philip's legitimacy was founded on the hereditary succession of his dynasty. Not only had the Chanter contested the king's right to separate himself from an undesirable spouse, but Pierre had even questioned the fundamental legitimacy of hereditary succession—indeed the crowning achievement of the Capetian dynasty. In his questions he preferred the ecclesiastical and imperial procedure of election to the royal procedure of birth, asserting that the latter often produced wicked monarchs. Although he recognized the hereditary principle in the choice of Biblical kings, he preferred election by the people, signified by popular acclamation. To shout the scriptural shibboleth "woe to the realm whose king is a child" in the Capetian capital was foolhardy because dynastic succession frequently produced heirs who were minors.[28] So Philip's deflection was benign: "if election works so well, how do you explain the disappearance of saintly bishops?" Because the Chanter's longer response is more relevant to the section on bishops, we shall defer consideration until Chapter Four, simply noting here that the two ended in proximate harmony.[29]

This harmony between the two dominating personalities was sheltered under the lofty and commodious vaults of Notre-Dame. When Philip was consecrated at Reims on 1 November 1179, the coronation was followed immediately by a mass in which the *laudes regiae* were chanted. Every Easter Sunday thereafter, these lauds were chanted at Notre-Dame of Paris during mass when the king ceremoniously took annual communion. They could also be intoned anytime the king wore his crown in the church. It was Pierre the Chanter's responsibility to choose three canons to leave their stalls after the reading of the Epistle and chant this litany in praise of the king antiphonally with the choir boys. At Notre-Dame the words and music have survived in a notated manuscript from the early thirteenth century (Paris, BnF 1112, fols. 309ff). As the Lord's anointed (*Christus*), the Capetian, like Christ, conquers, reigns and rules. A roster of saints from the church, ranging from Mary and Peter at the top and descending to the local bishops Marcel and Germain, are called on to help him, his queen and his ministers:

> Christ conquers, Christ reigns, Christ rules. [sung three times by the canons and repeated by the choirboys]
> . . .

[canons:]	[choirboys:]
Savior of the World	thou help him
Saint Peter	thou help him
Saint Paul	thou help him

> . . .
> [canons] Hear O Christ
> [choirboys] To the most serene, great and peaceful king Philip, crowned by God, life and victory

[canons:]	[choirboys:]
Redeemer of the World	thou help him
St. Michel	thou help him

> . . .
> [canons] Hear O Christ
> [choirboys] To Bishop Maurice and the congregation of Notre-Dame, salvation and life

[canons:]	[choirboys:]
St. Stephen	thou help him
St. Denis	thou help him

> . . .

[canons] Hear O Christ
[choirboys] To the queen [Ingeborg], salvation and life

| [canons:] | [choirboys:] |
| Ste. Marie | thou help her |

. . .

| Ste. Geneviève | thou help her |

[canons] Hear O Christ
[choirboys] To all of the judges and the whole army of the French, life and victory

| [canons] | [choirboys] |

. . .

| St. Marcel | thou help them |
| St. Germain | thou help them |

Christ conquers, Christ reigns, Christ rules [sung three times by the canons and repeated by the choirboys]

[canons:]	[choirboys:]
King of Kings	Christ conquers
Our glory	Christ conquers
Our mercy	Christ conquers

To the sole empire, glory and power; through the immortal age of ages. Amen [sung first by the canons and repeated by the choirboys and the same for the remaining strophes]
To the sole force, bravery and victory through all the ages of ages. Amen.
To the sole honor, praise and rejoicing through all ages of ages. Amen.
Kyrie eleison, Christ eleison, Kyrie eleison.[30]

Whatever his qualms about hereditary monarchy, Pierre as chanter of the choir was responsible for the performance of this powerfully hypnotic and martial litany, chanted at Notre-Dame in support of Capetian kingship.

Another manuscript from the second decade of the thirteenth century detailed the causes and names for which prayers should be offered at the cathedral. Heading the list was naturally the construction of Notre-Dame itself, followed by the Hôtel-Dieu, Saint-Victor and other hospitals, abbeys and churches in Paris, and then the ecclesiastical hierarchy headed by the pope, the archbishops and other bishops. The royalty included not only the king's family, represented by Philip himself, his wife, prince Louis, his son and other children of the king, but also the business of Jerusalem and Constantinople and the conversion of the Albigensians. Among the dead to be prayed for were Louis VII, his wife and queen Isabelle (Philip's first spouse buried at Notre-Dame) as well as Bishops Maurice and Eudes; but the list concludes with the name of Pierre the Chanter. It can be readily understood why the royal family and the prelacy were included within these worthy names and good causes, but the case was different for the Chanter, who was singled out alone from the many departed chapter dignitaries. Once again he had a rendezvous with his monarch under the vaults of the great church.[31]

Perhaps the best measure of their reunion at Notre-Dame is the verse in their honor that was set to music (in one voice) at their deaths. (Only the opening stanzas are offered here.)

> Pierre the Chanter (d. 1197):
>
> Having suffered eclipse so often,
> let the world renew its sorrow;
> suffering the setting of the bright light,
> let it unlock great sorrow;
> Paris shone
> when the light of the Chanter burned bright,
> whom death saw and envied,
> while he cared for the whole world,
> while he sowed the word of life,
> while his light shone not under a bushel;
> the sun, taken from our midst
> ends a happy life.[32]

> Philip Augustus (d. 1223):
>
> The alabaster box is broken
> and the lamp is extinguished
> when Philip dies;
> oil is poured out,
> Bethlehem is anointed, and
> Jerusalem breathes again;
> a comet presaging
> a change of the kingdom's throne
> obscures the world's sun.
> Syon, thus rising
> prefigures your destruction,
> and its hair, your baldness.[33]

Even quoted in full, it would be difficult to determine which of these verses was more poignant in beauty or more pertinent to its subject. In death both Pierre and Philip were honored by poetry and music under the vaults of Notre-Dame.

The Hidden Visages of Women

In the Paris of their day Philip Augustus and Pierre the Chanter give us public faces for the forces of government and the clergy, both masculine professions. If there were to be a public face of a woman in the year 1200, it would have been a queen, like Eleanor of Aquitaine from the preceding generation or Blanche of Castile from the following. For eighteen months in 1190–1191, Adèle de Champagne, the queen mother, had served as regent of the government along with her brother Guillaume, archbishop of Reims, but virtually nothing is revealed about her persona. In the year 1200, however, the reigning queen was the hapless Ingeborg, who was not even French; nor was she ever allowed access to the Capetian capital. Sequestered for two decades, she was imprisoned at the castle of Etampes in that year. The closest she ever came to Paris was the Benedictine monastery of Saint-Maur-des-Fossés upstream from the capital. The registers of Pope Innocent III, however, do contain for the year 1203 a poignant letter—probably dictated to one of her clerics—in which she bitterly complained of her treatment at Etampes. Among her misfortunes, she objected that her clothing befitted a queen neither in quantity nor in quality. Despite the complaint's plausibility, the royal financial accounts from the preceding year indicate that the king was spending more on her clothing than on his own. A sumptuous psalter was later composed and illustrated for her use, but it was made in the workshops of Vermandois, not of Paris.[34] In 1200 her rival Agnès de Méran was most likely lodged with her infant children at the royal nursery at Poissy downstream from Paris, but she too is only a shadow of a figure. The most that is known about her is the expense of her children's clothing, likewise recorded in the royal accounts of 1202.

The clerical population (*clerici*) of Paris excluded women by definition. Consisting of secular prelates, priests, clergy in the major and minor orders and simple clerics, it was further swollen by the multitude of students and masters in the schools. As much as 10 percent of the population may have been clerical. Except for the religious women who served the hospitals at the Hôtel-Dieu and Sainte-Catherine, the nunneries at Paris were limited to two and both located outside the walls. The abbey of Montmartre, founded by Louis VI to the north, was a house of Benedictine nuns; Saint-Antoine to the west was converted from a refuge for reformed prostitutes to Cistercian sisters by Bishop Eudes de Sully in 1204.[35] If we add the throngs of male workers who were brought in for the construction projects at Notre-Dame and on the walls, Paris undoubtedly had a sex ratio that was significantly skewed in favor of men. As in most preindustrial cities, there was also, to be sure, heavy migration of young females into the city to perform domestic service, and the least fortunate of them ended up as prostitutes. Because of the interest of the theologians, as has been seen, these women are the best documented of the poor female population, but only as a profession and not as individuals.

The bourgeoisie of Paris, however, most likely maintained an equal sex ratio reflecting a normal birth rate. As for the men so for the women; their names are revealed only when they produced documents treating the transfer of property. In most ecclesiastical charters recording these transactions and in most obituary notices detailing donations to churches, the name of the wife was joined to her husband's to indicate her approval of the transfer. Therefore we can identify, for example, Pernilla, the wife of Thibaut le Riche, as well as the sister of Gautier, the royal chamberlain; Sybille, the wife of Renaud Cheron; Heresenda, the wife of Jean Evroin; and Marie, the wife of Eudes Popin. But as individuals they remain only names. Of the seven tombstones that have survived from our period in the Jewish cemetery on rue Garlande, four belong to women, but they too are identified solely as daughters and wives of men.

If the visage of women in flesh and blood at Paris in 1200 remains concealed, it was nonetheless chiseled in stone and painted on parchment. Numerous faces of women were included in the sculpture on the west façade of Notre-Dame, which reached the level of the Kings' Gallery by the 1210s. Dedicated to the supreme woman, the mother of God, the edifice presented female situations that were accessible, visible and recognizable to all Parisians[36]. At the same time the workshops on the rue Neuve-Notre-Dame were producing the Bibles moralisées for the royal court. The first to emerge, the Codex 2554 of the Austrian National Library in Vienna (finished perhaps as early as 1215 but certainly by the early 1220s), was therefore an exact contemporary of the sculpture. More than one thousand painted medallions illustrate the opening books of the Old Testament and their moral interpretation, all accompanied by a running paraphrase and commentary in vernacular French. The familiar deeds accomplished by the women of the Biblical books (from mother Eve [Gen. 1] to the barren woman whom Elisha visited (IV Kings 4]) are illustrated according to the clothing fashions of the day.[37] In the accompanying tropological or moral commentary, the artists chose the same themes as were prominent on the façade of Notre-

Dame. An object of extraordinary luxury, this Bible moralisée was limited to the eyes of the royal court, especially the royal family and their chaplains and clerics who assisted them to decipher its message. Unlike the sculpture of Notre-Dame, therefore, the audience of this Bible was miniscule; nonetheless, since the artists availed themselves of the same iconography as the sculptors, the two monuments can be viewed together not for the faces of individual women but for feminine types and ideals that were fashioned according to ecclesiastical ideology.

The most comprehensive representation of the population at large was furnished at the central portal of the cathedral, in the tympanum of the Last Judgment (Figure 9). At the sound of angels blowing trumpets from either side, all the world's inhabitants are summoned on the final day. Twenty individuals arise from their tombs: seven identifiable males (a bishop, two mature men, a nobleman/bourgeois [? the figure carries a sword], a knight, a pope and a king), five identifiable females, and eight indeterminate figures who could be female or youthful males. Because there is a large margin of uncertainty, we can leave the sex ratio until the next scene. The five recognizable women are a crowned queen, a coiffed noblewoman/bourgeoise, and three veiled women. In the next register above the Archangel Michael and a devil separate the blessed and the damned at the center. To the left are the blessed, five crowned men and five women also crowned (three coiffed and two veiled), all robed and looking up to Christ above. (In this group the crowns doubtlessly signify the blessed elect.) To the right are ten damned whom devils drag with a chain to the mouth of hell. Six are men: a bishop, bearded male (either a nobleman or a bourgeois), monk, king, prelate, and knight. The remaining are four women: one old and veiled, a coiffed noblewoman/bourgeoise, and two others who are veiled. The sex ratio in heaven is symmetrical; that in hell is skewed toward the masculine. We shall see that in both sculpture and miniatures the headgear is important to identifying females. Although the crown undoubtedly designates queens (with the important exception of the crowns of the elect), the tightly tied coif points to matrons of high station. Whether they were noble or rich bourgeoise is difficult to determine, because the bourgeoisie were quick to imitate noble dress. The veil signifies virgins or the chaste, whereas uncovered hair may be indeterminate, but if it is long it bears negative connotations, especially that of sensuality. Although we can speculate endlessly over the members who are omitted (peasants, artisans, poor), these social indicators nonetheless display diversity within the population represented.

This diversity is found in similar depictions in the Bible moralisée, despite the constraints that the small medallions imposed on the artists (the medallions measure only 65 millimeters in diameter).

The first judgment scene appears in the moralization of the seventh day of creation and signifies that Jesus will rest on judgment day and embrace his friends and trample his enemies underfoot in hell (Figure 10). On either side in heaven, the friends are all male and clothed, including a monk, king and bishop. The enemies at his feet are all naked except for their headgear, which identifies a bishop, a coiffed woman and another woman with long hair (IVc; see note 37). The next occasion that assembles humanity together is Noah's ark, where one scene contains eight individuals of whom

Figure 9. Last Judgment, Notre-Dame, West façade, central portal, photo C. Rose, ©CMN, Paris.

four are women (one veiled, one coiffed, one with a cap and one bare headed [3rB]); another scene contains eight people of whom only two are women, both coiffed (3rC). The most significant representation of the diversity, however, occurs in the moralization of the fifth day of creation, when God fills the sea with many kinds of fish, signifying that Christ has filled the world with many kinds of people, of which the artist chose four: a mounted hunter with a falcon on his wrist followed by a man

Figure 10. Last Judgment, *Bible moralisée*, fol.1vc, Austrian National Library, Vienna, Picture Archiv+Signature.

with a stick to beat the bushes; a butcher cutting meat before three customers; a money changer weighing out coins on a scale before two male clients; and a seated cleric with a stick facing two seated males holding books in their laps (1va) (Figure 11). After recognizing the existence of the aristocratic class in the hunter served by a peasant, evidently the artist has succinctly identified three major segments of the contemporary Parisian population: tradesmen, bankers and scholars. Only one woman appears, placed among the butchers' customers. She is coiffed, showing that she is a rich bourgeoise.

One historical woman, the Blessed Virgin Mary, dominates the west façade of the cathedral, where she is found at least six times. Two of the three portals are dedicated to the events of her life. On the southern door (see Figure 25, in Chapter Four) she is the mother of Jesus, whom she holds on her lap, flanked by supporting column statues consisting of two prophetesses of the miraculous birth of her son, the Jewish widow Serepta (I Kings 17) to the left and the pagan Sibyl to the right. Below the tympanum

Figure 11. Four classes of people, *Bible moralisée*, fol. 1va, Austrian National Library, Vienna, Picture Archiv+Signature.

Figure 12. The woman healed by Elisha, *Bible moralisée*, fol. 58rC, Austrian National Library, Vienna, Picture Archiv+Signature.

unfolds the well-known story of the Nativity, beginning with a prophet, the Annunciation, Visitation, the birth, the shepherds, Herod and the three magi. The northern portal (see Figure 26, in Chapter Four) celebrates her coronation by Jesus, where they sit side by side in the upper tympanum, and below, her death and entombment performed by two angels. She also stands at the central trumeau, crowned and holding her child, flanked this time by only one female column statue to the right, Sainte Geneviève, the patron saint of Paris.

Mary's giving birth to Jesus celebrated the maternal function of all women at Notre-Dame. The Bible moralisée recalled and depicted the births of at least ten major Old Testament personages, beginning with Eve's delivery of Cain and Abel (2vA) and ending with the barren woman healed by Elisha (58rC). Two men, Moses and Samson, signified the nativity of Jesus himself. The most attractive depiction (Figure 12) was the last, where the barren woman of Elisha reclines in bed naked to her waist, displaying her full breasts while a maidservant holds the naked child for her to take (Figure 12). Giving birth was woman's foremost work in both the Bible moralisée and on Notre-Dame. With the exception of Eve's spinning while Adam digs (2vA; Figure 13), virtually no other female work is represented in the manuscript. Of the twenty-five scenes on the doorposts of the northern portal representing seasonal human labor, all but two concern men. The masculine tasks were multiple and

Figure 13. Eve spins while Adam digs, *Bible moralisée*, fol. 2vA, Austrian National Library, Vienna, Picture Archiv+Signature.

agricultural—for example, carrying grain, trimming vines, sharpening a scythe, treading grapes and sowing seed. On one occasion, a man is depicted warming his feet by the fireplace, but on two other occasions coiffed women perform the identical gesture—minimal recognition of the diversity of arduous female toil. We recall the single female customer in the Bible moralisée (also coiffed) waiting for the butcher to cut her meat.

Figure 14. Two couples of lovers, *Bible moralisée,* fol. 2rb, Austrian National Library, Vienna, Picture Archiv+Signature.

Most of the representation was didactic and stereotypic, offering examples to be avoided and ideals to emulate. The female body, for example, called attention not only to the maternal function but equally to a source of sensual danger. The artists of the Bible moralisée created at least ten scenes where women were depicted as exposing men to sexual temptation. The first is the scene where the serpent with a female head deceives Eve and Adam with fruit from the tree, which the commentator moralizes as the devil's enticements through bodily desires. The artist rendered the situation with two couples, a fully dressed man and woman lying in each other's arms, and a nobleman lying on top of a cleric (2rb; Figure 14). Although the latter was explicitly homosexual, the heterosexual couple equally shared erotic temptation. Thereafter, however, the dominant image is that of a woman with a cleric, suggesting the female danger to clerical chastity (3rC, 31rb, etc.; Figure 15). Biblical temptresses such as Potiphar's wife (8vCD) and Delilah (63rBC), of course, embody this female

Figure 15. A woman seduces a cleric, *Bible moralisée,* fol. 31rb, Austrian National Library, Vienna, Picture Archiv+Signature.

Figure 16. Lot's wife, *Bible moralisée*, fol. 5rA, Austrian National Library, Vienna, Picture Archiv+Signature.

function, and when prostitutes are found in the scriptural narrative they are duly noted (60rB, 35vb, 46va). As scenes of sexual violence, the Biblical rapes likewise include the gang rape at Bethlehem that is rendered with brutal force (65rC). The naked bodies of Eve and Adam are rendered chastely by the artists, but when Lot's wife is turned into salt outside of Sodom they render her completely naked and with offensive sexual organs—pendant breasts and exaggerated pudenda (5rA; Figure 16). The vice of lust is appropriately depicted among the twelve virtues and vices surrounding the central portal at Notre-Dame. Incorrectly restored at Notre-Dame, *luxuria* was probably represented by two lovers, as it was later at the cathedrals of Amiens and Chartres.[38] The most violent image was appropriately placed in hell at the Judgment scene; the emaciated body of a naked and blindfolded woman is placed astride a trunk, where her anus is threatened by a man's serpentine genitals from below (Figure 17).

Suggesting maidenly chastity, the veiled female offered a positive stereotype at Notre-Dame. Of the twelve virtues in bas relief flanking the central portal, eleven are women bearing emblems on their shields. (Seven are veiled, and four have uncovered heads.) The sole male who is clothed in armor represents fortitude. Because the vices portrayed beneath each virtue are weathered, a full census of the vices is not possible; still, none of the women appears to wear the veil. At least six of the vices are female and with long hair (pride, foolishness, avarice, despair, idolatry and wrath), and one is coiffed (malignity). More compelling are the five wise virgins of the Gospels placed on the left door post of the central portal. Each is veiled, holds her lamp burning upright and gazes upon Jesus at the central trumeau. To the right the five foolish virgins in disarray hold their lamps askew. Three are coiffed and two wear their hair long and uncovered. Long before the days of *laïcité*, Parisian women were evidently free to cover their heads.

Figure 17. The dead in Hell, Notre-Dame, west façade, central portal, photo. C. Rose ©CMN, Paris.

Virginity and humility are likewise depicted as veiled females in the Bible moralisée (4vc), but the most frequently occurring veiled woman is the image of the Synagogue, representing Jewish religion both in the Old Testament and in contemporary time. Although the commentary vaguely suggests that she may be saved in the last days, her present value is negative. Depicted at least nine times, she first appears in the incident of Judah rejecting his wife, thus signifying that Jesus has rejected the synagogue. Here she is veiled (as she will be, with only one exception), seated and conversing with three miniature Jews (8ra). Elsewhere she associates with Christ and the Church. In the next depiction she talks with ancient philosophers and wears a blindfold because she has spoken ill of Christ (31rd; Figure 18). In a scene representing Queen Jezebel, who threatened the prophet Elijah, she is likewise blindfolded, unveiled with long hair and flimsily clothed (53vd). This last image comes closest to that sculpted on Notre-Dame. On the buttress to the right of the central portal, the Synagogue is likewise portrayed as blindfolded (Figure 19). Inclined to the

Figure 18. The Synagogue, *Bible morali-sée*, fol. 31rd, Austrian National Library, Vienna, Picture Archiv+Signature.

Figure 19. The Synagogue, Notre-Dame, west façade, photo. P. Lemaitre, ©CMN, Paris.

right, her head is askew; her long, flowing hair is surmounted by a tiny toadlike demon; her bliaut and mantel have come unfastened, revealing her chemise; tablets of the Jewish law slip from her right hand; her left hand holds a broken staff; and at her feet lies a crown—all emphasizing blindness and disarray, a pathetic rival to the triumphant Church on the buttress to the left.

Except when she gives birth to Jesus and lies in her tomb, on the west façade of her church the Blessed Mary always wears a crown, proclaiming her as Queen of Heaven. Except in the Nativity scenes that appear in the moralizations, Mary is naturally absent from the Bible moralisée because only the Old Testament is treated. Her place, however, is taken by a female figure who is always crowned and haloed, thereby identifying herself as the Church. She first appears below a scene where God unites Adam and Eve in marriage (2ra) (Figure 20). In a posture that nearly replicates one on the north portal of Notre-Dame (see Figure 26), the Church is seated next to Christ, who takes her hand and points to her (but does not place the crown on her head). The crown and halo are her identifying markers; she wears a red mantel held with a golden clasp over a blue bliaut. Eight more times she appears with Christ, the Synagogue and the clergy, whom she shelters with her mantel. In the Bible moralisée, the juxtaposition of the Synagogue with the Church suggests a rivalry between the two women that inflicts pain on the Church, but on the façade of Notre-Dame her victory is assured. On the buttress to the left she holds her head erect, crowned and haloed as it should be (Figure 21). Her mantel is fastened over a bliaut; a broach is affixed to her chemise; her right hand holds a chalice; her left, a stout crozier to which a pennant is attached, announcing her triumph. Together with Mary, the figure of the Church offered a feminine imagery of victory to the Parisians who observed them from the Parvis below. If they were the celibate clergy, they might draw inspiration from an idealized female who compensated them for the real women of whom they were deprived. If they were Parisian women, they might have taken comfort in imagery that valorized their sex, but they must also have known that these high ideals masked the somber realities of their individual and earthly existence. In either respect, at the heart of Paris Notre-Dame stood as an isle of femininity within a sea of men.

Figure 20. The Church and Christ, *Bible moralisée,* fol. 2ra, Austrian National Library, Vienna, Picture Archiv+Signature.

Figure 21. The Church, Notre-Dame, west façade, photo. P. Lemaitre ©CMN, Paris.

CHAPTER THREE

King Philip and His Government

Government in a Baggage Train

By encircling Paris with walls and fortifications, paving the streets and squares and stimulating construction, Philip endowed the city with features that befitted a capital. Of the complex factors that contributed to this process, politics was undoubtedly preeminent. The king needed a permanent center to situate his new experiments in government. As the location, however, Paris had already been established. Although his grandfather and father had traveled incessantly throughout their lands, Louis VI nonetheless placed and dated 26 percent of his surviving acts at Paris and Louis VII 35 percent of his acts. By contrast Orléans, their next preferred city, was the site of only 6 percent and 4 percent of their charters respectively.

From his forebears, Philip inherited a small royal domain that was administered by two rudimentary devices, stationary agents called prévôts in the domain and an ambulatory court of the king.[1] In 1179 Philip received from his father scattered lands in the Île-de-France with a concentration forming a rough triangle among Mantes, Sens and Orléans. Included were sizable towns such as Paris, Orléans, Bourges, Étampes, Poissy, Compiègne,

Senlis and Laon. The lands were divided among about forty prévôtés that were overseen by thirty to thirty-five prévôts. Some of the small hamlets shared the same official; larger cities such as Paris, Orléans and Bourges had two or more. These agents manned the royal castles, executed the king's commands, held courts and most important, collected the revenues of the domain. Often this income was delivered in kind (wheat, oats, wine, capons, hens, eggs), but it was expressed in fixed sums of money known as farms, normally set low to guarantee a profit to the prévôt.

To supervise the prévôts the king took to the road. In addition to the demands of warfare, his court performed the functions of justice, hearing cases as it passed through the domain and overseeing collection of farms and other revenues. At times it was simpler to consume the produce en route or receive the monies directly as the court passed by. For example, when stopping at Compiègne in 1186, Philip confirmed the city's privilege that the inhabitants were not obliged to leave their city to account for their revenues; instead they needed only to wait for the king's arrival.[2] Who accompanied the king on these journeys is more difficult to determine. The witness lists to his grandfather's and father's early charters had offered glimpses of those present at court, but by the end of his father's reign they were standardized to the five household officials—seneschal, butler, chamberlain, constable and chancellor—who were staffed mainly by lords from the Île-de-France. The most prestigious was the seneschalcy held by Thibaut, count of Blois, occasionally accompanied by men of high rank—such as Guillaume, archbishop of Reims and Thibaut's brother; and Philippe, count of Flanders—who because of their notoriety caught the chroniclers' notice. Rudimentary administration required that the king's court be mobile. Like most early medieval monarchs Philip passed his days in a tent, transported by pack horses and a baggage train. When he appeared, for example, at the old Capetian palaces of Orléans, Bourges, Compiègne and Laon, his chamberlains unpacked bedding, unfolded chairs and hung tapestries on the bare walls, but these were minimal luxuries. It was easier to bring the king to the countryside than the reverse. On the road he saw and was seen, asserted his authority and intervened. During the first decade of his reign he issued only 24 percent of his charters at Paris, less than his father and grandfather.[3] Such mobility and personalized administration was made possible by the smallness of the royal domain, which could be crossed in a matter of days. Through negotiations with the great barons, Philip did acquire Amiens, Montdidier and Roye to the north of Paris before 1190, but these added only ten prévôtés and increased the revenues by 20 percent.

The Challenge of the Crusade

After the fall of Jerusalem in 1187 to the Saracens under the leadership of Saladin, a new crusade became the urgent business of Western Christendom. Philip refused to join the summons and leave the kingdom until 1190, when he was assured of the company of his archrival, Richard, king of England. Before his departure he drew up a testament, in the event that he might not return, but most important he attached an ordinance regulating the government of the kingdom during his absence.[4] This document became, in effect, the first written constitution of the Capetian monarchy. Although it contained provisions that were temporary, it introduced permanent novelties that contributed to a more stationary, centralized and bureaucratic administration. Alongside the prévôt a new local official, called a bailli, was recognized and his operations clarified. Primarily involved in justice, the bailli was instructed to hold monthly assizes or sessions throughout the domain. Three times a year, the baillis were to come to Paris and report on the affairs of the realm and the conduct of the prévôts. At the center of administration the king's court was replaced by two regents, the queen mother, Adèle de Champagne, and her brother, Guillaume, archbishop of Reims. Little inclined to travel, they remained for the triennial sessions at Paris, where they received the reports of the baillis and any complaints against them, as well as hearing appeals of justice from anyone of the realm. Most important, at these triennial sessions all of the prévôts of the domain were convoked to the Temple (see Chapter One) outside the walls of Paris, where they rendered account of their finances in the presence of six Parisian bourgeoisie, who were identified only by their initials. Adam, a royal cleric, wrote down the results. During the king's absence, therefore, the rudiments of a centralized bureaucracy were created in which the important functions of justice and finance were conducted at Paris three times a year.

These arrangements lasted no more than eighteen months because Philip found urgent reasons to return home as quickly as possible. The excuses included the nearly mortal illness of Prince Louis, his only heir; his own illness in the Holy Land; and settlement of the succession of Flanders, occasioned by the recent death of Count Philippe at Acre. Many of the provisions of the ordinance were allowed to lapse. Resuming the duties of the regents' court at Paris, his own court began to travel again, stimulated by acquisition of Artois and Vermandois from the Flemish succession. Nonetheless Paris began to play a more prominent role in his administration. During the next decade Philip issued 32 percent of his charters from the royal city, a sizable increase from the pre-Crusade period. Most important, however, the innovation of the triennial visits of the baillis and prévôts to the royal capital was retained, where they reported to an accounting bureau at the Temple. The seeds of centralization and bureaucracy had taken root.

Paris, the Hub of Government in 1200

The king's absence in 1190 produced the first series of governmental records, the financial accounts that the cleric Adam drew up at the Temple. A military misfortune in 1194 produced a second series, the establishment of the royal archives. After King Richard returned from the Crusade to defend his continental holdings against Philip in the spring of that year, the two kings skirmished in the Loire valley. By chance the English king caught the Capetian in an ambush at Fréteval near Vendôme and captured his baggage train. The chroniclers who reported this embarrassment noted that Philip lost not only his bedding and valuable treasure but also his seal and numerous documents. The latter included the charters of barons who had deserted Richard for Philip and his brother Count John, as well as various domain accounts that the chamberlain Gautier the Young was commissioned to restore. The extent of Gautier's work is uncertain, but what is clear is that after 1194 a royal archive was established permanently at Paris. Known subsequently as the Trésor des Chartes, it was deposited at the royal palace on the Cité and later housed in a special building next to the Sainte-Chapelle during the reign of Philip's grandson, Louis IX. It consisted exclusively of incoming charters, beginning with the charter of 1194 of Count John's treasonous terms with Philip, and continuing with other sealed agreements between the Capetian and barons such as the counts of Boulogne and Flanders, including King John's version of the recent treaty of Le Goulet in 1200. The contemporary chroniclers paid no attention to the foundation of these archives, but it is clear that Rigord, the royal historian at Saint-Denis, enjoyed access to them because he refers to the very documents that can be found in the Trésor des Chartes to this day. Alongside the financial accounts, therefore, Philip possessed a second documentary collection permanently located in the royal city.[5]

Whatever was inaugurated at the Temple by the royal cleric Adam, these documents were lost in a catastrophic fire that destroyed the Chambre des Comptes on the night of 26–27 October 1737. Fortunately, an antiquarian who frequented the Chambre before the disaster had borrowed one of the financial rolls, which he published ten years earlier as an appendix to his study on fiefs. As a result, his action miraculously preserved a record of the triennial accounting for the complete fiscal year 1202–1203. Just as a bolt of summer lightning illuminates the surrounding landscape in a momentary but brilliant flash, this account reveals the wheels of Capetian government turning with exceptional clarity. At no other time in Philip's reign are we better informed on the workings of his administration than at this date. Although the bolt misses the year 1200 by two years, it sheds light back in time and presents a reliable picture of the preceding years, in which we see the operation of government in unaccustomed detail. Given the fortuity of surviving records, we could hardly ask for a better source for our purposes. Following the instructions of the ordinance of 1190, the roll accounts for three terms: All Saints, 1 November 1202; Purification of the Virgin, 2 February 1203; and Ascension, 15 May. Each term is further divided into three chapters—prévôts, baillis and marches—reflecting the three elemental functions of finance, justice and warfare.[6] We shall turn first to the regular operations of justice and finance.

Baillis and Justice

Although the ordinance of 1190 stressed the judicial functions of the baillis, the accounts of 1202–1203 naturally revealed the financial aspects of these duties. Most helpfully, the accounts identified the personnel. The ordinance states somewhat ambiguously that the baillis were placed in lands "that were identified by their own names." The accounts resolve this ambiguity by identifying the baillis not by territory, as was the case of the prévôts, but by personal name. Ten chief baillis were named as working out of Paris. For example, at the center was Robert de Meulan, surrounded by Aleaume Hescelin and Mathieu Pisdoë; to the south were Hugues de Gravelle, Guillaume de la Chapelle, and Thierry de Corbeil; and to the north were Renaud, Guy and Pierre de Béthisy, along with Nevelon the Marshal. As can be seen from the map, since the areas of their activities overlapped, there were no distinct *bailliages* with defined boundaries, with

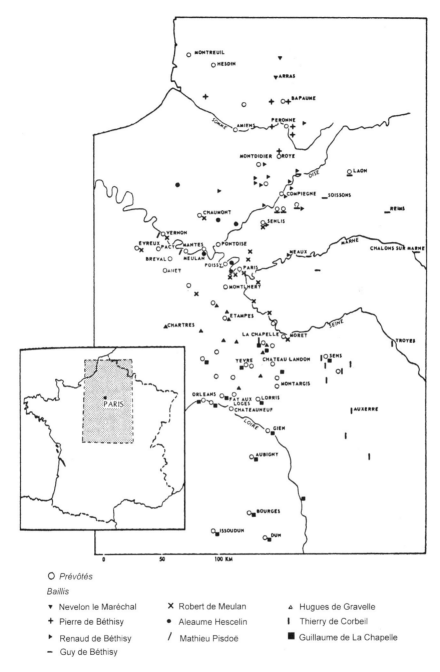

O *Prévôtés*

Baillis

▼ Nevelon le Maréchal   ✗ Robert de Meulan   ▵ Hugues de Gravelle

✚ Pierre de Béthisy   ● Aleaume Hescelin   ❘ Thierry de Corbeil

▸ Renaud de Béthisy   ╱ Mathieu Pisdoë   ■ Guillaume de La Chapelle

— Guy de Béthisy

Map 2. Royal baillis. *Source: The Government of Philip Augustus,* by John W. Baldwin, © 1986 by the Regents of the University of California. Published by the University of California Press.

the possible exception of Artois. The royal charters moreover show that the baillis frequently worked in pairs—again with the exception of Nevelon, who often acted alone in Artois. This collaboration can be best seen in the north, where the baillis operated as a team of four. When one dropped out, a new member quickly replaced him. This fluidity is further illustrated by the transfer of a bailli from region to region. Pierre du Thillay, for example, first appeared at Paris, showed up in the accounts as collaborating with Guillaume de la Chapelle at Orléans and finally became the bailli of Caen in Normandy after 1205.[7]

The accounts also reveal their salaries. In 1202–1203, for example, Robert de Meulan received 1 livre a day, Mathieu Pisdoe 15 sous and Hugues de Gravelle 10 sous.[8] Ten sous was nearly twice the highest wage for a merce-nary knight and equaled one-quarter more than the wage of the highest-paid artisan. In addition, Hugues was bestowed with gifts from the wardrobe, and other baillis received precious stones. Evidently the baillis were well paid, thus offering a strong incentive for their loyalty. As revealed by their place names, some baillis were recruited from the same family (the Béthisys, for example) and many originated from the royal domain (Meulan, Corbeil, and Le Thillay), where loyal agents were accessible. They offered the king many years of trusted service. Ten baillis remained in the records for twenty years or more; a Guillaume Menier was active for at least thirty-two years. In an age when life expectancy was fifty-five, these careers were completely devoted to the Capetian monarchy.

As outlined in the ordinance of 1190, the chief duty of the bailli was to hold monthly assizes at which they received appeals, did justice, defended royal rights and recorded judicial fines due to the king. They were also to supervise the conduct of the prévôts. From these courts the baillis were of-ten called assizors (*assessores*). Hugues de Gravelle was one of five assizors at Étampes, and Pierre du Thillay was designated by that title when he at-tended the assizes of Orléans in 1203. Other evidence suggests that they con-tinued to correct local officials, but the baillis' chapters in the accounts of 1202–1203 naturally furnish the best evidence of their collection of judicial fines and confiscations. In that year Guillaume de la Chapelle and Pierre du Thillay accounted for 346 livres from the assizes of Orléans, and the four northern baillis 256 livres from their combined jurisdiction. Counted up, they collected 6,870 livres, or about 7 percent of the ordinary annual income. That figure is undoubtedly too low because it does not take into account the hundreds of receipts in the baillis' chapters that mention only the name of a layman, a cleric, or a church in accordance with Capetian accounting practice. As in the Anglo-Norman records, these names represent sums for charters or for "offers" to facilitate or resolve judicial business. For example, Mathieu de Montmorency was in litigation with the abbey of Saint-Denis from 1200 to 1204, which was heard in the king's court. When Mathieu paid the bailli Robert de Meulan 50 unspecified livres in November 1202, he may have been seeking a favorable judgment. When the monks, in turn, gave Robert 20 livres "for a certain charter," that may have been payment for a royal charter they received the same year confirming their rights over Boissy-Laillerie. In 1203 the king decided a dispute between the canons of Saint-Aignan of Orléans and Aubert and Jean de Santilly over freeing the latter's serfs. Payment of 200 livres by the canons and of 54 livres by Jean in November 1202 may have facilitated the settlement.[9] Items amounting to 11,633 livres in the baillis' accounts are identified only by proper names. A proportion of that sum, impossible to determine, was profit from the judicial business of the baillis. Because money specifically designated for justice occupies only a small part of the baillis' chapters, we shall see that they record other activities as well.

The regents' central court, stationed at Paris with a triennial schedule, was superseded in 1191 when Philip returned from the crusade and his court resumed its traditional habit of itinerating throughout the domain and meeting at irregular times. Its routine can be best detected in a celebrated case of 1202 that decided a dispute between the king and the vidame over the regalia of the bishopric of Châlons-sur-Marne, occasioned by the death of the bishop in December 1201.[10] The details of this case are worth examining to understand the operations of the royal government. After preliminary hearings, Philip fixed a day at Paris for a judgment to which he convoked three bishops (Beauvais, Paris and Meaux), four learned clerics, three barons (the counts of Beaumont and Ponthieu, and Simon de Montfort) and five familiars of the king's entourage. The seven ecclesiastics were designated as "wise" (sapientes), and the four learned (litteratos) clerics were identified as Lothair of Cremona, doubtless an Italian expert on Roman law, the archdeacon of Bourges and two clerics who bore the academic title of "master." The five familiars included Gautier the Chamberlain, Barthélemy de Roie, Guillaume de Garlande, Guillaume des Barres and Philippe de Lévis, all well known from the royal entourage. Because none of these names, except those of the familiars, reoccurs in court decisions before or after 1202, we can conclude that the king's court did not as yet possess a core of permanent judges. The court finally ruled that the regalia should be rendered to the king and based its decision on two elements: legal arguments and testimony from practice. Benefiting from the counsel of the learned clerics, it evoked four reasons: (1) that the common law of the realm established from other regalian sees granted the regalia to the king in principle; (2) that a charter of Philip's father, Louis, likewise confirmed it specifically to the king; (3) that Roman law (*ius scriptum*—here Lothair's advice was pertinent) prevented prescription of such *fiscalia*; and (4) that the seventeen witnesses or jurors convoked to testify to the vidame's claim had, in fact, offered evidence against it. Placed under oath, the jurors (*jurati*) were identified by name, position, age, and party for whom they testified. At least five were age fifty or older and had witnessed the deaths of several bishops—a centenarian claimed to have witnessed ten—but none could testify that previous vidames had proved their right to the regalia, despite persisting in the practice of taking what they could. This jury, therefore, conducted an inquest into past practice following the procedures of canon law. Unlike the Norman inquests in which the jurors rendered their decision collectively, orally and independently of the parties, this canonical inquest took the depositions of each juror separately in writing and noted the party for whom the juror was giving testimony. Undoubtedly the depositions were taken at Châlons and were read to the court at Paris, where the decision was made. As a result, a certain Jean Paalé acknowledged receipt of 2,047 livres de Provins (1,527 livres parisis) for the regalia of Châlons in the baillis' chapter of November 1202.[11]

Adjourning wherever the king was found, following no regular calendar and possessing no permanent judges, the royal central court nonetheless began to acquire bureaucratic characteristics. It recruited trained personnel (learned clerics) and availed itself of the counsel of royal familiars to hear arguments; it followed established procedures such as the canonical inquest. When it settled at Paris with a fixed schedule and a permanent judiciary, as the *parlement de Paris* under Louis IX, it achieved the status of bureaucracy.

Prévôts and Finance

Although lacking spectacular acquisitions, Philip had nonetheless continued to increase the royal domain during the preceding decade.[12] The inheritance of the count of Flanders benefited him Artois and Vermandois when he returned from the crusade. The treaty of Le Goulet with King John in 1200 brought the county of Evreux, and parts of the Vexin. Montargis and Gien in the Gâtinais were annexed to the south. Totaled up in the accounts of 1202–1203, the number of prévôtés rose to sixty-two, administered by about forty-five prévôts, bringing in farms amounting to 34,719 livres. These figures represent an increase of 72 percent since the beginning of Philip's reign and of 50 percent in the last decade—certainly an indication of growth in the royal finances. In 1202–1203, therefore, some forty prévôts, identified only by the names of their posts, arrived three times at Paris, where they accounted their revenues, deducted their normal and recurring expenses and paid the balance to the treasurer, Brother Haimard of the order of the Templars, thus indicating that these transactions continued to take place at the Temple. Except for the disappearance of the six bourgeoisie, the accounting regime established in 1190 remained in operation.

These triennial exercises were divided into three chapters (prévôts, baillis and marches), of which the first two became permanent features of Capetian accounting into the thirteenth century. Within each chapter the prévôts and baillis accounted separately, most likely in the order of their appearance at the Temple. Although the prévôts' chapter was limited exclusively to these officials, the baillis' chapter included much more than the ten active baillis but were actually an assemblage of accounts. They included half of the prévôts who had already accounted in their own chapter and scores of other persons who were responsible for specialized tasks. Jean de Betefort, for example, was the keeper of the king's wardrobe and always accounted directly after the bailli Robert de Meulan, who operated out of Paris. Jean de Paalé and the bailli Guy de Béthisy accounted directly for the regalia of the bishoprics of Châlons-sur-Marne and Reims, which happened to be vacant at the time. Jean Cherchelarron was responsible for the Jews and a certain Godard for the forests. Whereas the prévôts account for regular income such as the farms and normal expenses such as alms and fiefrentes in their chapter, some twenty to thirty individuals identified by their personal names (except for the prévôts) are responsible in the baillis' chapter for sources of income that are mainly occasional. Even within the accounts of the ten active baillis, the revenues are of an occasional and irregular nature and the expenditures are varied in comparison to the standardized expenses of the prévôts.

Thanks to the survival of the accounts of 1202–1203, we have for the first time hard information on the finances of the Capetian monarchy around the year 1200. Brother Haimard wrote down the accounts, not to arrive at a budget of the total revenues and expenses of the government but to supervise and control the fiscal activities of the local officials. Using an abacus, he added up the revenues, subtracted the expenses and arrived at an excess or deficit for each prévôt, bailli and other agent; but he did not compute the total income, expense or balance in the treasury, although he possessed the means to perform these exercises. After performing this audit, however, we may extract enough information to arrive at an overall estimate of Philip's revenues and expenses, which can best be seen in tabular form in Table 1.[13]

In 1202–1203, therefore, Philip's prévôts and baillis brought him 115,000 livres in ordinary annual income. (The ordinary revenues from the marches were minimal.) As can be seen at a glance, the revenue from the prévôt chapters, depending heavily on the farms, did not fluctuate much from term to term, but the bailli receipts varied greatly. The distinction between the two chapters was apparently an auditing decision to separate fixed regular income from occasional income. We shall call both chapters "ordinary" income, that is, to be expected over time and to be distinguished from "extraordinary" income such as the 20,000 marks received from King John in 1200, or the large reliefs from the succession of great baronies, or wartime revenues, which, as shall be seen, were the result of unusual circumstances. These fortuitous "windfalls" were most likely collected and accounted for at the chamber of the king's household.

The accounts also enable us to perceive the sources of Philip's revenues and for the first time quantify them and estimate their importance. Again, the results can be best seen in Table 2.[14]

In a predominantly agrarian economy, the agricultural domain yielded about half the king's revenue. About 33,000 livres (or 32 percent of total income)[15] came from the farms, which were usually divided into three equal installments, thereby producing a steady revenue throughout the year. They

TABLE I

Annual income for the three terms of 1202–1203 in livres parisis

	November	February	May	Totals
Prévôt chapters	10,554	9,983	11,244	31,781
Bailli chapters	15,102	26,460	33,122	74,684
March chapters				8,671
Total ordinary income	25,656	36,443	44,366	115,136

SOURCE: *The Government of Philip Augustus*, by John W. Baldwin, © 1986 by the Regents of the University of California. Published by the University of California Press.

TABLE 2

ources of ordinary income in 1202–1203 in livres parisis.

	Income (in _livres parisis_)	Percentage of total income
⌐LTURAL DOMAIN		
.ôt farms	33,164	32%
.roduce outside farms	10,353	10%
Gîte	1,215	1%
Forests	7,432	7%
Total	52,164 =	50%
TOWNS AND COMMERCE		
Tailles	6,848	7%
Other urban revenue	4,186	4%
Exchange and minting	256	
Money taxes	8,150	8%
Jews	1,250	1%
Total	20,690 =	20%
CHURCH REGALIA	4,747	5%
JUSTICE	6,807	7%
MILITARY		
Vavassores	770	1%
Sergeants	1,037	1%
Total	1,807	2%
UNDIFFERENTIATED NAMES	11,633	11%
MISCELLANEOUS	4,986	5%
Grand Total	102,834*	100%

SOURCE: _The Government of Philip Augustus,_ by John W. Baldwin, © 1986 by the Regents of the University of California. Published by the University of California Press.

* 102,834 = 89% of 115,000. SOURCE: _Budget_ pp. 1–205.

ranged from 35 livres at Vitry-aux-Loges to 3,700 livres at Paris. The prévôts and baillis often sold off produce of wheat, oats, wine, chickens and eggs, which they accounted for separately amounting to about 10 percent of the annual revenue. Because the right of hospitality or _gîte_, realized so little this year, it was probably consumed on site as Philip's court circulated throughout the royal domain. About half of the forest revenues (7,432 livres or 7 percent) were collected by Godard, custodian of the forests around Paris. Those of Vincennes and Saint-Germain-en-Laye produced the other half.

Despite the expanding commercial economy of towns such as Paris and

Orléans, the urban conglomerations of the domain produced only 20 percent of the royal income in 1202–1203. The most reliable and profitable revenues were the money taxes (8,150 livres or 8 percent), which, although masquerading under various names (*tallia panis et vine* at Paris, for example), were collected once every three years from the towns in exchange for the king's promise that he would maintain the currency without debasement, and the taille (6,848 or 7 percent), a traditional but arbitrary tax that the king levied on the towns of his domain. In 1202–1203, for example, the two chief cities of Paris and Orléans paid out 2,995 and 1,500 livres respectively. Money exchange and the Jews yielded little this year—testimony that new policy toward the Jews, established in 1198, was too recent to bear much fruit (1,250 livres or 1 percent).

Revenues from his regalian churches depended on the death of the bishops. In 1202–1203 Châlons-sur-Marne, Laon and the great archiepiscopal see of Reims were vacant, the last due to the death of Philip's maternal uncle Guillaume de Champagne. We have seen that Jean Paalé collected 1,527 livres from Châlons, after the regalia had been adjudged to the king, and the bailli Guy de Béthisy received 500 livres from Laon, obviously a down payment in round figures, but Guy was likewise responsible for administering the vacancy of Reims. In February he accounted for the rents, tailles, profits of justice and the sale of wood, grain wine and so on. After expenses and obligations were deducted, he estimated that Reims had netted 2,260 livres for the first twenty weeks. The regalia yielded the king 4,747 livres in 1202–1203, but it could be more profitable. Since Reims remained vacant for one year and ten months, it may have produced as much as 12,000 livres for the king. Items that we have classified as military revenues were too small to account for Philip's buildup of a war machine against John, as we shall see; rather, they appear to be regular levies. Finally, we have noticed that the 6,807 livres realized from the exercise of justice, was likewise insufficient to account for the profits of the royal courts. Most likely, judicial proceeds were included in the sum of 11,633 livres that we have categorized as "undifferentiated names" and that certainly masked all kinds of operations, including military ones as well.

As each prévôt and bailli accounted before Brother Haimard three times a year, he not only acknowledged his revenues but also deducted expenses from them before turning over the balance to the treasury.[16] The prévôts' expenses were routine: local repairs, maintenance, wages for artisans, services and supplies, as well as fixed obligations owed by the king for alms to churches and fief-rentes for knights. Although the baillis acknowledged

aimilar expenses, their expenditures were more diversified and often in
volved sums that were not true expenses but internal transfer of sums for
judicial and military purposes. Moreover, since most of the prévôt and bailli
expenses were ostensibly for local needs, no accounts exist for the central
court or the royal household, as may be found later in the century. The closest to a household account is that of Jean de Betefort in the bailli chapters,
who received 500 livres from the Temple and 100 in a loan, from which
he deducted expenditures for the robes of the king, queen, Prince Louis
and his wife, Blanche, and the "children of Poissy" (that is Philippe and
Marie, the infants of the recently deceased Agnès de Méran), along with
royal chamberlains, baillis and other court personnel. The total paid out
amounted to 558 livres, certainly nowhere near the expenses (21,698 livres
for three months), for example, of the royal hotel in 1227. Obviously, the expenses of the central court were not included in the accounts of 1202–1203.

Since this fiscal year saw the opening of Philip's military campaign against
King John, the possibility of war expenditures cannot be excluded from the
prévôt and bailli accounts. Although precision is not possible, some sums
can be subtracted from ordinary expenses as war expenditures and roughly
estimated. In addition, the prévôts and baillis deposited large sums with
Brother Haimard at the Temple and with Brother Guérin, who, we shall
see, was Philip's chief agent at the central court. Since these disbursements
were free from expenses, they may also be considered positive balances. The
approximate totals of ordinary and war expenses and of deposits to Brothers
Haimard and Guérin are found in Table 3.[17]

TABLE 3
Ordinary and war expenses and deposits in 1202–1203 in livres parisis

	Prévôts	Baillis	Totals
Expenses			
Ordinary	6,400	6,000	12,400
War	3,600	13,500	17,100
Total	10,000	19,500	29,500
Deposits			
To Brother Haimard at Temple	18,000	37,000	55,000
To Brother Guérin		5,000	5,000
Total	18,000	42,000	60,000

SOURCE: *The Government of Philip Augustus*, by John W. Baldwin, © 1986 by the Regents of the University of California. Published by the University of California Press.

What becomes immediately apparent from the two elements of expenses and deposits is that the ordinary revenues of Philip's government (115,000 livres) were producing a substantial surplus. Ordinary expenses consumed only 12,400 livres, or 11 percent of royal income. When military expenses are added, they still expended only 26 percent of the budget. A balance of 85,500 livres remained, or if that figure is too optimistic, Brothers Haimard and Guérin received in cash at least 60,000 livres for the king's court and warfare. Although well situated for our purposes, the account for the year 1202–1203 became available only by chance survival, but the habit of spending less than the income appears to have been a regular feature of Philip's government. In November 1221 (we know from another account that survived by hazard), the king enjoyed a surplus of 131,826 livres from the previous term, and the current accounting revealed that the government spent only 66 percent of its income, again passing on a favorable balance. These parsimonious traits were replicated in the same proportions in a third surviving account of 1227, from the opening years of Philip's grandson, Louis IX.[18]

On the eve of Philip's military campaign against King John, therefore, the accounts of 1202–1203 suggest that the ordinary revenues and expenses of Capetian government allowed Philip the means to wage war. To this point we have been concerned only with routine operations of Philip's government; we shall see that he further reinforced his favorable position with additional war revenues.

The accounts of 1202–1203 show us the prévôts and baillis arriving three times a year at the Temple before Brother Haimard to account for their revenues, from which they subtracted their expenses and deposited the balance in the treasury. These features accommodate well with the description provided by Richard Fitz Nigel in the *Dialogue of the Exchequer* in England a generation earlier.[19] From this treatise we may surmise that the accounting took place around a table on which was spread a cloth marked with columns like a chessboard. Each column was assigned a unit (denier, sous, livre, 20 livres, 100 livres), so the table could be employed as an abacus to add, subtract and compute the balances. Like the English sheriffs, the prévôts and baillis faced judges who supervised the accounting. Performed by the six bourgeoisie during the king's absence on the crusade, after his return their replacement remains unidentified. Nonetheless, the accounting sessions at the Temple possessed all the features of a bureaucratic organ: regular times, rules, specialized personnel and current records.

Two Bureaucrats

During the 1190s, the contemporary chroniclers were unaware of the governmental transformations initiated by the ordinance on the eve of the crusade, but the flash of illumination of 1202–1203 remarkably illuminates the turning of the bureaucratic wheels. Clearest in view are the forty-some prévôts and ten baillis who descended on Paris three times a year, leaving a detailed record of their activities. As examples we shall examine closely the prévôt of Paris and his colleague, the bailli Robert de Meulan. The prévôt who accounted in 1202–1203 remains unidentified in accordance with Capetian practice, but he acknowledged receipt of 1,233 livres, 6 sous, 8 deniers, which was exactly one-third of the annual farm of 3,700 livres from Paris.[20] In addition he collected 1,000 livres from the money tax (the taille of bread of wine). From this income, he deducted expenses that appear to be regular because they often recur throughout the succeeding terms. He was responsible for paying the fixed alms the king owed to ten neighboring churches, among them the abbeys of Chaalis, Montmartre, Saint-Martin-des-Champs and Saint-Lazare, the Knights Templars at the Temple and the parish church of Saint-Merry on the right bank. The royal chaplain Evrardus was likewise reimbursed, as were the royal familiars, Gautier the Chamberlain and Guy, the king's butler, in the form of fief-rentes. The newlywed royal couple, Prince Louis and Blanche, received allowances as well. Administration of the royal city required that the prévôt remunerate at least a dozen artisans with wages ranging from 4 deniers to 7.5 sous a day. They included smiths, hatters, helmet makers, falconers and skilled workers who were identified by name and the title of *magister*. The prévôt procured supplies such as wine, coal, rope, candles and crossbow bolts. He was occupied with the transport of money and letters, making of barrels, procurement of horses and construction and renovation of prisons, because he was in charge of policing the royal city.

Involving occasional revenues and expenses, Robert de Meulan's accounts in the baillis' chapters were longer.[21] More than fifty sources of income were acknowledged. The most important were the taille of Paris (2,960 livres) and a transfer from the prévôt of Paris (372 livres), but there were also revenues from the Jews (including exchange of currency), debts from Senlis and Champagne, scutage for knights from Melun and Corbeil, Châteaufort, and Senlis, sale of wheat from Gonesse, proceeds from the forest of Yvelines and scores of other sources identified only by proper names.

Certain expenditures indicate activities that overlapped with the prévôt, such as transport of money and prisoners and building a jail. Even more than his colleague, he supervised construction projects: new royal stables, a butlery, towers, turrets, various houses for the king, adding pillars to a hall and refurbishing the chambers of the royal court. The chaplain Evrardus, first seen in the prévôt accounts, received funds to install stained-glass windows (*verrinis*) in his chapel. Although it is difficult to locate where this work was performed, much may have taken place at the royal palace. Artisans likewise received wages from the bailli, including those already in the employ of the prévôt. Even more than the prévôt's, the bailli's activities were oriented toward warfare. He bought horses and saddles, paid knights and procured catapults, tents and other equipment, all military measures in which Brother Guérin figured prominently. Our perceptions of the nature of these activities naturally depend on the fortuity of a single year, but the three available glimpses of the prévôt of Paris and the bailli Robert de Meulan show them to be busily at work, taking responsibility for their tasks under the supervision of the regular accounting sessions directed by Brother Haimard at the Temple.

The King's Entourage

In addition to leaving a record at the Temple, the prévôts, baillis and other agents no doubt rendered a visit to Île-de-la-Cité, where they conferred with the king or his entourage if they were in town. This took place in the large Salle du Roi of the royal palace. Because the court of the king kept no regular records, its composition has to be determined from other sources. During the opening decade, the chroniclers recognized noteworthy figures such as the great barons of the houses of Flanders and Champagne, who overshadowed the young Philip. Insisting that they all accompany him on the crusade, the king left many of these magnates buried in the Palestinian sands when he returned in 1191, including the influential Philippe, count of Flanders; the royal seneschal Thibaut, count of Blois; and his brother, Étienne, count of Sancerre, all of his father's generation. Thereafter the royal charters ended with the phrases *dapifero nullo* and *cancellaria vacante*, indicating that the king had not replaced the seneschal or chancellor at his court. Furthermore, by 1202 Guillaume, the aged archbishop of Reims and third brother of the Champagne party, had died in disgrace over the marital negotiations.[22] It was not until 1213, when Philip was contemplating an expedition to England, that a chronicler, the Anonymous of Béthune, writing in the vernacular, identified the inner core of the king's trusted counselors: a cleric, Brother Guérin; the knights Barthélemy de Roie and Henri Clément; and the chamberlain, Gautier the Young.[23] The reason for their obscurity in the intervening period is apparent. Unlike their baronial predecessors, they were all young and of modest status, and therefore less worthy of notice, but they emerge around 1200 in the new governmental records. They cannot be distinguished fully by function because, resisting specialization, they performed many kinds of duties; nonetheless each may stand for a separate category within the royal entourage.

Royal Clerics

The royal charters that had indicated for more than a decade that the chancery was vacant, suddenly in 1201–1202 began to add the phrase, "given by the hand of Brother Guérin."[24] This was a precipitous introduction to a personage who was to dominate royal administration for the remainder of the reign. In the accounts of the following year, he appeared at least fifty times, more than any other name with the exception of Brother Haimard. The succeeding documentation afforded by the archives and other sources cite him with accelerating rapidity. By 1213–1214, when he was noticed by the chroniclers, Guillaume le Breton identified him as "the special counselor of King Philip because of his wisdom in the royal hall and his incomparable gift of counsel . . . so that he handled the affairs of the kingdom and the needs of churches as if he was second to the king."[25] *Secundus a rege* was the stock phrase for designating the king's chief minister. It was justified because Brother Guérin had, in fact, replaced the recently deceased Archbishop Guillaume of Reims. Of humble origins, Guérin was called "brother" because he was a member of the crusading order of the Knights Hospitalers, making him both a cleric and a knight. The crusading connection may suggest how the king first found his loyal servant in the years after 1190. By 1213 he was rewarded with the bishopric of the nearby see of Senlis, undoubtedly because of royal favor but also with the support of the pope, who appreciated Guérin's efforts to bring about a public, if not private, reconciliation between the king and Queen Ingeborg.

As the king's chief minister, Guérin's duties were wide-ranging and omnicompetent. Drafting the royal charters and signing them with the phrase "by the hand . . . ," he remained in the chancery throughout the reign; we find him in 1220 commissioning the drafting of the third and last of the chancery registers. In the accounts of 1202–1203, his financial dealings extended from the Norman marches north to Soissons and south to Bourges; they consisted mainly of expenditures and disbursements of monies ranging from 50 sous to 2,000 livres. Military concerns are prominent in these transactions, as would befit a member of a military order. When the king faced the major military challenge of his career in 1214 at the battle of Bouvines, Guérin was close by as the chief strategist. After the conquest of Normandy, Guérin journeyed to Falaise twice a year to preside over the judicial sessions of the Norman exchequer. From the scattered royal charters, no other person was more active than he in conducting inquests, arbitrating disputes and rendering judgments. As cleric and later bishop, he assumed particular responsibility over ecclesiastical matters.

Brother Guérin was only one of a score of clerks of the king (*clerici regis*) who surfaced repeatedly in royal documentation.[26] Brother Haimard, the Knight Templar who supervised the triennial accounts at the Temple, was another, but he specialized in fiscal and monetary matters. The remaining clerics performed many and varied services: often traveling on missions as envoys, conducting negotiations, frequenting Rome to treat with the pope over the interminable business of the king's matrimony and administering the regalia of vacant bishops, as did Eudes Clément, or punishing the vidame of Châlons-sur-Marne, as did Master Guillaume de Saint-Lazare. Master Gautier Cornut, a royal cleric at Orléans, performed the more pedestrian task of dispensing funds from a vineyard. The king's clerks often received prebends (a living) from royal churches such as Saint-Martin de Tours or Saint-Frambauld de Senlis, whose chapters appear to have been designated for that purpose. Some were recruited from loyal families, notably the Cléments and the Cornuts, who regularly furnished personnel for royal administration. About twelve identified themselves by the title magister, indicating that as clerics they claimed an advanced education. Philip's employment of masters from the schools increased distinctly over his father's practice (only two or three appear under Louis VII), but considerably fewer than the scores if not hundreds who appear in contemporary Anglo-Norman records. It is clear that although the schools of France were the dominant producers of educated men in western Europe, the Anglo-Normans were the chief consumers. Like Guérin, a few French royal clerics were rewarded with a bishopric. Master Guillaume de Saint-Lazare became bishop of Nevers, and Master Gautier Cornut was dean of Paris before he

was finally elevated to the archbishopric of Sens. (His previous election
to the bishopric of Paris, however, did not succeed against the opposition
of the university masters and the papacy.) No more than five out of some
eighty elections, however, chose royal clerics to the French episcopacy. We
shall see that Philip's grant of freedom of election to the royal bishoprics
was apparently another contrast with the Anglo-Norman realm. Unlike
royal clerks serving Kings Richard and John, an efficient and loyal servant
of Philip Augustus could not expect promotion to high ecclesiastical office.

Royal Chancery

The principal contribution of clerics to secular government was their skills
of literacy. Although a few literate laymen could be found, most were unable to read and write Latin, the language of government. Philip Augustus
himself could not function in that language without the service of a cleric.
From Carolingian times, the clergy had furnished a secretariat for govern-
ments headed by an officer called the chancellor. The early Capetians relied
on local churches such as Notre-Dame, Saint-Denis and Saint Victor to
draft their documents and even entrusted the task to the recipient of the
charter if it was an ecclesiastical body. The major function of the royal chancellor was to append the royal seal. At the end of Louis VII's reign, however,
the chancellor began employing clerics of his own. When Philip's chancellor
Hugues du Puisset died in 1185, the king refused to replace him (thus the
phrase cancellaria vacante on royal charters), but these charters continued
to be drafted by a team of at least seven clerics, unnamed though distin-
guishable by their handwriting. After 1190 this number grew to seventeen,
usually working in groups of two or three and developing a scribal hand
that was characteristic of the royal chancery. By the time Brother Guérin
appeared on the royal charters (1201), the chancery had become a bureaucracy.[27] Not only did the chancery redact the royal charters and letters that
were sent out but as business multiplied there was need to keep copies. (Incoming letters, we remember, were routinely preserved in the archives since
1194.) The papacy had perfected a system of registers for that purpose by
the advent of Innocent III in 1198, and King John instituted the practice of
transcribing copies on chancery rolls by 1199 in England. By 1204–1205 the
Capetians followed suit in initiating a series of three registers (named A, C
and E) that, among other matters, recorded the most important of the out-
going documents. We have seen that Étienne de Gallardon was entrusted

with the responsibility of transcribing register E before he left the chancery for Bourges.[28]

As a cleric at Notre-Dame, Pierre the Chanter was acutely aware of chancery practice. He was familiar, for example, with the distinction between "letters of grace" and "letters of justice" issued by the chancery at Rome. In commenting on the Biblical passage of the Apostle John's vision of a book closed with seven seals (Rev. 5:4), he exhibited his acquaintance with how seals were variously used on contemporary letters that were open, closed and forged.[29] His chief concerns about the secular chanceries, however, evoked two questions. How were chanceries to be remunerated, and under what conditions were the clergy permitted to participate? Both papal and royal chanceries were accustomed to charge beneficiaries for their letters. In 1191, for example, Philip Augustus exempted the Templars from these fees. In an attempt to gain favor on his accession to the English throne in 1199, King John rolled back the exorbitant rates his brother Richard had charged.[30] Just as a bishop is not allowed to raise the synodical fees of his priests, Pierre queried, may the prince double or triple the revenues of his seal at will? After an involved discussion he concluded that the rates should remain stable. In effect, therefore, John was to be commended for returning to the rates of his father.

As for the clergy's participation in the chancery, the chief obstacle was the danger that they would become involved in affairs that resulted in bloodshed. In general canon law decreed that clerics who were associated with "blood judgments" became unfit to handle the sacraments and could not advance in holy orders. More specifically, the Chanter and Robert of Courson observed that chancery clerics might be required to draft letters ordering execution, mutilation, imprisonment or unjust fines. To avoid endangering clerical status, the two theologians advised princes to assign such tasks to literate laymen. This counsel was adopted by Innocent III in the canons of the Lateran Council of 1215.[31] Because of the rarity of literate laymen and the profoundly clerical composition of chancery, this was surely difficult to enforce. The Chanter modified the categorical principle by permitting clerics to copy commands that punished malefactors in general terms, or even specific individuals with monetary fines.[32] Because this narrowed the prohibition to individual sentences decreeing death or mutilation, the theologians thereby authorized most of the routine business and would not have depleted chanceries of their clerics.

Royal Knights

Barthélemy de Roie and Henri Clément were designated the "king's knights" (*milites regis*), a term that accented their military functions.[33] This was particularly the case with Henri, who bore the sobriquet marshal bequeathed by his father Robert Clément, the former tutor of the young Philip. Henri's brother Aubry, like so many of his contemporaries, died at the siege of Acre in 1191; Henri first appears in the accounts of the marches in 1202–1203 confided with military duties. In the culminating battles of 1214, he was at the side of Prince Louis at La Roche-aux-Moines. Expiring from wounds shortly after, he was mourned throughout France for his heroism. Like his brother, the cleric Eudes, he could also be found conducting administrative tasks. The Cléments may be associated with two other families, the Garlandes and the Barres, who had long supplied the Capetians with illustrious and loyal knights, all bearing the forename of Guillaume. The contemporary chroniclers celebrated their feats in combat, but governmental documents reveal them serving at the king's court as well. A Guillaume from each family, for example, assisted Philip in judging the regalia of Châlons in 1202.

Although his knightly prowess was not negligible, Barthélemy de Roie's service was chiefly administrative. The agreement of 1194 between Philip Augustus and John, count of Mortain, the first to be retained in the newly founded archives, contains the name of Barthélemy, the king's knight and pantler, who swore to guarantee the terms. A younger son from the modest family of Roie in the newly acquired Vermandois, he was the most richly rewarded in the accounts of 1202–1203, with gifts of clothing and a payment of 100 livres. This was followed by promotion to the grand chamberlainship in 1208, succeeding Mathieu, count of Beaumont. Barthélemy lacked sons, so his daughters were given in marriage by the king to important lords in Normandy and the north, and royal favor bestowed on him an impressive patrimony of lands. Although he conducted himself honorably on the battlefield of Bouvines as befitted a knight, his career centered on the royal court. He too did not miss the judgment of Châlons, received and disbursed funds on the military marches of 1202–1203, traveled to Falaise and later to Caen to sit on the biennial sessions of the Norman exchequer and participated in numerous inquests, arbitrations and judgments. Of all the king's new *familiares*, none appeared as early, was more constant in attendance or lasted as long as he. He became, in fact, the lay counterpart of the omnicompetent cleric Brother Guérin. Among the royal knights, Barthélemy was joined by Aubert de Hangest, also from Vermandois, but the earliest of these knights was Philippe de Lévis from the castellany of Montlhéry. Surviving the crusade with the king, he began as a royal assizor working with the bailli at Etampes. On him and Gautier the Chamberlain the king conferred the delicate task of punishing Thomas, the royal prévôt of Paris, in 1200, as has been noted.

Royal Chamberlains

Until assumed by Barthélemy de Roie, the grand chamberlainship of the royal court was held by Mathieu, count of Beaumont.[34] He left virtually no trace in the records, so his position was undoubtedly honorific. The principal duties in the chamber, which consisted of looking after the bedroom, storing treasure and managing the domain, had long been undertaken by Gautier the Chamberlain. Having served Louis VII since the 1150s and an old man in the 1190s, he drew up his testament in 1198 and died in 1205. Despite his humble origins, the contemporary chroniclers noted the destinies of his numerous sons, especially those who rose to high ecclesiastical office. Three became bishops: Étienne, of Noyon (1188); Pierre, of Paris (1208); and Guillaume, of Meaux (1213). Three lay sons followed their father into the royal court, but the life of Philippe (the oldest) was cut short in 1191, when, like so many, he fell at the siege of Acre. Ours, the second son, participated on and off in the royal court throughout his career. The accounts show him receiving funds with Barthélemy de Roie for military actions in the Vexin, receiving a daily wage of 1 livre, the highest wage paid to a bailli, but soon after he transferred to Prince Louis and served at La Roche-aux-Moines in the crucial year of 1214.

His absence from Philip's entourage was filled by his brother Gautier (called "the Young" while the elder was called "the Father"). As befitted a chamberlain, Gautier the Young's attendance was constant and his tasks broad. Guillaume le Breton attributed to him reconstitution of the royal archives after the embarrassment of Fréteval. Because this consisted also of restoring the lost fiscal and domain documents, like his father he attended to finances in the chamber. He too participated in punishing the vidame of Châlons. The accounts of 1202–1203 picture him receiving monies for unspecified tasks as well as helping with military preparations on the Norman marches. (After Guérin, he received the most mention.) He accompanied Guérin to preside over the sessions of the Norman exchequer and undertook missions to Rome. With Ours at the side of Prince Louis, Gautier the Young rode with Philip at Bouvines. When Gautier died in 1218, Ours returned to the royal court. The more routine tasks of the royal household were performed by a swarm of cupbearers, squires, pantlers, cooks and falconers. Remunerated for domestic services, few of them were engaged in administrative tasks; nonetheless, the bailli Guillaume Poucin and the powerful Barthélemy de Roie entered court service as domestic servants.

Although the chroniclers caught sight of them as individuals from time to time, Philip's four familiares were not noticed as a team until the eve of Bouvines; yet they had been working together since 1195, when Ours and his brother Gautier, Henri the Marshal and Barthélemy de Roie witnessed a transaction at Amiens.[35] We see them at their greatest activity in 1202–1203, thanks to the financial account's brilliant beam. Like the baillis, they performed a great diversity of tasks, accepted important responsibilities and worked efficiently. Of modest station, they were completely dependent on royal patronage; well paid, their loyalty was unquestioned, and being young, they offered many years of service.

Finance and the War Machine

The survival of financial accounts for this fiscal year comes at a propitious moment. On the eve of Philip's campaign against Normandy, Haimard added to the prévôt and bailli chapters a third set devoted to the military preparations on the Norman marches. The triennial accounts of the marches furnish remarkable evidence for both the workings of Capetian bureaucracy and the fueling of Philip's war machine.

Both Philip Augustus and John exchanged concessions in the treaty of Le Goulet in May 1200.[36] The Capetian recognized John as Richard's heir for his continental possessions and forced Arthur to submit to John as vassal for Brittany. For this recognition, John not only conceded the territory of Evreux and a payment of 20,000 marks but explicitly acknowledged the French king as his overlord for the fiefs of Normandy, Anjou and Aquitaine. With the legal relation between the two monarchs reestablished, Philip could amicably entertain John at Paris in the summer of 1201 and depend on the unstable character of the English monarch to make a mistake. He did not have long to wait, because in the same year events moved rapidly. Hugues, count of Lusignan, proposed to marry Isabelle, heiress to the county of Angoulême, thus creating a powerful coalition of Aquitainian barons that blocked John's

vital route between Poitiers and Bordeaux. John's riposte was swift and inge-
nious. Swooping into Angoulême, he seized the heiress and promptly married her himself, professing a passion for the twelve-year-old Isabelle that
subsequent conduct, in fact, confirmed. This bold move would have been
successful if John had taken care to compensate the outraged fiancé, but instead he added insult to injury by challenging the victim to a duel and attack-
ing his lands. Hugues' response was to apply for redress to John's overlord,
the Capetian king. As confirmed in the treaty of Le Goulet, Philip had the
right to summon his vassal John to Paris to answer charges, but John refused
to meet anywhere except on the Norman borders, as was customary for the
dukes of Normandy. What John neglected to acknowledge was that he was
being summoned as duke not of Normandy but of Aquitaine. When John
failed to appear on the appointed day of 28 April 1202, "the court of France,
being assembled," the chronicler Ralph of Coggeshall reported, "adjudged
the king of England to have forfeited all the lands which he and his ancestors
had before that time held of the king of France, for the reason that he and
they had long neglected to render all the services due from the lands and had
nearly always disobeyed the summonses of their lord the king."[37]

Now having a clear judgment, Philip's next task was to enforce it. Two
campaigns were prepared, one led by the king down the Seine against the
Norman Vexin, and the other by Arthur, supported by the Lusignans and
other southern barons, against John's positions in the Loire valley. When Arthur learned that John's mother, the aged dowager Eleanor of Aquitaine, was
at Mirabeau, the temptation to capture her was too great. Eleanor resisted
long enough to allow John time to arrive on the scene, and in one stroke he
captured Arthur, the Lusignans, and his major southern enemies. Faced with
this defeat, Philip had as his only recourse to abandon his campaign against
Normandy and descend to the Loire to repair the damage. From November
1202 to May 1203 (the period when the Capetian accounts were casting light
on royal finances), Philip Augustus was absent from the Île-de-France and
the Norman frontier. The triennial accounts of the marches that were established to manage the Norman campaign therefore depict the operation of
the French war machine as a bureaucracy without the king's presence.

The march chapters are organized around five clusters of castles in the
Vexin (in all about seventeen) that protected the border of the Île-de-France
against Normandy (Map 3).[38] They may be identified by a chief castle in
each cluster, stretching across the Seine from the northeast to the southwest. To the east of the river they consisted of Gournay, Lyons-la-Forêt, and

Gisors; to the west, Vernon-Evreux, and Anet. Shifting about frequently, four to six war treasurers supervised the castles at any particular moment. Their principal task was to account for the wages of the military personnel. From the mass of information supplied for the three terms of November, February and May, we may distinguish two particular phenomena: the movement of troops, and the cost of raising an army. By detailing soldier's wages, the treasurers also record troop deployment on the Norman frontier. Most of the payments went directly to knights, crossbowmen and sergeants, but Eudes the Chamberlain designated five captains of foot sergeants, including Marshal Henri Clément, Guillaume de Garlande and Cadoc, this last the infamous mercenary captain, who received lump sums.

Although the movement between castles was constant, it is clear that the king concentrated most of his troops to the west of the Seine. The presence of Prince Louis and his companies at Le Goulet from November through February likewise confirms that Philip intended to launch his attack down the river toward Normandy from the west bank. No clear pattern emerges in the shifting of foot sergeants from castle to castle, but a striking decline

Map 3. Philip Augustus's castles in the Vexin.

of knights from all of the garrisons in the region becomes evident (for example, from fifty to sixteen at Evreux, twenty to twelve at Vernon, thirty to twenty at Gisors, and fifty-eight to nineteen at Lyons). After the disaster of Mirabeau, the king was moving his mobile cavalry into the Loire region. That major commanders such as Henri Clément and trusted familiars such as Barthélemy de Roie disappear from the accounts after November confirms this new deployment.

Shifting troops and removing contingents to the Loire naturally complicate the task of estimating the effectives that Philip had amassed for the aborted campaign into Normandy, but these estimates can be offered: 257 knights, 245 mounted sergeants, 71 mounted crossbowmen, 101 crossbowmen on foot, and 1,608 foot sergeants, for a total of 2,282.[39] These figures do not include the auxiliary personnel (miners, engineers, artisans, etc.) who accompanied the combatants, nor the band of mercenaries for whom Cadoc was paid 3,290 livres angevins by the treasurer Thibaut de Chartres. At the going rate for foot sergeants, this would have added 300 men to that category. An army of 2,300 to 2,600 effectives, of which only 250 were knights, was not large by contemporary standards, but it was an army that was completely salaried and unencumbered by the constraints of feudal service. In 1197 King Richard had attempted to convert his feudal levies into a standing army of 300 knights that would be available at all times. Whereas Richard failed in his project, Philip Augustus succeeded in raising a standing army, including 250 knights, who would fight as long as the money lasted.

The cost of warfare comprised, to be sure, more than soldiers' wages, but the latter component is the one factor for which the accounts of the marches furnish serial information. The normal daily wages can be determined for five categories of combatants: knights (72 deniers parisis), mounted sergeants (36 deniers), mounted crossbow men (48–54 deniers), crossbowmen on foot (12–18 deniers), and foot sergeants (8 deniers). The contemporary Norman exchequer accounts show that John was paying his troops about 30 percent less. From the Capetian accounts, we can calculate that Philip paid 27,370 livres parisis in wages to these five categories of troops in the marches. The total did not include the lump sum that was given to Cadoc for his *routiers* (mercenaries).

The figure of 27,000 livres is of interest because it echoes a comparable figure from a designated war tax, called the *prisée des sergents*. In 1194 Philip Augustus levied on the towns and royal abbeys of the royal domain specific quotas of foot sergeants accompanied by wagons. According to a copy

included in the register, seventy of eighty-three towns and abbeys were as-
sessed 7,695 sergeants and 138 wagons.[40] (The wagons were apportioned at
the rate of one to every fifty sergeants or fraction thereof.) Fifteen towns
and abbeys commuted their obligations into money, for a total 16,463 livres.
How these levies of sergeants, wagons, and money were deployed is not
clear, but by 1202–1203 they had all been commuted to money payments.
Inserted between the prévôt and bailli chapters for the November term, a
special chapter entitled *servientes* reported that sixty-four towns and abbeys
were assigned sums of money for their sergeants to be collected by four
baillis for a grand total of 26,453 livres.[41] In twenty-five cases, the number
of sergeants was given on which the money assessment was based, and the
term of service was specified at three months. It is apparent that the daily
wage was the normal rate of 8 deniers and the wagons brought 13 livres,
10 sous for the three months. Some of the items missing from the 1194 account can be found in subsequent prévôt and bailli chapters for the sum of
another 1,037 livres, bringing the grand total of the prisée des sergents of
1202–1203 to 27,490 livres, or a figure close to that actually paid in wages in
the marches accounts (27,370 livres).

The closeness of these two figures may not have been a coincidence but
rather the result of fiscal budgeting. On the demand side, the war treasurers
reported the number of troops deployed and the wages paid, which could furnish estimates of how much money was needed. On the supply side, the prisée des sergents appears to have been set at arbitrary rates. When the items in
1194 that overlap with those of 1202–1203 are compared, we see that the rates
were rarely the same, suggesting that the accounting bureau could have fixed
them. In this way the bureau had the power to raise the money to cover the
military wages on the marches. To be sure, the evidence for a military budget
rests on a comparison of two sums, but whether or not it was a coincidence
it is nonetheless true that the bureau possessed the data and accounting tools
to produce such a budget. We have seen that budgets were, in fact, created for
calculating revenues and expenses of the entire government at the end of the
reign. Although the troops' wages did not constitute the full costs of war, there
was logic in using money raised for recruiting sergeants to pay the wages of
an army composed largely of sergeants. In all events, Philip Augustus could
count on a permanent army of 2,500 men of which 250 were knights.

In addition to wages, the war treasurers on the marches accounted for
construction and repair of fortifications (since castles had been recently
captured); procurement of grain, bacon, wine and other supplies for the

garrisons; and compensation for horses and equipment lost in combat. The treasurers make no mention of armaments—crossbows, bolts and coats of mail—although such items can be found elsewhere in the prévôt and bailli accounts and in specialized inventories copied into the royal registers. Summed up, the treasurers reported expenses on the Norman marches for the fiscal year 1202–1203 of 65,931 livres, to which another 17,100 livres, earmarked for war in the prévôt and bailli chapters, may be added, resulting in a grand total of 83,000 livres. We recall that the prévôt and bailli chapters reported a surplus of 60,000 to 85,500 livres, to which should be added the prisée des sergents of 27,000 livres, for a total of 87,000 to 112,500 livres. Thanks to the good state of Philip's finances, the treasury had ample reserves to cover the costs of war reported on the Norman marches. Again, we should remember that the war was not limited to the Norman frontier but extended to the Loire campaign, led personally by the king, and to other theaters of combat for which we have no figures. Nor are the full expenses of the king's "hotel" known. Of equal importance, the fiscal accounts ignore significant revenues as well, such as the despoiling of the regalian churches during the interdict and, most important, King John's relief of 20,000 marks sterling (36,230 livres parisis). These expenditures and receipts were undoubtedly handled in the royal chamber that followed the king on his travels but left no trace in the accounting bureau in Paris.

What is now clear from the fiscal accounts of 1202–1203 is that on the eve of the attack against Normandy the finances of the Capetian monarchy were adequate to the task. The regular expenses of administration consumed no more than one-eighth to one-quarter of the ordinary revenues, allowing large surpluses, which, combined with a war tax, more than covered the known expenditures on the Norman border. Most likely unreported expenses elsewhere were also met by unrecorded but significant receipts in the royal chamber. Moreover, the king enjoyed a permanent mercenary army whose wages were financed by a budgeted war tax. This war machine was the product of an effective administration—indeed a bureaucracy—staffed by prévôts, baillis, and war treasurers who regularly reported to a central accounting bureau stationed at Paris. With the king absent in the Loire valley, his trusted familiars, Brother Guérin, Barthélemy de Roie, Henri Clément, Gautier the Young and the bailli Robert de Meulan, can be seen in the march accounts busily receiving monies and disbursing them to the treasurers. Barthélemy and Henri soon disappear to join Philip, but Guérin, Gautier and Robert remain active throughout the year. Brother Guérin surfaces at least a half-dozen times handling large sums of 2,360, 1,760, and 1,340 livres frequently designated as "from the Temple by letter" (*de Templo per litteras*). Specialized personnel, defined duties, regular procedures, assigned localities, supervision from a fixed center, and records kept in accounts and by letter are all salient hallmarks of an established bureaucracy.

Military Victory and Expansion of the Realm

With tanks full, by the summer of 1203 the war machine assembled by the treasurers in the Vexin was ready to push down the Seine toward Normandy.[42] The major obstacle was the imposing Château-Gaillard, halfway between Paris and Rouen, the key to Richard's defenses of the duchy. The castle was invested in September and succumbed to Philip's siege engines by March 1204. Thereafter the towns of Falaise, Caen, Bayeux and Bonneville capitulated in rapid succession; Rouen, the principal city of the duchy, held out until June 1204 before it succumbed. Simultaneously, Guillaume des Roches, John's former seneschal of Anjou and now in Philip's service, led the Capetian armies in the Loire valley in Arthur's absence. By the spring of 1205 Loches and Chinon, the two key castles in the region, had also capitulated. When a campaign in the summer of 1206 brought few results, a truce was signed in October in which John conceded all of his territories north of the Loire to the Capetian, plus the castles of Loches and Chinon. Normandy and Brittany fell in one short season; in another, the Loire fiefs of Anjou, Maine and Touraine. The explanation for John's sudden loss of the kernel of his father's continental holdings, which his brother Richard had defended so successfully in the 1190s, is surely complex, but John himself must certainly share in the responsibility. His capricious treatment of the prisoners taken at Mirebeau, culminating in the murder of Arthur, precipitated a wave of defections in Normandy and in the Loire fiefs, of which Guillaume des Roches was only the most notorious. Moreover, John's refusal to come to the aid of Château-Gaillard, preferring to remain in the west of the duchy, discouraged his Norman barons from resisting. When he precipitously abandoned the duchy in December 1203, taking with him his new bride, it was clear that he could no longer be counted on to defend his possessions. Against John's deficiencies and inaction, Philip's preparations nonetheless add an essential factor to the equation. A standing army of 2,500 troops, including 250 knights, and a full treasury certainly contributed to the victory.

Yet John vowed to return and recover his fiefs.[43] When he finally arrived in February 1214, he was well prepared. Through subsidies and alliances he had formed a coalition of allies to the north, composed of his nephew, Otto of Brunswick, emperor of the Germans; the counts of Flanders and Boulogne; and other important barons from the Lowlands. His strategy was to catch Philip between a pincer movement, one wing composed of the allies advancing from the north on Paris and the other from the south led by himself with recruits from Poitou and surrounding territories. The coordination of the two prongs was successful. At the last moment Philip was forced to divide his troops and dispatch his son, Louis, to oppose John's southern thrust. When they met at La Roche-aux-Moines outside of Angers on 2 July, John declined battle for reasons that are not entirely clear, but he nonetheless succeeded in splitting the Capetian army at a crucial moment before Philip faced the allies on 27 July at Bouvines, on the northern frontier near Lille. Because a small force of paid troops was no longer sufficient, the king called on his *fideles* throughout the realm to raise an army of about 1,300 knights and 4,000 to 6,000 foot sergeants. The allies brought somewhat larger contingents to the field, but they were hindered from deploying all their effectives because Brother Guérin, who directed Capetian strategy, forced them to engage in combat as soon as they arrived on the field and before all of their companies could be drawn up for battle. The strategy succeeded, bringing Capetian victory to completion. When the day was over, the counts of Flanders and Boulogne were taken prisoner, and Emperor Otto barely escaped with his life.

The battle of Bouvines confirmed Philip's conquest of the fiefs of Normandy, Brittany, Anjou, Maine and Touraine. Assessing the extent of territory gained, modern historians have estimated that these victories increased the royal revenues from two to four times. The recently discovered fragment of a fiscal account from November 1221 enables us to calculate the gains with greater precision.[44] Since the account was a true "budget," that is, computation of both the total annual revenues and expenses, we can now estimate the ordinary revenue as 195,000 livres parisis for that fiscal year. This was 80,000 livres more than the 115,000 livres in 1202–1203, or an increase of 70 percent—not quite a doubling of income as has been claimed. However we interpret the accounts, the impression of Philip's wealth nonetheless remains strong. The Capetian government recorded a surplus of 132,000 livres in November 1221 and again of 107,650 livres in February 1227. When the king drew up his testament in 1222, his legacies totaled 790,000 livres. Whether or not that amount was actually distributed, a cleric who attended

Philip's funeral reported hearsay that it was more than 2 million livres. The picture remains confused, but it cannot be denied that Philip had augmented his revenues significantly.

The increase in territory and income continued to stimulate improvements in the bureaucracy, of which recordkeeping is the surest sign. When Caen fell into Philip's hands in May 1204, the clerics of the royal chancery found an inventory of Norman fiefs drawn up by King Henry II in 1172, which they copied into their Register A.[45] This information prompted Philip's baillis to conduct further inquests into the Norman feudal holdings; they were likewise copied into the register until the entire duchy was surveyed. Similar investigations were begun into the fiefs of the old Capetian domain as well. Other information of interest to the royal court was recorded: charters of urban liberties, inquests into forests, domain accounts, debts to Jews, all kinds of lists of castles, bishoprics and abbeys and so on. As the information swelled, the books were recopied and reorganized in 1212 and again in 1220, thus allowing the chancery portable handbooks of information useful to the royal court as it traveled about. Of greatest concern, we remember, were the royal charters dispatched by the chancery and incoming letters received in the archives, of which the most important were likewise copied into the registers.

Acquisition of Normandy also contributed to the growth of royal documentation. Although financial records had been kept since 1190, none were drawn up for the justice exercised in the courts of the king and of his baillis. Prior to the Capetian conquest, however, the Anglo-Norman dukes kept records of the judgments rendered by the exchequer as it met twice a year in Caen. By 1207 Philip had moved the exchequer to Falaise, closer to Paris; dispatched two justices, Brother Guérin and Gautier the Young (later replaced by Barthélemy de Roie), to preside over the biennial sessions; and continued the practice of writing down a summary of the decisions taken.[46] Thus the Capetians instituted their first judicial records, which were later perpetuated by those of the parlement of Paris, or the first stationary, royal court of justice during the reign of Louis IX, Philip's grandson.

1200, a Turning Point in Capetian Bureaucracy and Centralization

Like his father and grandfather before him, Philip Augustus opened the first decade of his reign by carrying his government around in his baggage as he traveled throughout the small royal domain. This permitted him to attend personally to his affairs, judge, collect revenues, wage war, oversee his lands and be seen by his subjects. It was easier to carry the government to the countryside than the reverse. These ambulatory habits, to be sure, persisted into the remaining decades of his reign. During the second decade (1191–1203) 32 percent of his charters were issued at Paris, increasing to 39 percent in the third decade (1204–1214) and returning to 28 percent in the last (1215–1223).[47] By comparison to the first decade (24 percent) and to Philip's forebears, Paris saw more of the king than at any other time previously. Thanks to the establishment of a bureaucracy in the capital, moreover, the royal presence was no longer required. In 1190, on the eve of departure for the Third Crusade, Philip issued an ordinance that established a government to operate without his presence. His mother and uncle set up a provisional court at Paris, but most important, his prévôts and baillis were summoned three times a year to Paris, where they could be supervised by an accounting bureau at the Temple. With a fixed place, a regular schedule, established procedures and a continuous record, this organ constituted without question the nucleus of a bureaucracy, but it may not have been the first time. From 1144 to 1147, while Louis VII was away on the Second Crusade, Suger, abbot of Saint-Denis and regent for the king, brought similar financial business to Paris, where he was the first to make use of the services of the Temple. Whatever the innovations, however, they were abandoned on the king's return. In contrast, Philip's return, although it allowed the regents' court to lapse, permitted the accounting bureau and the triennial visits of the prévôts and baillis to continue. The accounts of 1202–1203 show them functioning in accordance with the ordinance of 1190. This decade was a true turning point, a reversal in the flow of government. Now the countryside converged on the center, rendered increasingly necessary by the growth of the royal domain. This decade also brought improvements in the bureaucracy so that it could function without the immediate presence of the king. The accounting bureau rolls, archives and recent chancery registers furnished accurate records. The old magnates were replaced by teams of familiars who operated out of the king's court and by teams of baillis who circulated throughout the domain. Of modest origins, they depended on the king's favor; handsomely remunerated, they remained trusted agents; and young, they outlived the king himself. Along with the war treasurers, these men constructed a war machine that was amply financed with the surpluses from an efficient administration and an astutely budgeted war tax. Philip's small but permanent army of knights and foot sergeants created on the Norman marches was the spearhead of his military success, which cleared northern France of his English enemies and so remarkably added to the royal lands. Implantation of an accounting bureau at Paris was a small beginning, to be sure, but it initiated a process that has been irreversible to this day. Paris was the center where the great magnates followed the royal officers, to erect residences so they could better treat with the king's government. In the following reigns, the courts of justice likewise took the path of finance. Thanks to these bureaucratic achievements, Paris became irreversibly the capital of France. The foundations of the Jacobean state were laid.

CHAPTER FOUR

The Church, Clergy and Religious Life

Between January and September 1200 the interdict levied on Philip Augustus's lands deprived the inhabitants of Paris of the church's services. Throughout the city the doors to churches and the gates to cemeteries were closed, and the sacraments were withheld from the faithful. Only baptism was administered to the newborn and the consecrated host given to the seriously ill. These draconian measures affected all levels of the clergy and the laity. Regular observance of mass and confession ceased; the special occasions of confirmation, marriage and the conferring of holy orders were suspended; and the stench of unburied bodies infected the air. Most noticeable was the great hush that descended over the city as the bells of scores of churches no longer marked the canonical hours or pealed out the festivities that enlivened Parisian life.[1] This being the Middle Ages, of course there were exceptions. The exempt abbeys of Saint-Germain-des-Prés and Saint-Denis, for example, were allowed to continue their routine services behind closed doors and with muffled bells. Nonetheless, by the brutal suppression of the services most Parisians were suddenly reminded of the overwhelming role the church played in their lives.[2] Although in the past French kings had been punished with excommunication for their marital foibles, this was the first time Paris

had suffered a general interdict levied by the papacy. In addition to the dev-
astating effect on religious life, the interdict also powerfully illustrated the
hierarchical nature of the contemporary church. Claiming the fullness of
power (*plenitudo potestatis*), Pope Innocent III in Italy could assert his authority over the church in France and the spiritual life of the faithful with no
exception for kings. Configured as a great pyramid, with power descending
from God through the pope to the bishops and the secular clergy and from
them to the laity below, this simple schema, now given practical effect in the
interdict, suggests an approach to the church at Paris in the year 1200.

Pope

Pope Innocent was no stranger to Paris, where he had studied theology
for a few years between 1180 and 1187 and "had sweated over scholastic
studies," as his biographer recalled. When he mounted the papal throne
in 1198, he announced the event to all the bishops of Christendom, but
the papal chancery enregistered only those letters addressed to the bishops
of France, the king and Eudes, bishop of Paris.[3] Months later, as Innocent
fondly reminisced over his earlier studies, he sought to emphasize that he
was especially bound to Philip and his kingdom (*tibi et regno tuo specialiter
nos teneri fatemur*).[4] His immediate purpose was to persuade the king to
dismiss Agnès de Méran, Philip's concubine, but the special relationship
between the papacy and the Capetian kings had roots deep in the past. In
the same letter, he exhorted Philip to continue in the footsteps of his father,
Louis VII, whom Pope Alexander III had designated as the "most Christian" (christianissimus) king of France, a title that had been bestowed since
the eleventh century.

The interdict of 1200 was only the first of Innocent's numerous interventions into French affairs, but the pope sought to force Philip to submit
his marriage to papal judgment, thereby underscoring the papacy's supreme
jurisdiction over the sacrament of marriage to which the king as a Christian was obliged to submit. Papal authority was again asserted in 1202 when
Innocent legitimized Philip's children born to Agnès. When the pope attempted to mediate between Philip and John over the Normandy in 1204,
he admitted that it was a dispute over fiefs normally under the purview of
kings, but in this case his intervention was justified "by reason of sin," over
which he had jurisdiction.[5] These interventions were simply attempts to define and extended the claim of "fullness of power" over the entire church.

Bishop

If the pope was the supreme fount of authority, the practical ruler of the church at Paris was without doubt the bishop. The archbishop of Sens in whose province Paris was located was distant and claimed only honorific and procedural precedence. In the year 1200 the office of bishop had just shifted from Maurice to Eudes, both originating from Sully-sur-Loire to the southeast of Orléans. Maurice died on 11 September 1196, after an unprecedented episcopacy of thirty-six years; Eudes succeeded him from 1197 to 1208. (Pierre de Nemours [1208–1219], son of Gautier the Father, the former royal chamberlain, followed him.) The toponym "de Sully" was all that Maurice and Eudes held in common. Rigord, the royal historian, commented cryptically that Eudes was different from his predecessor in both morals and style of living.[6] Maurice's family was obscure (only his mother, Umbergie, can be identified); Eudes came from the powerful lords of Sully-sur-Loire, who were cousins of the kings of France and England.

Maurice first appeared as canon of the chapter of Notre-Dame, then archdeacon of Josas, and master of theology with a reputation as an effective preacher.[7] Later anecdotes suggest that the chapter had difficulty in choosing a bishop after the death of Pierre the Lombard in 1160. According to the most credible story, when the canons approached King Louis for advice, he asked who the two best candidates were. They proposed Master Pierre Comestor and Master Maurice de Sully. When he further queried as to who was best in caring for souls, the canons replied that Pierre was learned in Scriptural studies but Maurice's ability to preach and conduct practical affairs especially qualified him to care for souls. The canons followed the king's advice and gave the post to Maurice, allowing Pierre to supervise the schools.[8] Maurice's enduring achievement as bishop, as has been seen, was the construction of Notre-Dame, but his long episcopacy enabled him to be active in diocesan affairs and a close counselor of Kings Louis and Philip. Sensing the end to his life approaching, he retired to chambers at Saint-Victor, where edifying stories were told about his last days, including his ability to detect the unconsecrated host and his firm faith in the resurrection.[9]

The transition between the episcopates of Maurice and Eudes in 1196, however, was clouded by questions that have not yet been resolved. The English chronicler Ralph of Coggeshall, who was well informed about Paris, related that at Maurice's death all the clergy and people with the consent of the king elected Pierre the Chanter to succeed as bishop, but the latter declined, citing its great burdens. It is true that the Chanter was approaching the end of his days as well (he died the following year), but he did in fact accept election to the deanship of Reims. In all events, Adam, the abbot of the Cistercian house of Perseigne in Normandy, chided Eudes for not regretting the recent death of the Chanter just as he would not have welcomed the Chanter's presence if he were alive.[10] Our fullest information about Eudes comes from a letter by Pierre de Blois, archdeacon of Bath, who responded to a request from the abbot of Gloucester to report on the election and character of the new bishop. While the chapter was considering a replacement for Maurice, Pierre explained, the threat of simony reared its ugly head, but it was repulsed by prudent members of the chapter, who elected Eudes by common assent. Pierre had known Eudes personally both at Paris, where the young man studied the arts and theology under the tutorship of a certain Pierre de Vernon (otherwise unidentified), and at Rome, where Eudes attended the papal curia after 1187. In his praise of Eudes, Pierre paid little attention to his scholarship but emphasized his vigils, fasting and alms, despite an unnamed temptation at Rome. Although Eudes's former life was beclouded, there was no doubt that his chief virtue was his princely lineage, now transplanted to Paris.[11]

Eudes de Sully's first position was chanter of the archbishopric of Bourges, where his family was well established (his brother Henri had been archbishop since 1183.) At Paris his administrative abilities were best demonstrated in the synodical statutes that regulated the activities of the diocesan clergy. He was reputed to be Philip Augustus's ecclesiastical liaison to give advice on episcopal appointments. At least five bishops were chosen on his recommendation, all of whom he had known at Paris.[12] The chapter no doubt chose Eudes because of his close ties with royalty, but Philip was disappointed to the point of fury with his cousin's part in the interdict of 1200. Of the nineteen regalian bishops for whom information exists, thirteen sided with the king and refused to publish the papal decree in their dioceses. The six who obeyed the pope, we remember, included Eudes, the bishop of the royal capital. Philip seized the lands and goods of the observant bishop with such vehemence that he was obliged to compensate Eudes with special privileges after the interdict was lifted. The king exempted "his dearest cousin Eudes for whom he had a special love" from all personal military service for the duration of his life.[13]

Both Maurice and Eudes were elected to the bishopric of Paris by the canons of the chapter, but with the participation of the king as well. The delicate problem of how these two authorities should work together was resolved by

Philip's father, Louis VII, after his return from the Second Crusade in 1149 and reconfirmed by Philip in the ordinance testament of 1190. When a regalian bishopric (a bishopric under royal control) fell vacant, the canons of the chapter approached the king for a license to elect a new bishop, which the king issued without objection. After a bishop was chosen and canonically consecrated by the archbishop, the king returned the regalia (the temporal possessions) he held during the vacancy. The formula of the ordinance testament that made such collaboration workable was this: the canons should choose a candidate "who was both pleasing to God and useful for the kingdom" (*qui Deo placeat et utilis sit regno*). Both sides were free to interpret the precise qualifications of the candidate, but they must agree that their mutual interests were satisfied.[14] Apparently the system worked well not only for Maurice and Eudes but for most other candidates because few elections were contested.

We remember (see pp. 78–79) that the conversation between Philip Augustus and Pierre the Chanter inserted into the cartulary of Bourges by Étienne de Gallardon addressed precisely the question of selecting suitable bishops. After enduring the Chanter's harangue over monarchs, the king passed to the offensive by asking his interlocutor how it can be explained that in ancient times saintly bishops were chosen, such as St. Marcel at Paris and St. Sulpice at Bourges, whereas today scarcely any bishop has been canonized as a saint. At this point it is appropriate to quote Pierre's response in full:

> Lord King, I shall demonstrate that my answer is well considered. In the ancient elections the electors called upon the Holy Spirit, who is both wise and wisdom itself, by fasting, not two or three days, but continually for weeks, accompanied by effusion of tears, contrition of hearts and humiliation of spirits. Thus supplicated by humility and spiritual affliction, the Holy Spirit guided the deliberations of the electors and enabled their agreement to elect those who sought utility more than preeminence. Following not their own will but that of Jesus Christ, the precious life of those elected ended in more precious deaths.
>
> In our modern elections, on the contrary, it is not the great wise man but the most stupid mentor, the devil, who arrives without being called, following banquets, drinking parties and secret meetings, convoked by his servants named "Pride," "Shame," "Anger," "Greed," "Simony," "uncontrollable Ambition" and others. It follows that he who is chosen by such negotiations does the work of him whose counsel has been accepted, living in pride, greed, exaltation and pomp. Such a life is survived not only by a wicked death but also by maledictions of his people.

The Chanter's response was received by the king with goodwill and entire agreement.

Pierre's reply, therefore, was simple: the difference lies in the attitude of the electors. In ancient times the canons implored the Holy Spirit for guidance prepared by weeks of fasting, prayers, tears, contrition and humility of spirit, whereas today the Devil operates through banquets, drinking parties and secret sessions dominated by pride, avarice, simony and inordinate ambition. Pierre's stance in this conversation finds resonance in his writings as well.[15]

Although purported to have been held during the Chanter's lifetime, this conversation was applicable to an election that, in fact, took place three years later in 1200 and involved Bishop Eudes of Paris. After the death of Henri, archbishop of Bourges and Eudes's brother, in 1199, the canons were not able to agree on a candidate. Inspired by the Holy Spirit, they decided to resort to the procedure of "compromise" by which they entrusted the choice to Eudes de Sully, whose family had been long associated with the bishopric and whose good relations with the king were now restored. They further stipulated that the candidate should be a Cistercian like the deceased Henri and proposed three abbots from the order. Eudes wrote the names of the three on slips of parchment and sealed and placed them on the altar of a neighboring church at Bourges, Notre-Dame de Salis. Spending the night in vigils, tears and prayers, he selected the name of a candidate, Guillaume, abbot Chaalis, whom the chapter unanimously elected the next morning. To shorten a long story, the exemplary piety of this Archbishop Guillaume was, in fact, recognized as befitting sainthood when he was canonized in 1218, eight years after his death.[16] The story survives, to be sure, in a saint's life composed for St. Guillaume's canonization, and in his writings the Chanter explicitly opposed the procedure of drawing lots to choose a bishop. Nonetheless, Pierre could not have been surprised with the results: fasting, tears, prayers and humility had produced at Bourges a bishop worthy of canonization, a rare occurrence in thirteenth-century France. King Philip's sly reproach was answered.

The bishops of Paris presided over their cathedral and diocese from the episcopal palace constructed by Maurice de Sully between Notre-Dame and the southern arm of the Seine. As temporal lords, they held houses, lands and rights throughout the city and the Île-de-France as any great magnate did, but as bishops they also received income from designated churches. As was common in the twelfth century, they reinforced their hold on their temporal possessions by feudal bonds, claiming lordship over vassals who were both laity and churchmen. Bishop Eudes, for example, designated as vassals the distant counts of Brittany, Saint-Pol and Bar-le-Duc as well as the prominent lords of Montmorency, Beaumont-sur-Oise and Senlis in the vicinity, and the castles at Corbeil, Montlhéry and Ferté-Alais. His lordship likewise extended to the dignitaries of the chapter of Notre-Dame, the collegiate churches of Saint-Marcel, Saint-Germain-l'Auxerrois and Saint-Cloud and numerous individuals.[17] As a great baron the bishop of Paris managed his household with pantlers, butlers, cooks, stablemen, marshals, chamberlains and doormen; prévôts, mayors and sergeants oversaw his rural estates.[18]

To help him with the ecclesiastical tasks, the bishop relied on another corps of agents. The parochial duties of Notre-Dame were confided to an archpriest of Paris. When the construction made it impossible for the cathedral to serve as a parish church, the archpriest moved to various churches around the town before settling at the church of Sainte-Marie-Madeleine on the Cité. As Paris grew, a second archpriest was designated by 1205 at the church of Saint-Séverin on the Left Bank.[19] Archdeacons and chancellors, who were likewise dignitaries of the chapter of Notre-Dame, were enlisted to aid the bishop in administering the diocese. Although the bishop retained authority to ordain priests to churches and supervise their spiritual ministry, three archdeacons were delegated to oversee the material wealth of the parish clergy. By Maurice's time the diocese had been divided into three archdeaconries, titled Paris, Josas and Brie, but already the three archdeacons had begun to assert their independence and encroach on the bishop's jurisdiction. They made themselves particularly unwelcome among the parish clergy by insisting on heavy fees when they made their annual visits.

The chancellor, equally a member of the chapter, functioned as the bishop's secretariat by drafting letters and documents, in addition to other duties in the library and the schools. When Pierre the Chanter considered the governmental function of the chancery, as we have seen in the previous chapter, he and Robert of Courson devoted most of their attention to the bishop's chancery. Because the suitableness of clerics working for bishops was not a problem, they concentrated on the issue of remuneration. If the chancellor was adequately endowed with a prebend, could he charge the recipients of his charters for his services? Was not this a selling of spiritual goods that amounted to simony? Even the appurtenances to the office, such as wax, parchment, ink and notarial skill, could become implicated in simony. Pierre and Robert argued the question at length, but the clinching argument was the example of their hero, Thomas Becket, archbishop of Canterbury. When Becket previously served as royal chancellor, he grew

disgusted with the venality of the English chancery. As archbishop, therefore, he strictly forbade his own chancellor, Master Arnulph, to accept the
slightest remuneration for his office—not even a knife. Apparently the restriction was effective, because Master Arnulph was deeply in debt to the
notorious Flemish usurer, William Cade. But what if the chancellor lacked
a prebend, and the bishop was forced to hire a scribe at a daily wage? In that
event, the Chanter conceded, the bishop could charge for parchment, ink
and labor, but he could not demand a fee for the seal because that would be
equivalent to selling his miter, crozier or other priestly insignia.[20] Courson
further developed his teacher's concession by permitting moderate fees to
chancery clerics without regular income, provided they did not contract
for them at the beginning but received them as gifts after the work was
completed.[21] These ideals, however, exceeded the realities of the practical
world. The papal chancery at Rome was notorious for excessive fees, even
after an attempt by Innocent III to regulate them, and in 1215 the chancellor
of Notre-Dame, Étienne de Reims, was obliged to reduce his fees at Paris.[22]

Feeling competition from the archdeacons and chancellors, the bishop of
Paris began to look for an escape. Around the turn of the century a new "official" was created in northern France who was completely dependent on the
bishop and performed the diocese's legal and secretarial business. This *officialis* appeared in Paris by 1204, subsequently presiding over the bishop's court
and drafting the bishop's letters and documents. Apparently he was trained
in canon law because his writings were composed according to standardized
formula, and he authenticated the bishop's decisions and documents by his
own seal. Formerly members of the chapter or his household witnessed the
bishop's letters by appending their names at the bottom of the charter. By
1201, these witness lists began to disappear from the episcopal documentation and were replaced simply by the official's seal. By 1211 the designation of
official of Paris was invariably accompanied with a master's degree (*magister
officialis*), thus confirming the learned qualifications of the new personage.
From then on, most of the bishop's documents were produced by the new
official in formulaic language and authenticated with his special seal. He not
only became the bishop's sole notary but also made his notarial services available throughout the city.[23]

The emergence of the official and the change in drafting letters was also
accompanied by a new interest in documentation that paralleled the contemporary royal collections of accounts and inventories. The traditional
collections of church documents in cartularies continued. A small volume

called the *Livre noir* was completed at the end of the twelfth century, and materials were collected for the series of great cartularies of the thirteenth for use by the bishop and the chapter. Obituaries were likewise compiled, culminating in the chapter's large obituary of the thirteenth century.[24] Bishop Eudes, however, began to draw up inventories of his own resources, just as the royal chancery had done in the king's registers. A list of all of the bishop's fiefs and vassals was compiled for the episcopal cartulary to which was appended the first pouillé that organized all the parishes of the diocese by deaneries and those of Paris according to the jurisdiction of the two arch-priests.[25] Most important, as shall be seen, the newly established statutes of Eudes's annual synods for the diocesan clergy were carefully recorded and preserved. Like the king, the bishop felt the need to collect information on which his duties depended.

The Chapter of Notre-Dame

Although the bishop's seat (*sedis*) was located at Notre-Dame, he was none-theless obliged to share the cathedral with the chapter. If, in fact, the chap-ter chose the bishop with the concurrence of the king, it also became the bishop's chief competitor. The recorded history of most bishoprics consisted of interminable disputes between the bishop and chapter because of the independence of the latter. Only Maurice de Sully's skillful diplomacy re-duced these conflicts during his long episcopacy.

The chapter consisted of a little more than fifty churchmen, called can-ons, including a leadership composed of seven dignitaries.[26] More than half resided in the cloister of Notre-Dame, which was a designated territory con-sisting of individual houses, gardens and lands situated to the north and east of the cathedral. A ford connected the canons' cloister with the Île-de-Notre-Dame upstream on the Seine, which was largely uninhabited and served mainly as pasture. Protected by an enclosure with a limited number of gates, the cloister enjoyed immunity from the jurisdiction of both the bishop and the king. The chapter acknowledged the pope as their spiritual superior, and in 1200 Philip Augustus confirmed that anyone who violated the sanctity of the cloister was liable to a fine of a hundred livres.[27] Re-membering his happy boyhood spent in the cloister of Notre-Dame, Philip's father, Louis VII, exempted the chapter's lands from paying for the king's hospitality as he traveled about.[28]

At the head of the dignitaries of the chapter was the dean, who was elected by the canons and was responsible for the leadership and spiritual care of the canons. His stall was on the right (or Gospel) side of the choir to underscore his preeminence. Hugues Clément, from the family of royal marshals who enjoyed the king's favor, was dean at the turn of the century (1195–1216), but he was preceded by Hervé (1185–1190) of the powerful lords of Montmorency to the north of Paris and was to be followed by Gautier Cornut (1221–1224), from another family indebted to royal patronage. Backed by prestigious family lineage and independence, the dean was a prelate in his own right and a formidable rival to the bishop. For this reason Bishop Eudes de Sully listed the dean, along with the chanter, chancellor, and all the archdeacons, as his liege men and required that they swear to him fealty (except for the fealty they owed the chapter).

It is most likely that the bishop chose the chanter, the second-ranking dignitary. He occupied the stall opposite the dean on the left (or Epistle) side of the choir. In 1200 Pierre the Chanter, whose renown was acquired as a theologian, had just died three years earlier. He was preceded by a certain Gautier (1177–1180) and was succeeded by Robert de Villeroy (1198–1225). Holding a staff as sign of his office, the chanter had as his principal duty to preside over the activities of the choir, correcting the books of chant and disciplining unruly behavior among the other clerics and choirboys. Pierre the Chanter's voluminous writings evidence little interest in the liturgical duties of the choir, and only few mentions of disciplinary problems. On one occasion, for example, he recounted a fight that broke out among the clerics of the choir; on another, he noted the antics of the choirboys during the Feast of Fools.[29] Concentrating on his teaching, he no doubt delegated the liturgical functions to subchanters such as Gallo (1186–1198) and Pierre (1207–1238), who were elected by the chapter.

The bishop appointed the remaining dignitaries. Although they were delegates of the bishop, the three archdeacons of Paris, Josas and Brie increasingly competed with their master over supervising the secular clergy of the diocese. In addition to supplying the secretarial services for the chapter, the chancellor maintained the library and corrected the nonliturgical books, but his duties had long included supervision of the schools of the cathedral. We shall treat this function in the following chapter but merely note here that most of the men who held the position were appropriately theologians and usually claimed the master's degree.

Like the bishop, the chapter of Notre-Dame was rich in lands and dependent churches throughout the city and the diocese. Grouped into twelve regions outside Paris, the domains were managed by as many prévôts, aided by mayors, deans and sergeants, as those who served the bishop's lands.[30] Like the bishop also, the chapter claimed specific jurisdictions throughout Paris and a special relationship to particular churches. The collegiate church Saint-Merry and its neighbor Saint-Sépulchre on the right bank and the collegiate church Saint-Benoît and Saint-Étienne des Grés on the left were titled the "four daughters of the chapter." Saint-Jean-le-Rond, Saint-Denis-du-Pas, Saint-Christophe, Saint-Aignan and the Hôtel-Dieu, all on the Île-de-la-Cité, submitted to the spiritual jurisdiction of the canons. The abbey of Saint-Victor enjoyed the privilege of sharing prebends with the chapter of Notre-Dame.[31]

Named by the bishop, each of the fifty canons was assigned a prebend that drew its income from the chapter's domain and conferred wealth, thus elevating the canon to the elite clergy of Paris. His chief function was to serve in the choir of the cathedral, chanting the daily round of services with the help of chaplains, clerics and choirboys. Because the remuneration was attractive but the duties onerous, the canons' besetting failing was absenteeism and lack of attention to the offices. With proper permission, a canon could take leave of absence to depart on pilgrimages, attend to legal business and even further his own education in the schools, but many were astute in finding other excuses. By 1173 Pope Alexander III had decreed that any canon absent for more than half the year would no longer be considered resident and eligible to receive income from his prebend.[32] Even dignitaries like the chancellor were asked to submit to an oath of residence.[33] We shall see that donors to the chapter inserted financial inducements into the canons' daily routine to ensure their attention to chanting the liturgy. It was in the choir of the cathedral, however, whose soaring vaults furnished an impressive stage, that the canons performed their essential tasks at Notre-Dame.

Worship in the Choir of Notre-Dame

Although the bishop and chapter might cooperate or compete over the cathedral, in the fullest sense Notre-Dame itself belonged not to them but to the saints, and most particularly to its supreme patroness, the Blessed Virgin Mary.[34] Like most churches, it doubled as an architectural reliquary for safeguarding and exhibiting the hallowed remains or relics of these heroes and heroines of God. The relics were kept in the treasury to the east of the cathedral and displayed on the altars during feast days. During the Viking invasions of the ninth century, many of the relics of the region were brought to the cathedral for safekeeping behind the walls of the Île-de-la-Cité. The most prominent were listed in a sacramentary (Paris Bnf lat. 2294) from the tenth century, but new donations were continually added.[35] The constructions at Notre-Dame in the 1160s, however, prompted their removal to Saint-Étienne-des-Grés on the Left Bank, where they were "recovered" early in the reign of Philip Augustus, who ceremoniously transferred them back to Notre-Dame once the completed choir was ready to house them again. The occasion was recorded in the king's obituary and celebrated with a new feast day, the *Susceptio reliquiarum*, to be held annually on 4 December. At that time the most noteworthy of the treasures consisted of a lock of hair of the Virgin, the present patroness; stones from the slaying of St. Stephen, the former patron of the ancient cathedral; a piece of the true cross, a thorn from the crown of thorns, three teeth of St. John the Baptist and the arm of St. André.[36] In addition, the clergy had been assiduously collecting relics from saints venerated locally, such as St. Geneviève, the patroness of Paris; St. Denis; St. Germain and St. Marcel, former bishops of the city; and St. Gendulph.

As a reliquary Notre-Dame had to compete with equally prestigious treasures found in surrounding monasteries, such as the body of St. Geneviève at her church, that of St. Vincent at Saint-Germain-des-Prés and especially the relics of St. Denis. According to the royal historian Rigord, who was a monk of the abbey, Saint-Denis's prized relics consisted of a nail from the crucifixion, a thorn from the crown, and the arm of Saint Simeon, which the monks paraded through the city during the catastrophic floods of 1196 and 1206 with propitious results. The true test, however, came in 1191, when the infant Prince Louis and royal heir fell deathly ill during his father's absence on the crusade. The monks brought out their celebrated relics and proceeded to the church of Saint-Lazare to the north of Paris, where they were met by Bishop Maurice in company with the canons, clerics, students and populace of Paris. Not to be outdone by the powerful abbey, the bishop brought his own relics from the cathedral. Joining forces, they proceeded to the royal palace, where the abbey's relics were applied to the boy's stomach in the form of the cross, and he was delivered immediately from danger.[37] Because it is Rigord who narrates the story, the victory was naturally accorded to Saint-Denis. The capture and sack of Constantinople in 1204 by the Western crusaders released a flood of new relics in the West. When the king received a consignment in 1205 procured from the Latin emperor Baudouin (formerly the count of Flanders), they were bestowed on the abbey. The most important included an impressive piece of the true cross (measuring a foot in length and a width that could be grasped by the hand joining the thumb to the index finger), another thorn from Christ's crown, a lock hair from the baby Jesus and a rib and tooth of St. Philip.[38]

As prestigious as were these relics, they possessed one potential function that raised the alarm of Pierre the Chanter and Robert of Courson. Although the saints' virtues could be used for healing, could the relics also be enlisted for financial gain? Just as the Paris theologians had balked at the practice of soliciting alms from usurers, so they were equally suspicious of relics being pressed into service for fundraising. Saints who had abhorred money while alive were enlisted into promotional schemes when dead. Although Pierre was uncertain about the remedy, Robert resolved his master's hesitations. Because the casket of the Parisian St. Gendulphus split open when it was overlaid with silver, Robert concluded that this was due to the saint's contempt for money. Similarly the body of St. Firmin of Amiens refused to budge, when it was about to be transported on a fundraising campaign. Relics should never be displayed for the purpose of raising money. Echoing the misgivings of the Chanter and Courson, Pope Innocent III turned to the issue at the Lateran Council of 1215. Rather than outright prohibition, he preferred regulation. Newly found relics cannot be venerated without papal authority, and ancient and attested relics should not be exhibited outside the reliquary. To correct abuses from displaying relics for collecting alms, the council forbade all such preaching campaigns without explicit permission from the pope or bishop.[39]

Unlike the abbey of Saint-Denis, which sought to become the royal necropolis of the Capetians (Abbot Suger succeeded in having Louis VI interred there), the cathedral of Notre-Dame was not as prominent as a burial church. When Geoffroy, count of Brittany, was killed in 1186, reportedly in a tournament, Philip Augustus not only deeply grieved over the loss of a friend but had him incongruously buried in the choir at Notre-Dame, as will be seen. When Queen Isabelle died four years later, the king also interred her in the choir (behind the Eagle lectern) and founded two chaplains each to say daily prayers for the souls of the count and the queen. Pierre the Chanter noted these two examples when he discussed procedures for creating prebends in his questiones.[40] Whereas Bishop Maurice preferred Saint-Victor, Eudes placed his tomb in the middle of the choir of the cathedral.[41]

The locus of worship at Notre-Dame was unquestionably the choir of the new cathedral, completed in 1182.[42] Enclosed from the ambulatory that encircled the perimeter of the apse, it was also completely separated from the transepts on the west by the jubé, which consisted of a carved stone screen pierced by a gate surmounted by a crucifix. In effect the choir constituted a church within a church. The bishop entered the choir by a gallery from the episcopal palace to the south, the canons by a door from the cloister to the north at the emplacement of the present *portail rouge*. Within, the choir was divided between the sanctuary and the chancel. The former was the easternmost portion, raised and separated by a railing and containing three altars: the high altar, behind which were the altar of St. Marcel and finally the altar of the Trinity, or Notre-Dame des Ardents, so named because of its reputation for curing those afflicted with the "sacred fire." On three sides (except on the east), the western part or chancel was lined with two levels of wooden stalls or seats that had been supplied by the chanter Master Albert, at his death in 1177. When the seat of each stall was raised, it was fitted with a small perch or *misericorde* that supported the occupant as he stood before the stall.

Pierre de Roissy, chancellor of Chartres and former member of the Chanter's circle at Paris, composed a "Manuel on the Mysteries of the Church"; it opened with a section that addressed the question, "What do the individual features [*singula*] of the material fabric of the church signify?" Although Pierre was concerned with the metaphorical meaning of the building, under the influence of the Biblical school of Saint-Victor he believed that all metaphors must be grounded in the material realm of the *visibilia* to be valid. In other words, only through the visible can the spiritual be perceived. The church that he envisaged was, of course, generic, but because he was well acquainted with Notre-Dame after years of residing at Paris, many of the features he observed were those of the cathedral as well. His manual indicates that the choir stalls were furnished with pillows, cushions and padded backrests, and carpets were spread across the floor. Above the wooden stalls hung white linen curtains, and above them silken panels colored red, white, cerise, and green. They could be figured with animals and birds, but the human form should not be depicted realistically.[43]

The bishop and all members of the chapter were assigned specific places in the chancel. Pierre de Roissy further noted that the seat of the bishop (*cathedra*) should be separate from the others but closest to the altar.[44] Accordingly he was placed on the right or Gospel side and to the east end

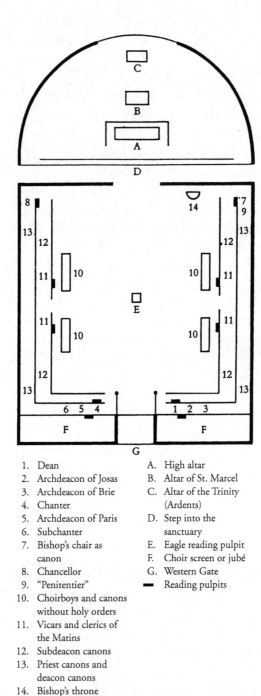

1. Dean
2. Archdeacon of Josas
3. Archdeacon of Brie
4. Chanter
5. Archdeacon of Paris
6. Subchanter
7. Bishop's chair as canon
8. Chancellor
9. "Penitentier"
10. Choirboys and canons without holy orders
11. Vicars and clerics of the Matins
12. Subdeacon canons
13. Priest canons and deacon canons
14. Bishop's throne

A. High altar
B. Altar of St. Marcel
C. Altar of the Trinity (Ardents)
D. Step into the sanctuary
E. Eagle reading pulpit
F. Choir screen or jubé
G. Western Gate
━ Reading pulpits

Plan 1. Diagram of the choir of Notre-Dame. *Source: Music and Ceremony at Notre Dame of Paris, 500–1550* by Craig Wright, © 1989 Cambridge University Press. Reprinted with the permission of Cambridge University Press.

of the chancel. He also possessed a canon's stall immediately to the right on the second level. Directly across from him to the left was the chancellor. At the western end of the chancel the gate was flanked on either side on the upper level by the dean (to the right) and the chanter (to the left) with their backs toward the nave. To the right of the dean were the archdeacons of Josas and Brie; to the left of the chanter were the archdeacon of Paris and the subchanter. Since the death of the chanter Master Albert, in 1177 chanters such as Pierre the Chanter and Robert de Villeroy did not participate directly in the activities of the choir. Although they were ultimately responsible, they assigned direction to the subchanter Galon or Pierre, who oversaw the liturgy of the choir from his seat on the left. To the left and right at the second level of the stalls were the canons who attained the orders of priest and deacon, that is, the senior members of the chapter. Beneath them at the first level on both sides were the subdeacon canons and the clerics and vicars of churches associated with Notre-Dame who participated in the cathedral's liturgy. In front on both sides at the ground level were the choirboys, who were directed by a rector walking back and forth. The bishop and the chancellor to the east and the dean and chanter to the west were given lecterns; at the exact center of the chancel was the Eagle lectern. In perfect symmetry, the chapter and their associated clergy were divided into two camps to the south and north, facing each other across the chancel under the watchful supervision of the bishop and chancellor to the east and the dean, chanter and subchanter to the west.

Attendance at the daily services varied greatly. Only the subchanter swore an oath to guarantee his presence. The bishop and the dignitaries were often absent on business; individual canons had their own excuses. Attendance varied further according to the solemnity of the feast or occasion, but financial inducements were deemed necessary to secure the canon's presence. In fact it became regular procedure to pay each canon along with the other attending clergy for each service attended. These "distributions," as they were called, were normally counted in deniers, but occasionally in sous, payable at the end of the office. The higher the rank of the occasion, the more lucrative the payment.[45]

Of the missals that were composed for the cathedral, some twenty-five survive from the twelfth and thirteenth centuries and show that the liturgy of Notre-Dame achieved its definitive form during this period. The routine duty of the chapter was to chant the eight canonical hours and celebrate a high mass each day.[46] At a cathedral like that of Paris, the hours were grouped in three sections: nighttime beginning at midnight (matins and lauds), morning from eight to noon (prime, terce and sext) and evening from three-thirty to six (nones, vespers and compline). During the eight canonical hours all 150 psalms of the psalter were chanted each week. Most of the canons and other participating clergy would have learned the psalms by heart, but the performance of this enormously time-consuming task naturally encouraged the participants to chant the text as rapidly as possible. In addition, between terce and sext in the morning the canons celebrated high mass according to the Roman rite, which they had performed since the ninth century.

Superimposed on this daily *opus dei* were the feast days that celebrated the saints and special events.[47] Most missals contained a calendar appended to the beginning of the manuscript. The manuscript Paris Bnf. Lat. 1112, which was compiled for Notre-Dame between 1212 and 1218, illustrates the feasts that were celebrated at the cathedral around the year 1200. In the format of a small portable manual, six folios contain the calendar, one page for each month. The ancient Roman calendar is correlated with the ecclesiastical chronology on the left of the page in red and blue ink, to which the feasts are listed in black to the right at the appropriate date and with notation of the liturgical rank of the celebration. The most solemn are the four annual (*annum*) feasts of the Christian calendar: Christmas (25 December), Easter, Pentecost and the Assumption of the Virgin (15 August). Because Easter and its dependant Pentecost are moveable feasts, they sweep back and forth across the months of March and April (Easter) and May and June (Pentecost) every year. These annual solemnities required the highest level of celebration in vestment, word, song and ceremony. We shall see that the Advent season, culminating in Christmas, was the busiest and most joyful for the clergy of Notre-Dame because it included the feasts of the Holy Innocents and Circumcision assigned to the lower clergy. At the end of the long Lenten season, Easter was also important. (We remember that the *laudes regie* were sung for the king at that time.) The Feast of the Assumption in honor the Virgin was, appropriately, a popular occasion at Notre-Dame.

Other feasts were privileged by granting them the status of duplex or semiduplex (arbitrary terms meaning literally "double" or "less than double"). For example, at Notre-Dame duplex status was accorded not only to important occasions such as the Nativity of St. John the Baptist (24 June), the Nativity of the Virgin (8 September) and All Saints Day (1 November) but also to local saints such as Marcel (3 November) and Geneviève

(26 November), as well as to feasts important to the cathedral: Reception of the Relics (4 December), St. Stephen (26 December), Holy Innocents (28 December) and Circumcision (1 January). St. Germain (28 May) and St. Gendulph (13 November) were assigned semiduplex status. More recently canonized saints were added, such as Thomas Becket (29 December) and Bernard of Clairvaux (25 August). Bernard was inserted at the initiative of Bishop Eudes in 1207, no doubt in memory of his Cistercian brother; Becket was a particular favorite of the clergy, especially the theologians around Pierre the Chanter.[48] On the feast day of a saint, the treasury was opened and the relics were produced for veneration.[49] The higher the status of the feast, the more numerous the clergy, the greater number of candles, and the more sumptuous the vestments. (As many as 120 clerics crowded the choir for the highest remuneration of the annual feasts.) Special liturgies were created for individual feasts, and elaborate processions were added. Of greatest importance was the music that accompanied the liturgy.

Music at Notre-Dame

The vaults of the choir reverberated with the sound of music rolling into the newly constructed nave. Although work on the two bell towers on the west front had not yet begun, Pierre de Roissy observed that bells pealed incessantly throughout the church to mark regular celebration of matins, high mass and vespers, as well as the special feast days and the preparations for them. They tolled also for the death of individuals: three times for a man, twice for a woman, and as many times for a cleric as his rank in holy orders.[50] The prevailing sound that issued from the choir of Notre-Dame, however, was that of the vocal plainsong. Since ancient times the canonical hours and the mass were chanted by the clergy in unison with traditional melodies and in a meter that followed the accentuation of the words. Although ancient chants were sung for most of the liturgy, music particular to Notre-Dame was written for the five standard chants of the ordinary mass (Kyrie, Gloria, Credo, Sanctus and Agnus dei). The notation for this music first appears in the missal Paris Bnf. Lat. 1112, which also provides the Parisian calendar and enables us for the first time to hear this plainchant as it was performed in the chancel around 1200.[51]

The turn of the century at Notre-Dame, however, was also marked by an extraordinary innovation in the history of music in the Western world, the emergence of polyphony. As early as the opening decade of the twelfth century, a certain Adam, chanter of Notre-Dame and canon of Saint-Victor, began to write new poetry and plainchant for the liturgy of the cathedral.[52] Master Albert d'Étampes, chanter at Notre-Dame from 1146 to 1177, followed him. He not only bequeathed the choir stalls to the cathedral but, more important, contributed to its music. A collection of liturgical books and composition of a conductus (processional music) for the feast of St. James, not for one voice but two and perhaps three, was among his legacies.[53] In the midthirteenth century, an anonymous English cleric who knew Paris well chronicled the spectacular arrival of polyphony at Notre-Dame, now technically labeled the *organum*:

> And note that Master Leoninus . . . was the best creator of organum, who made a great book of organum for both the mass and canonical hours to adorn the divine service. And this was in use until the time of Perotinus the Great, who abbreviated it and made many better substitute sections or passages, because he was the best composer of discant, better than Leoninus. . . . This Master Perotinus composed the best four-voiced works, such as *Viderunt* and *Sederunt*, with an abundance of artful harmonic color; and similarly he composed the most noble three-voice works, such as Allelluia, *Posui adiutorium, Nativitas*, etc. . . . The book or books of Master Perotinus were in use in the choir of the cathedral in Paris . . . until the present day.[54]

Of the two composers named, Master Leoninus was canon of Saint-Benoît and of Saint-Victor on the Left Bank before he became canon of the cathedral by 1192 and disappeared from the records in 1201. In addition to his contribution to the music of Notre-Dame, he was a celebrated poet, having written a verse rendition of the first eight chapters of Genesis. Gilles de Paris included him among the great poets of Paris in 1200. The name Perotinus is the diminutive of Petrus and most likely designates Pierre, subchanter of Paris from 1207 until 1238, canon of Saint-Victor as well. This Pierre was well documented for his services as a judge delegate and contributor to the cathedral's liturgy. The book containing the polyphonic compositions identified by the anonymous English cleric is called the *Magnus liber organi*.[55] This is an enormous repertory of more than a thousand items, which shows that Masters Leoninus, Perotinus and their followers wrote scores of compositions in two to four voices for all of the major feasts celebrated at Notre-Dame. Privileging the annual, duplex and semiduplex solemnities, they also furnished polyphony for the saints' feasts whose relics were important to the church as well as for processionals on these occasions. Their earliest production and most creative energies were lavished on the Christmas season, when in rapid succession they wrote polyphony for the feasts of the Nativity (25 December), St. Stephen (26 December), St. John the Apostle and Evangelist (27 December), the Holy Innocents (28 December) and the Circumcision (1 January). Their creativity was so buoyant that Bishop Eudes and the archbishop of Sens, Pierre de Corbeil, were forced to intervene to curb the excesses of the younger clergy to whom the performance of the feasts was entrusted. (We shall return to these festivities in Chapter Six.) Pierre the Chanter was perhaps too old to appreciate the importance of this phenomenal activity, but his student Robert de Courson did recognize the novelty of the situation. In a questio he asked whether these masters of the organum could legitimately hire out their services if they offered scurrilous and effeminate works for the youthful and uncultivated. His response was that a lax prelate does commit simony if he confers a benefice on a master who only seeks to show off his exhibitionist music, but if the polyphony is soberly sung on feast days according to the custom of the land, the master is worthy of his hire.[56]

Because the cathedral possessed no organ until the fourteenth century, and other instruments were not permitted in the church, all music was produced *a capella* by the male voice.[57] The canons of the chapter and the vicar priests of the associated churches surely chanted the plainsong in the choir, but the more difficult musical tasks were entrusted to professional singers. Most of the singing was performed by sixteen unbeneficed clerics of matins supported by choirboys. The latter could be as young as ten years of age in accordance with Psalm 8:3 ("Thou hast performed praise with the mouth of infants and sucklings"). By 1208 a master of the boys of the choir was required.[58] Two to six soloists performed the polyphonic pieces, and the higher the feast day, the more the soloists. Since lighting was dim within the church, most of the music was sung from memory. The choristers were to sing *corde* (from the heart); to know a piece by heart was therefore termed *cordetenus*. Again, the higher the feast, the more the candles, the better the notes could be read, and the more difficult the polyphony that was performed. Since there appears to be differences between the notated texts of the repertories and the actual performance, allowing scope for the singer's virtuosity, it is difficult to imagine how they were actually sung. The acoustics, moreover, were different than what is found today within the bare walls of Notre-Dame. Around 1200 the choir was insulated with tapestries, drapes, banners and rugs all of which softened the reverberations. Polyphony may have sounded different from plainchant because wall hangings and banners were added.

The most spectacular polyphony was sung at Christmastide, to which we shall turn later, but a more modest example is the polyphonic conductus composed to memorialize the death (in 1186) of Geoffroy, count of Brittany, performed in the choir where he was interred. His anniversary was celebrated on 21 August of each year, supported by foundations from his sister, Agnès the countess of Blois, and the king. These affluent donations may have financed the two conductus that were written and set to music for the occasion. One piece composed for two voices begins:

> The splendor of the warring host
> suffers an eclipse,
> for today the sun's
> ray is extinguished,
> and the world's light has fallen,
> when the flower of Brittany
> is sent from the way
> and enters the father's abode.
> Death in this harsh lot,
> treating all men equally,
> knows not how to spare.[59]

Worship in the Nave of Notre-Dame

All of the foregoing liturgy, chant and music that we have considered took place exclusively in the chancel of the choir, sealed off from view of the rest of the church by a stone jubé that guarded its western end. In an exposition on the form of a church building, Pierre de Roissy explained that

> the church is divided into two parts, that is, into a chancel and a nave (or ship). The nave/ship signifies the subjects who are in the sea of this world, whence "they go down to sea in ships . . ." (Psalm 106:23). The chancel signifies the prelates, whence "they are holy and the holy of holies . . ." (Dan. 9:24, Ex. 30:29). The chancel should be more humble because Christ, bowing his head, gave up the spirit (John 19:30), and signifies that the cleric should be more humble than the people. . . . The chancel and the nave of the church are joined together in a certain middle section [*medium*], which is called the crossing (or crucifix) because with the mediation of Christ's passion we are joined together. . . . Between the clergy and the people is a certain middle section, which in certain places is always closed and in others open and especially on feast days which signifies that on feast days the clergy should open the Scriptures to the people through preaching.[60]

In this passage, which resonates the Chanter's aversion to lofty churches, his student Pierre de Roissy clearly evoked the separation between the clergy and the laity marked architecturally by the jubé at the division between the chancel and the nave; but he also indicated a middle section, a crossing or crucifix that signified Christ's redeeming passion. How this middle section was closed in some places but open in others is not clear, but it suggests that in some way the separation between the chancel and the nave may have been relaxed on feast days to allow entry to the laity, or it may simply have implied that the laity could circulate around the choir in the ambulatory. Although the clergy were the fishermen in the Biblical metaphor, the laity were the fish, submerged in the sea of the nave. As they stood in the nave or at the crossing on ordinary days, they could hear the words and music of the chant coming across the jubé from the chancel, but what could they see?

By the early thirteenth century the clergy left the chancel at the end of vespers on certain feast days, filed in procession to chapels where the saints of the day were honored, performed a service at the station and returned to the choir chanting an antiphonal. While these processions moved within the cathedral or at times outside to a neighboring church, the singing was performed in monophonic plainsong. But as polyphony was added to the repertory, the procession often sang a piece composed in multiple parts, standing still in station to inspire further devotion from the spectators. Eventually the tradition was established that in exiting and entering the chancel the procession paused outside the gate under the crucifix and sang an antiphon or response in polyphony.[61] The higher the solemnity, the more elaborate the performance.

In addition to observing processions on feast days, the laity also attended services held in the chapels situated around the choir off the ambulatory. These chapels were dedicated to particular saints, or to votive commemorations. For example, in 1204 Adam de Montreuil, canon of Notre-Dame, endowed four priests to chant prayers and services in a votive chapel for the repose of his soul and those of his family.[62] By this time, more than fifty chaplains were employed to serve saints' chapels and sing votive services. As the construction of Notre-Dame progressed, doubtless these chapels spread into the nave, where they were eventually inserted between the buttresses as side chapels by the end of the thirteenth century, as they now can be seen. But these saints' and votive chapels encircling the choir off the ambulatory and into the nave could not accommodate large crowds and were not designed to serve as the principal or parish altar of the nave. Because the construction of the nave was still in progress during the year 1200, the parish duties of the cathedral were suspended for decades. Bishop Maurice divided the island into thirteen parishes to replace the former parochial functions of the cathedral and transferred the archpriest to the Right Bank, and later to the Île-de-la-Cité. The principal parish duty that remained in the nave, therefore, was that of preaching, as Pierre de Roissy's text suggests. (He later treated the symbolism of the pulpit.)[63]

The parochial service missing for the faithful in the nave of Notre-Dame was, surprisingly, the celebration of the Eucharist. The doctrine of transubstantiation was well established by the end of the twelfth century, and the Eucharist received increasing devotion from the laity. According to current theology, when the priest pronounced the words of consecration ("This is my body" and "This is the cup of my blood"), the elements of bread and wine became, respectively, the actual body and blood of Christ. The faithful began to demand to see the host or bread after it was consecrated—thus raising the liturgical issue of when the host should be displayed, which in turn opened the theological question of the precise moment at which the bread and wine were transformed into the body and blood of Christ. At Paris the debate was lively. Pierre the Chanter and his disciple Robert of Courson argued that the transformation was not complete until the words of consecration of both the bread and wine were pronounced. That is to say, only after the cup was blessed could the priest display the host. Against this position Stephen Langton and the two chancellors of Notre-Dame, Pierre de Poitiers and Prévostin, argued that the bread and wine were transformed separately with the respective consecrations. In short, the priest could show the bread immediately after pronouncing "This is my body." The debate was significant enough for Pierre de Roissy to copy the leading opinions of both parties, although he himself did not take a position. Bishop Eudes, however, sided with his two chancellors against the Chanter and Courson. His synodical decrees declared:

> Priests are enjoined that when they have begun the service of mass, they should not hold the host too high so that it can be seen by the people, but in front of their chest until they pronounce "This is my body." Then they can raise it [above their heads] so that it can be seen by all.[64]

(It should be recalled that the priest stood facing the altar with his back to the congregation.) Because of the celebrity of the bishop and the schools of Paris, this liturgical usage was accepted throughout Western Christendom, but we must keep in mind that the custom of elevating the host during mass at Notre-Dame satisfied only the desires of the canons and the accompanying clergy in the choir. In the nave, the masses of the faithful who could not see through the jubé into the chancel would have had to be satisfied with their imagination, or seek the experience in their parish church.

Figure 22. Interior of the nave of Notre-Dame, photo, C. Rose, © CMN, Paris.

In the year 1200, as the desire to satisfy the visual senses was mounting, how did Notre-Dame itself look to the faithful from the nave? Pierre de Roissy's contemporary treatise, "Manual of the Mysteries of the Church," helps to give a rudimentary answer. Although the "mysteries" of the church were symbolic, they can be understood only by observing what is seen. His recounting of the visible therefore enables us, in a rough sense, to perceive the elements that Parisians saw. For example, the foundation of the church signifies Christ, the walls the two people of God, the gentiles and Jews, who meet in the keystone of the vaults, which is again Christ. The stones represent the virtues and the mortar, love. Not only does this evoke the basic elements of the church, but he also noted that the foundation of the church is oriented east, toward the rising of the sun at equinox and not at the summer or winter solstices. Of other visual interest, he noted that the glass windows of the church, signifying sacred Scripture, repelled the wind and rain but transmitted the brilliant sunshine and were fragile. The lower quadrangular windows were wider than the upper circular windows. Within the building he drew attention to the supporting pillars of the nave and choir; without, to the rooster perched on the roof that was mounted on a globe and an iron cross, facing the wind like a weathervane.[65]

Because construction of the nave was approaching completion around 1200, contemporary Parisians could imagine its basic shape and features. If we subtract later and relatively secondary alterations, we too can ascertain how it looked to contemporaries from the present building. Following the established tradition in cathedrals and monasteries, the nave of Notre-Dame is long. It is surmounted by five sexpartite vaults, as opposed to three in the choir. At the level of the vaulting (which is most apparent), the distance from the west portal to the beginning of the choir (including the western atrium and the crossing) measures twice that of the choir. Since the view into the choir and chancel was blocked by the jubé on the ground, one was obliged to raise his or her gaze to the upper stories, where the choir becomes the focal point of the entire church. The whole nave prepares one optically for the eastern end of the edifice. The seven massive columns on either side of the nave that appear to bear the weight of the upper tribune, windows and vaults facilitate this visual effect. The harmony of their profiles admits no distraction to this eastward perspective.[66] As the largest cathedral of its day (5,500 square meters at ground level), Notre-Dame could accommodate 7,500 spectators in the nave and an additional 1,500 in tribunes, according to the estimates of the nineteenth-century restorer Eugène Violet-le-Duc.

Its record height of 33.1 meters produces an overwhelming sense of verticality. The towering vaults direct one's attention along the upper tribune and windows of the nave and above the jubé toward the tribune and windows of the choir. The levels of the ground and the tribune are illuminated by windows that pierce the outside wall, but those that compete for attention are the upper windows of the clerestory. The present large clerestory windows were added in the second half of the thirteenth century to admit more light, but Violet-le-Duc restored the previous fenestration in the two corners where the northern and southern transepts meet the nave. Here we see the upper windows of the early thirteenth century consisting of a small rose surmounted by a clerestory not as high as the replacement.

The only glass that has survived from the late-twelfth- and early-thirteenth-century windows are fragments embedded in the present western and southern rose windows. These pieces display gemlike artistry that employed brilliant red, green and yellow against a background of deep blue with red edging.[67] The combination of deep blue and brilliant red produced a pervading cast of purple. Since Notre-Dame lost its windows in the eighteenth century except for the three large roses, we must turn to another example, the interior of Notre-Dame at Chartres, which in all probability replicated Paris's glass and whose original windows remain essentially intact. Here we encounter windows of brilliant luminescence piercing the darkness of a generally somber church. With its original glass and smaller clerestory windows, Notre-Dame de Paris was likewise dark. It is true that the exterior buttressing was designed to leave the interior free and unencumbered for these vast expanses of glass, but the function of the glass was less to illuminate the interior than to generate brilliant color. For this reason the "enlightened" spirits of the eighteenth century found them gloomy and gothic and substituted translucent grisails that admitted more light.

Prayer in the Nave of Notre-Dame

Secluded in the holy of the holies of the choir, the clergy were the active force at Notre-Dame, in contrast to the laity in the nave who were largely passive, like the fish of the sea according to Pierre de Roissy's metaphor. With their eyes the laity admired the colors of the windows, and with their ears the harmonies of the chant and polyphony. They attended services in the chapels in the ambulatory, imagined the mysteries of the mass hidden behind the choir screen and, as will be seen, reflected on the sermons from the pulpit. But the principal form of worship permitted to them in the nave was that of personal prayer. After completing the *Verbum abbreviatum*, Pierre the Chanter composed another treatise on penance with the same incipit, but containing a large section on prayer titled *De oratione et speciebus illius*. Devoted to the mechanics of praying, this treatise outlined seven postures of prayer accompanied by illustrations. Although the eight extant manuscripts circulated only in eastern and southern Europe (none has surfaced in France), the work draws heavily on his former treatise and its authorship is clearly attributed to the Chanter.[68]

Composed in Latin, it was addressed, of course, to the literate clergy as the *oratores* of society, but Pierre insisted that the audience also include the Christian faithful of every sex, age, status and profession for whose instruction the clergy were responsible.[69] The focus was not on recitation of collective prayers in the liturgy performed by the canons in the choir, but on private and individual prayer that could be voiced by laypeople as well. As general advice, Pierre proposed it was better to pray in churches than at home, better at night than in the day; that one direct prayers to the east toward Jerusalem or the altar; that one should not pray too fast and take care of pronunciation; that men's heads should be uncovered and women's veiled; and that men should avoid feminine distractions.[70]

More specifically, Pierre prescribed seven postures for praying, six explicitly authorized in the Bible and one recommended by tradition. They included standing, kneeling and reclining. The Chanter made provision for illustrations of his text not only to convey mental images to the clergy but, more important, to facilitate the illiterate laity's understanding, as Pope Gregory had taught. Eight manuscripts were furnished with figures, of which the Pegau copy from the thirteenth century depicted the postures of young men garbed in elegant lay attire as well as a woman.[71] The first three postures positioned the man standing erect to distinguish him from beasts. In the first the hands are clasped and extended above the head as far as the arms can reach (Figure 23). The most universal of postures, it was recommended for women as well and not limited to the church but suitable for the home, street, field, marketplace and elsewhere. In the second the arms are extended sideways to form a cross, a position more appropriate for church or other sacred places. In the third the hands are extended forward, together and directed toward the eyes as if reading a book. The fourth posture places the supplicant on both knees on the ground (Figure 24). (The position of genuflecting on one knee is never mentioned.) The fifth fully prostrates the supplicant with his face turned squarely toward the earth, thus representing the penitential humility implied in an animal position. The sixth (and last Biblical posture) is a bow from the waist with the head directed toward the altar. It was prescribed for recitation of the *Gloria patri* and for the moment of transubstantiation during celebration of the mass. In the last and traditional posture (and the only one figured by a woman), the supplicant carries her weight on her knees and elbows without touching her stomach to the ground, in the manner

Figure 23. Praying while standing, ms. Pegau, Bibl. Univ. 432, Bibliotheca Albertina, Universitätsbibliothek Leipzig.

of a camel. It was attributed to Tarsilla, Pope Gregory's aunt, and appropriate for severe penance.[72] Throughout this extensive discussion of corporal configurations, no allowance is made for the sitting or leaning of supplicants in good health, and no exceptions are granted to clerics or the cloistered.[73] As supervisor of the choir at Notre-Dame, Pierre the Chanter was a severe disciplinarian, permitting his fellow canons little accommodation from the misericordes in the choir stalls.

As for recitation of specific prayers, Pierre enumerated a sequence beginning with the *Pater noster*, prayers to the Trinity (for the great festivals) and to the Blessed Virgin Mary, and ending with the *Credo* (proposing examples to be employed).[74] Although this list served the clergy, it was less useful for the illiterate laity, to whom he prescribed massive repetitions of the Pater noster (one hundred for matins, thirty for lauds, twenty for prime and fifty during the mass).[75] He even prescribed a schedule of prayers and postures for visiting a church. On entering, for example, one prostrates oneself or genuflects three times, reciting the

Figure 24. Praying on knees, ms. Pegau, Bibl. Univ. 432, Bibliotheca Albertine, Universitätsbibliothek Leipzig.

Pater noster or the *Te invocamus* to the Trinity. Instructions are then offered for adoring the cross, praying to the Virgin, frequenting the altars and venerating the relics of saints special to the particular church.[76] Because the *De oratione* was a prescriptive treatise representing the Chanter's personal advice, it ensures, to be exact, little guarantee of actual practice, but given Pierre's position at the cathedral it nonetheless affords us a glimpse into how the faithful might have prayed in the nave of Notre-Dame.

Sculpture on the West Façade

Before the nave was completed, around 1200 the third architect began laying the foundations and raising the buttresses for the west façade, which was to contain three portals adorned with sculpture. (We have already examined this sculpture in a search for the female visage.) The portal to the south (now called the portal of Sainte-Anne; Figure 25) was already completed because it was decided to make use of a portal sculpted for the former cathedral in the midtwelfth century. Begun in the earlier style of Saint-Denis and the west front of Chartres, this portal was joined with contemporary but archaized sculptures to harmonize with the original. The portal to the north (Figure 26) was made early in the century and dedicated to the Coronation of the Virgin. Although savagely mutilated during the Revolution, it has been skillfully restored to recapture its former splendor as a chef d'oeuvre of the period. The central portal depicting the Last Judgment (see Figure 9 in Chapter Two) is more difficult to date, but it is roughly contemporaneous to the other two.

Undoubtedly the profuse sculpture of these three portals was created to convey meaning to the clerics and the bourgeoisie who entered the nave. Commissioned by the bishop or chapter with the advice of the learned chancellors and resident theological masters, the imagery may have sought to express sophisticated theology. Certainly it has intrigued modern art historians, who have ingeniously employed superior resources and erudition (unavailable to medieval contemporaries) to devise astute iconographic programs that often link the sculpture to contemporary events. But the bourgeois and even the majority of the clerical public were not so well prepared; what they thought about what they saw is difficult to grasp today. For this reason it is appropriate to begin by simply identifying the major imagery according to explicit categories.

From the antecedents at Saint-Denis and Chartres, the south door may be designated as that of the Virgin and Child or the Incarnation. In the central panel of the tympanum, the Madonna holds the infant Christ in her lap, flanked by two angels; to the left a bishop and a scribe who writes on parchment, and to the right a kneeling king holding a long scroll. On the lintel below is portrayed the story of the Nativity beginning with the Annunciation and concluding with the visit of the Magi. On either side of the door are eight column statues that include David, Solomon, Isaiah, the Sibyl, and Sts. Peter and Paul; in the middle is a bishop.[77]

The tympanum of the Coronation of the Virgin of the north portal depicts a seated and crowned Christ next to a seated Virgin who is crowned

Figure 25. Notre-Dame, west façade, south portal, photo. C. Rose, ©CMN, Paris.

Figure 26. Notre-Dame, west façade, north portal, photo. C. Rose ©CMN, Paris.

by an angel from above. They are flanked by angels holding candles. Below is the resurrection of the Virgin from her tomb, and below that three prophets and three kings holding continuous scrolls. To the left of the portal are column statues of St. Denis holding his head in his hands, flanked by two angels, and to his left a king; to the right of the portal are John the Baptist, St. Stephen, St. Geneviève, and a bishop or pope. A standing Virgin and child occupy the middle trumeau. The door itself is lined with representations of the six ages of man, the signs of the zodiac and the labors of the seasons.[78]

We have already examined (in Chapter 2; Figure 9) the central door that offers a classic representation of the Last Judgment. On the lower level of the tympanum, two flanking angels blow their trumpets to summon from their tombs the dead who represent diverse segments of society. At the center of the second level, St. Michael the Archangel and the Devil weigh out the merits of each soul on a scale. Those chosen to be saved are to the left, wearing crowns and gazing upward; to the right the damned are drawn in chains to perdition by a devil. Above them, seated over the heavenly Jerusalem, is Christ, who displays his redemptive wounds while flanked by two angels holding the instruments of the crucifixion, and again flanked by a sainted cleric and a sainted queen, no doubt the Virgin. At the ground level at the middle of the trumeau is the beau Dieu (Christ) flanked on either

Figure 27. Notre-Dame, west façade, the kings' gallery, photo. P. Muller, ©CMN, Paris.

side by the twelve Apostles. The doors are lined with images of the wise virgins, with their vessels full of oil, and the foolish virgins, whose cups are empty. Beneath all are medallions representing the virtues and vices.[79] We remember from Chapter Two that the two buttresses to either side carry statues of a crowned lady representing the church and a blindfolded, disheveled lady representing the synagogue; the outermost buttresses carry St. Stephen and St. Denis.

Contemporaneous to the three western doors, the sculptors mounted a gallery containing twenty-eight kings of Judah but robed in contemporary garments, wearing crowns and bearing scepters. At the end of the eighteenth century they were pulled down one by one by a Revolutionary crowd convinced that they portrayed the detested kings of France. Apparently a pious royalist secretly gathered the heads of the statues and gave them a Christian burial because he considered them sacred as part of a consecrated building. Miraculously they were rediscovered in 1977 in the course of excavating a bank and now can be viewed in their full, if mutilated, majesty at the Musée national du Moyen Age (Figure 28). Equally remarkable, they bore unmistakable traces of polychrome, which confirms the theory that much of the sculpture of the west façade up to the kings' gallery was painted in brilliant colors. Consisting of yellows, red, black, blue, green and gold, these colors helped to render the sculpture more vivid. The hues of red and ocher, for example, accentuated the torments of hell at the perimeter of the last judgment.[80] Unlike the white limestone surface darkened periodically by pollution to which we have become accustomed, color dominated the exterior of Notre-Dame as it did the interior. The central rose window with its flanking lancet windows, the superior arcade of stone tracery and the two western towers that are familiar features of today were yet to come in the later decades of the century.

As Parisians approached the west façade of Notre-Dame along the rue Neuve-Notre-Dame, opened by Bishop Maurice de Sully, or stood in the parvis (then smaller than today) before the three portals, how did they understand the images that were placed there on view? In the sixth century Pope Gregory the Great pronounced (and it has been profitably repeated ever since) that the artistic images of the church serve as the Bible of the illiterate. We may expect that all but the most rustic onlooker could recognize the Biblical stories and legends of the life and miracles of the Virgin to whom the cathedral was dedicated. They could follow the Biblical accounts of the Savior's nativity and his coming again at the end of time to judge

Figure 28. A king's head from Notre-Dame, Musée du Moyen Âge, photo. C. Rose, ©CMN, Paris.

the world. They may have been able to recognize Biblical figures such as David, Solomon, Isaiah and John the Baptist as well as famous saints such as Peter, Paul and Stephen (one of the early patrons of Paris). They may have known local saints such as Denis, Geneviève, Germain and Marcel, whose relics were treasured at Paris. And they must have been impressed with the abundance of bishops and kings in the south and north portals of the west façade, not to speak of the gallery above. Whether the bishop and king on the door of St. Anne were meant to be the contemporary Maurice de Sully and Louis VII, Étienne de Senlis or Louis VI, or St. Germain and the Merovingian Childebert did not much matter. Whether the lofty gallery contained the kings of Judah or those of France was equally not important; in fact they could represent different things at the same time, as Pierre de Roissy endlessly demonstrated in his manual on ecclesiastical metaphors. The dominant message was that Notre-Dame served its patroness the Virgin and was shared by both bishops and kings.

No text has survived of what laymen thought about the sculpture on the west façade around 1200, but an account has nonetheless been preserved of what a king said. In 1201 King John of England, recently crowned and at peace with Philip Augustus after the treaty of Goulet, visited Paris as the French king's guest and was festively entertained. Since John was housed at the royal palace, there is no doubt that he visited the new church on the other end of the island. In 1201 he could have admired the sculpture of the door of St. Anne, but the other two portals might not have been finished. He was surely familiar with the theme of the Last Judgment, which would soon be sculpted on the central portal. Shortly before his coronation in 1199, however, he was at the abbey of Fontevraud in the Loire valley in the company of the sainted Hugh of Avalon, bishop of Lincoln, who took the opportunity to show him a Last Judgment in stone on the abbey portal. There the bishop pointed out that on the right side among the damned dragged off to Hell were kings in full regalia, as at Notre-Dame. Such would be John's fate if he were not careful of his conduct. But John immediately took the good bishop to the left side where he presumed to find kings among the blessed, made conspicuous by their crowns. We may wonder whether, in fact, kings could have been identified by their crowns among the blessed at Fontevraud or whether John had mistaken for kings the blessed all of whom wore crowns at Paris. In any event Bishop Hugh drew the moral that such images were placed at the church entrance for a purpose. Those who entered to pray to God in their need should be ever mindful of the final judgment and ask forgiveness of their sins.[81] This anecdote indeed evokes the role that the sculpture at Notre-Dame was to play for the laity of Paris.

Monastic Rivals

We recall that at Paris the bishop was both a great temporal lord with lucrative lands and rights and the spiritual lord over the churches and parishes of the diocese. This latter authority, however, was contested by the great monasteries in and around the city. They included the ancient Benedictine abbeys of Saint-Denis and Saint-Germain-des-Prés, as well as the ancient abbey of Sainte-Geneviève, now a house of regular canons, to which the regular canons of Saint-Victor and the Cluniacs of Saint-Martin-des-Champs may be added. These religious houses claimed not only temporal lands and rights like the bishop but also spiritual authority over their parishes. Most important, the ancient houses of Saint-Denis, Saint-Germain-des-Prés and Sainte-Geneviève claimed long-established exemption from episcopal authority, which was confirmed by numerous papal letters. This exemption prevented the bishop from ordaining the abbots, from pursuing them in his own court of law and from supervising the clergy in their parishes. Such exemption, in effect, transformed the abbots into bishops in their own lands, ritualized by the custom that the abbots wore the bishop's miter in their own churches. Bishop Maurice opposed the authority of Saint-Denis over the priory of Argenteuil and the parochial rights of Saint-Geneviève over the parish of Saint-Jean-du-Mont on the Left Bank, but with little effect. In 1163, when Pope Alexander III was invited to consecrate the new buildings at Saint-Germain-des-Prés, Maurice was excluded from the ceremonies because he arrived wearing his bishop's miter at a church where only the abbot could wear his.[82]

As a loyal member of the chapter of Notre-Dame, Pierre the Chanter vigorously defended the bishop's rights against the exemptions claimed by Saint-Denis and Saint-Germain-des-Prés. In a chapter of the *Verbum abbreviatum* devoted to excoriating monastic privileges, he marshaled arguments that included opinions voiced by Bernard de Clairvaux and Gilbert de la Porrée, revered figures of an earlier generation. In particular, he singled out the two Parisian houses. For example, the power to convoke a synod of priests is exercised first by the pope, then by the primate over his region, the metropolitan over his province and the bishop over his diocese. How does one reply to the question, In which (or of which) diocese is Saint-Denis located? If one could say in or of the diocese of Paris, why could it not also be under Paris? It is absurd for a church to claim that it is in or of such a diocese and not under the bishop of the diocese nor subject to him. What is the reason for mutilating the church of Paris of its members, Saint-Denis and Saint-Germain-des Prés, when these two monasteries are not even exempt from the king's jurisdiction? In fact, Abbot Suger of Saint-Denis called Thibaut, bishop of Paris, to his deathbed and confessed obedience to him as a son to a father, asserting that the devil himself had procured the abbey's exemption. The abbots who paraded their miters at the great Lateran council in 1179 only made themselves ridiculous.[83] Despite the Chanter's protestation, Bishop Eudes was forced to contend with the abbeys of Saint-Denis and Sainte-Geneviève over cases begun by Maurice de Sully, but the Lateran council of 1215 did seek to regulate monastic incursions on episcopal authority.[84]

The Multiplication of Parishes

Since ancient times the bishop's cathedral had served the sacraments and ministered to the laity of his city.[85] Notre-Dame remained the unique parish of the Île-de-la-Cité until the end of the eleventh century, but the steady growth of Paris resulted in creation of new parishes that changed and evolved in response to demographic pressure. The one or more priests who served each parish had the exclusive right to administer the sacraments of the Eucharist and penance and often baptism and burial. As parishes fell under the jurisdiction of other churches, particularly the great monasteries, as we have seen, their boundaries tended to approximate the temporal authority of their patrons. By 1205 Bishop Eudes drew up a pouillé or inventory of the patronage in his entire diocese. In Paris itself his patronage extended to only two churches on the Cité and one (Saint-Séverin) on the Left Bank, while Sainte-Geneviève, Saint-German-des-Prés, Saint-Martin-des-Champs and the collegial church of Saint-Germain-l'Auxerrois patronized parishes throughout the city. Even the small monastery of Saint-Eloi claimed four parishes on the Cité.[86]

The two great building projects exercised the biggest impact on the distribution of parishes around 1200. Construction of the new Notre-Dame closed the cathedral and forced the laity to resort to numerous chapels and oratories on the Cité, some of which had already served as parish churches. By 1183 Bishop Maurice created twelve or thirteen parishes on the small island. The most notable was Sainte-Marie-Madeleine, recently converted from a confiscated synagogue, but others such as Saint-Barthélemy, Saint-Germain-le-Vieux, Sainte-Geneviève-la-Petite and the miniscule Sainte-Marine carved out complex territories, some of which consisted of only one side of a street.[87] No doubt Pierre the Chanter had this new development in mind when he penned the chapter "Against the Multiplication of Churches and Altars" in his *Verbum abbreviatum*. Pierre longed for the simpler days when Paris was like the Biblical Israel, which had only one temple or tabernacle for an entire nation, whereas today we raise "altar against altar." Individual cities should be satisfied with only one church; populous cities should be limited to a few parishes, but all under the authority of the major church.[88]

The construction of the walls, as has been seen, not only stimulated demographic pressure to create new parishes but also contributed to their dismemberment and redefinition. On the Right Bank, where the largest and most populous parishes were located, the vast Saint-Germain-l'Auxerrois was particularly vulnerable. A sizable parish of Saint-Eustache was carved from its territory in the northwest corner of the walls, that of Saint-Jean-en-Grève from Saint-Gervais, and the boundaries between Saint-Gervais and Saint-Paul to the east were now redefined by the walls. In the center lay the populous parishes of Saint-Jacques-de-la-Boucherie and Saint-Merry. The latter was a collegiate church containing eight canon priests, as Pierre the Chanter noted, like the larger chapter of Saint-Germain-l'Auxerrois, which boasted twelve canons.[89] At the other end of the scale, the houses on the Grand-Pont were divided among no less than three parishes.[90] On the Left Bank the walls were responsible for creating the new Saint-Côme and Saint-André-des-Arts to the west out of the large Saint-Sulpice, but by 1202 the abbey of Sainte-Geneviève succeeded in protecting the integrity of its parish du Mont inside and outside the walls to the southeast despite Bishop Eudes's counterclaims. In the center Saint-Benoît remained stable, but Saint-Séverin was strangled by the new creations.[91] The accelerating population growth was signaled by creation of a second archpriest at Saint-Séverin between 1191 and 1205 and the rebuilding of parish churches at Saint-Gervais, Saint-Merry and Sainte-Opportune on the Right Bank and Saint-Séverin on the Left. The abbot of Sainte-Geneviève was obliged to replace the inadequate chapel of Saint-Jean-du-Mont within the abbey with a proper parish church at Saint-Étienne-du-Mont.[92]

The Parish Clergy

Despite these contested jurisdictions, the bishop of Paris, aided by two archpriests and three archdeacons, was responsible for overseeing the parochial activities and competence of the secular clergy of his diocese. Unlike the monks or regular clergy who were secluded, the secular clergy were those who lived in the world (*seculum*) and who ministered directly to the laity. They were divided into three major or sacred orders of priest, deacon and subdeacon with responsibility for the sacraments, and minor orders such as doormen, readers and acolytes performing lesser duties. Like the king, Bishops Maurice and Eudes acquitted their responsibilities in two ways, centrifugally or centripetally. They could travel throughout the diocese on "episcopal visitations" inspecting the clergy, or they could summon the diocesan clergy to annual synods held at the cathedral where they assembled to be supervised, instructed and inspired. To accomplish the last task, Maurice de Sully instituted the custom, for which he gained particular renown, of preaching a sermon at the opening of the synod in which he announced his program.[93] During the succeeding episcopacy, Eudes de Sully began to write down the statutes or regulations that the diocesan clergy should observe, paying particular attention to changes in canon law. His own statutes touched the clergy's preparation for the synod, administration of the sacraments and other miscellaneous matters. The Parisian example was followed by Archbishop Stephen Langton for Canterbury and Richard Poore for Salisbury in England, without doubt influenced by their residence in Paris. The Lateran Council enjoined the practice of written statutes on all dioceses in 1215.[94]

Maurice de Sully's inaugural sermon has survived in a Latin version, probably delivered before the clergy but also translated into vernacular French for the clergy whose Latin was less firm. It proposed a threefold program of a holy life, correct knowledge and continued preaching, a schema that was close to the heart of Pierre the Chanter and his circle. Striving for a holy life and pure conscience, the clergy should avoid all manner of wickedness, which the French version specified as the capital sins of lust, gluttony, pride, hatred, avarice and covetousness. Eudes's statutes counseled the clergy's preparation as they traveled to the synod; for, example, they should arrive with fasting and prayer, their clothing should be appropriate and they should frequent decent inns en route. Lust (luxurie) headed Maurice's catalogue of sins because sexual purity was unequivocally demanded of all those who administered the Lord's body at the altar.[95]

The issue of celibacy of the clergy was revived in Western Christendom in the eleventh century, when the papal reformers known as the Gregorians decreed that the clergy who served at the altar should refrain totally from all sexual activity. Since those in minor orders could legitimately marry, the line of battle was drawn at the level of subdeacon and raised the question, Was the subdeacon in major orders and prohibited from marriage or not? Enforcing celibacy on the clergy was further complicated by a papal practice that arose in the midtwelfth century by which the pope dispensed specifically named subdeacons or even deacons from celibacy and allowed them to marry. Eudes's statutes skirted the problem by merely stating that no priest or chaplain may have a woman in his house on any occasion unless she was his mother or sister.[96] The issue became intense in 1208, however, when the Cardinal legate Guala opened his council at Paris with a declaration of war: "We Guala . . . excommunicate all priests and any other cleric whomsoever who after legal warning introduce into their own houses or elsewhere domestics (*focaria*) or other women whereby evil suspicion can arise that would scandalize the people and the church."⁹⁷ It is true that the term *focaria* commonly referred to concubines who lived with priests, but the unqualified terminology ("any other clergy") raised such a commotion at Paris that Pope Innocent III was forced to allow French bishops to absolve their clergy who fell under the ban.

At Paris, however, opinion was divided. In opposition to the strict Gregorians was a group that sought reform. Although the latter vigorously excoriated clerics involved in prostitution, fornication, adultery, concubinage and sodomy, they argued that these ills were not the cause but the symptoms of a more basic dysfunction: indiscriminate application of celibacy to the clergy at the rank of subdeacon or below. In its place they advocated the regime of the ancient church by which only bishops and priests were required to remain unmarried. From the previous generation the learned Pierre le Mangeur was said to have advocated reduction of the rules of celibacy to his classroom. Around 1200 the most vocal advocate of this group was Robert of Courson, who addressed three fundamental issues in as many questiones. In the first he debated whether the subdiaconate belonged to sacred orders, and after reviewing conflicting arguments he concluded in the affirmative because it had been decreed in a general council. This being the case, he contested in the second question the pope's right to grant dispensations and offered a comment on contemporary conditions. He noted the case of a young deacon who was refused a dispensation to marry when he confessed fears that he would be unable to live continently. His condition had greater merit than for many older clergy who were far beyond temptation of the flesh but nonetheless enjoyed the comfort of wives. As a matter of fact, Robert noted, married deacons and subdeacons in the French church and in remote regions frequently claimed papal dispensations. Permission to marry could be offered only by a general council inspired by the Holy Spirit, instituted by the holy fathers and confirmed by the pope. Having raised the barrier, Robert then sought to surmount it in his third questio. A benefit to one generation can provide damnation to another. Just as the serpent of bronze saved the children of Israel in the wilderness but became the occasion of idolatry afterwards, so the former vow of celibacy was useful to holy orders in the past but has now become an excuse for license, sodomy and even nepotism. As the saying goes, "the Lord has taken away our sons and given us nephews." Robert concluded by calling for a general council that would restore the clergy to their original status in the ancient church.[98] With different nuances, Robert's position was seconded at Paris by Raoul Ardent, Gilles de Corbeil, Girard of Wales and also Pierre the Chanter (although this opinion was not expressly recorded). Robert, his closest student, nonetheless testified that the Chanter was accustomed to declare that a general council should be convoked to restore the church to its primitive state and revoke the vows of continence for sacred orders. The upcoming general council at the Lateran in 1215, however, did not respond with hoped-for results. In 1207 Innocent III confirmed that the subdeacon was in sacred orders and thereby subject to celibacy, and the council itself took no notice of the Parisians' arguments but reinforced the sanctions against clerical marriage.[99]

The second requirement of Maurice de Sully's synodical sermon for the diocesan clergy was correct knowledge (*recta scientia*). At first glance this may seem to have been the least of his concerns. If priests from the outlying reaches of the diocese were untrained, this could hardly be said of the urban clergy, who were recruited from the schools flourishing in the city. Robert of Courson noted that rude peasants in the countryside remote from teachers could be excused by ignorance, but not those at Paris where teachers were so numerous.[100] This comparison was even more pertinent to the clergy. Collegiate parish churches such as Saint-Germain l'Auxerrois and Saint-Merry were staffed by canons who bore the master's title. (For example, such scholars as Master Pierre de Louveciennes frequently held the deanship of Saint-Germain.)

Maurice's first remedy for clerical ignorance was to prescribe a list of liturgical and sacramental books to be possessed by each priest (for example, lectionaries, baptismals, computations and psalters). Eudes's statutes specified manuals and *ordines* for the services of extreme unction, catechism and baptism, as well as ordines for the divine offices to ensure that the parishes followed the cathedral's usage and liturgy. Furthermore, priests were to exhort their parishioners to recite frequently the Pater noster, the Apostles' Creed and the *Ave Maria* and to preach sermons on Sundays and other feast days in which they explained the Creed to the people with citations and reasons from Scripture.[101] For his part Maurice had already delivered sermons both in Latin and French that instructed the clergy on how to explicate the Creed and the Pater noster to the laity.[102] Finally, Eudes strictly enjoined his priests, under the penalty of heavy fines, to transcribe a copy of the synodical statutes in their parish handbooks and keep it up to date.[103]

Because the clergy's principal duty was to administer the sacraments to the laity, Maurice's list of prescribed works included a book on the sacraments and a collection of penitential canons; the main body of Eudes's statutes treated at length application of six of the seven sacraments. (Holy orders were omitted because they pertained only to the bishop.) The synodical statutes had been well prepared by decades of intense discussion in the theological schools of Paris. The hundreds of questions debated in the classroom of Pierre the Chanter and his students were collected and organized around the sacraments, such that his work is rightfully titled a *Summa de sacramentis et anime consiliis*. Beginning with baptism, the collection proceeds to the sacrament of penance. After Pierre's death, Robert de Courson produced a final version that attempted to complete the treatment of penance and fill in the missing sacraments. Benefiting from all this labor, Pierre de Roissy's *Manuale* includes a section on ecclesiastical sacraments that summarizes the conclusions of the Chanter's school.

Among the profusion of issues, a few examples may be raised to show the practical tenor of Eudes's statutes. Baptism should be celebrated not only with reverence and honor but also with great care, particularly in the pronunciation of the formula "*N. ego baptizo te in nomine Patris et Filii et Spiritus Sancti*," whether in Latin or in the vernacular. For that reason the laity should be instructed so that men (even women, fathers and mothers) could be called on to baptize in times of necessity. In his questiones Pierre the Chanter delved into the complexities of using different languages (Greek, Hebrew, French or English) and of making mistakes in vocabulary or grammar. His final conclusion was that good intentions overcame practical difficulties.[104] Eudes took particular interest in the practice of charging for baptism, marriages and burials. Following the current teaching of the theologians, he strictly prohibited fees if they were exacted before the ceremony but allowed free contributions to follow as alms.[105] To ensure respect and honor toward the Eucharist, utmost care should be observed in washing the linens and vestments of the altar and keeping the liturgical vessels clean and without cracks. Following after theological debate in the schools, as has been seen, Eudes issued instructions that the host should be elevated after the words of consecration of the bread so that the body of the Lord could be viewed by the congregations of the parish churches,if not at Notre-Dame itself.[106]

In Maurice de Sully's synodical sermon, correct knowledge (also termed *discreta scientia*) was useful for administering the sacrament of penance. Although he recommended that priests possess a book of penitential canons offering fixed schedules of penance for each category of sin, he preferred the new approach of casuistry, which considered each sin and sinner individually. A priest endowed with discerning knowledge should be able to distinguish between good and bad, venial and criminal. Penance was the sacrament that sought to deal with a Christian's sins committed after baptism. By the late twelfth century, the theologians had divided it into three parts: contrition of the heart, confession of the mouth and satisfaction by good works, or as Bishop Maurice expressed it in a vernacular sermon, *la repentance del corage, la confessions de la bouce* and *la penitance*.[107] In the synodical statutes, Eudes de Sully limited his attention to the practice of confession, delving into (as was his custom) practical applications. In hearing confessions, for example, the priest should choose an open place in the church where he was in public view, avoiding hidden corners and places outside the church except under extreme necessity. Moreover, the priest should keep a modest and sympathetic countenance, always look down, never directly at the penitent (especially if a female), but always with patience and benevolence in order to encourage a full and complete confession. Most important, the priest must exercise care and caution.

In confronting doubtful issues, he should consult his bishop or prudent men by whose advice (*consilio*) he may assign satisfaction with greater assurance.[108] By "prudent men" he undoubtedly referred to the contemporary theologians at Paris, and particularly to the school of Pierre the Chanter, whose *Summa de sacramentis* was expressly devoted to advice for the soul (*et anime consiliis*).[109] After opening his discussion of penance with the declaration that he would treat the theoretical questions found in the "Books of Sentences" less thoroughly than more practical issues, Pierre plunged into hundreds of cases, many of which arose from contemporary conditions in Paris. For example, at the parish church of Saint-Merry, which contained eight canons, to whom should the parishioners confess? Could they divide their sins among the eight?[110] So many were the cases discussed that the organization of the *Summa* broke down at the sacrament of penance, and Robert of Courson was obliged to devote three-quarters of his version to that sacrament. The *questiones* of the Chanter and Courson in turn inspired Robert of Flameborough, Thomas of Chobham and Pierre de Poitiers de Saint-Victor, among others, to compose manuals for confessors in which they summarized the conclusions of the Parisian schools. For their part Thomas and Pierre de Saint-Victor referred back to the synodical statutes, and the latter singled out the Parisian statutes for praise along with the works of Bishop Maurice and the Chanter of Paris.[111]

In effect, the bishop and theologians mounted a collaborative enterprise at Paris for putting the sacrament of penance into effect. Following ancient imagery, the priest/confessor was the doctor charged with healing the soul of sin. Just as a physician must know the symptoms and conditions of an illness, so the confessor must recognize the particular circumstances and how to deal with them. Investigation of the infinite complexity of *circumstantia*, or the science of casuistry, became the hallmark of

Figure 29. Celebrating mass at Easter, *Bible moralisée*, fol. 39va, Austrian National Library, Vienna, Picture Archiv+Signature.

their craft. A decade later, Pope Innocent III recognized their achievement and incorporated it into the famous statute 21 *Omnis sexus* of the Lateran Council, which projected the influence of these churchmen throughout Western Christendom for centuries:

> All believers of either sex after arriving at the age of discretion should faithfully confess all of his or her sins to his or her own priest at least once a year and strive to fulfill the enjoined penance so that he or she can reverently receive the sacrament of the Eucharist at least at Easter. . . . Like a skilled physician who applies wine and oil to the wounds of the injured, the priest should act with discernment and caution to inquire carefully into the circumstances of the sinner so that he can wisely understand the sins, how he should give advice and what remedies he should apply, because different techniques can be used for healing the sick.[112]

Preaching to the People

Assiduous preaching (*predicatio continua, la sainte predication*) was the third function that Maurice de Sully proposed to the diocesan clergy in his synodical sermon. At the outset he emphasized that preaching should always be preceded by a holy life and correct knowledge. In effect, as Pierre the Chanter had demanded of himself, the priest preached not so much by word as by example. Like Jesus, he should act first and teach later. Maurice, we remember, was chosen bishop of Paris because of his preaching skill. No doubt he preached from the pulpit in the nave of the old Notre-Dame at the opening of his episcopacy, but after construction began it is hard to say where he delivered his sermons. His influence on the preaching of the day was due both to his personal example and equally to a series of model sermons he composed in Latin during the first decade of his episcopate. They consisted of the synodical sermon, two sermons on the Credo and Pater noster, as has been seen, and sixty-four sermons divided into three series: for Sundays and feasts of the saints following the liturgical year, for the period between the first Sunday after Pentecost and Christmas and for particular saints' feasts. These were simple homilies to be used by the less educated priests—brief in length (even briefer in winter when it was cold), and founded on the literal and historical text of Scripture from which allegorical and moral lessons were drawn. Of equal importance, it may have been Maurice himself (but most likely a collaborator) who turned these model sermons into French. The French versions are longer because the adapter sought to elaborate and embroider them to be better understood by a lay audience. Although the Latin versions were directed to the priests to serve as the basis of their sermons to the people, the French performed this function directly. Numerous surviving manuscripts testify that Maurice's model sermons were of great service to the clergy of his diocese. They fitted into Eudes de Sully's program of the synodical statutes urging priests to preach to the people on Sundays and the feast days, supporting their explanations of the Creed with citations and reasons from the Scriptures.[113]

Preaching was also the third and crowning function of Pierre the Chanter's program. It constituted the roof to the edifice of theology, and the goal toward which all theological training was oriented. As Maurice declared, preaching should proceed from the preacher's exemplary life—more by example than by word—as the Chanter phrased it. Whereas Maurice gave the clergy sermon models, Pierre offered them the material and inspiration for their preaching. His *Verbum abbreviatum* was crammed with citations, arguments and examples useful for sermons. His *Summa Abel* was a collection of *distinctiones*, that is, a dictionary of multiple meanings and interpretations of the individual words of Scripture, all arranged alphabetically for quick reference. Like Maurice, he privileged the literal and historical sense of Scripture but preferred the tropological or moral interpretation over the allegorical.[114]

None of the Chanter's sermons has survived, but his inspiration to the preachers lasted long after his death. By 1221 the celebrated preacher Master Jacques de Vitry, who himself probably studied with the Chanter at Paris, penned his *Historia occidentalis*, which opened with the misfortunes of Paris at the turn of the twelfth and thirteenth centuries and the origins of the preaching movement that God ordained to meet the challenge. In Jacques's opinion, the movement began in the theological schools of the royal capital, specifically in the classroom of Master Pierre the Chanter. Pierre's first note-worthy disciple was Foulques, an unlettered priest from Neuilly-sur-Seine in the Parisian region, who attended the Chanter's lectures and preached to his parishioners on Sundays what he had learned in school during the week. His teacher invited him to address other students at the church of Saint-Séverin on the Left Bank, but the reception was disappointing. When his audience consulted their notes after the sermon, they discovered that his words had lost the effect that made them so exciting during delivery. Foulque's charisma found expression as a preacher and a wonder worker among the crowds of Paris. Preaching in the market of the Champeaux on one occasion, he generated a vast outpouring of emotion and repentance. He was particularly effective among usurers, prostitutes and incontinent clerics, as has been seen. To Foulques's example Jacques added other celebrated preachers, among them the Parisian Masters Stephen Langton, Robert of Courson, and Pierre de Roissy. Bishop Maurice's and Pierre the Chanter's work at Paris received further recognition from Innocent III at the Lateran Council of 1215. Lamenting the ignorance and negligence of bishops in the past, the pope commanded prelates to appoint men qualified in works and words to preach the word of God throughout the dioceses, particularly the large ones.[115] There is little doubt that these Parisian initiatives prepared the way for the mendicant friars who appeared in the thirteenth century and styled themselves specifically as orders of preachers.

In 1200 at Paris, however, not only the bells but also the city's pulpits were silent. What were the lay parishioners missing during those nine months of interdict? Maurice's sermons in French directly envisaged an audience of Parisian laity, and likewise Pierre the Chanter and the guides to confessors addressed the same public. Like the sculpture on the west façade of Notre-Dame, the sermons were pronounced to teach lay men and women about the Christian religion. But what did the laity see, hear and most important understand of the message? Because chairs were lacking in the naves of churches, they stood mutely before the preacher addressing them from the pulpit. They listened passively, and inarticulately because no response of how they received the message has come down to us. By reading the French adaptations of the Latin models, however, we may catch intimations of how the preacher suited his sermon to his audience, just as by paying close attention to the guides to confessors we may detect how the parishioners' concerns were received by their priests. If the vernacular adapter of the sermons went to unusual length to explain the Gospel text or liturgical formula, we may suspect that the audience was minimally instructed in Christian worship. If the preacher frequently scolded them for whispering, we may suspect that inattention was habitual to the services.[116] But since all our information is mediated through the clergy, no response comes directly from the laity themselves. It is true that contemporary vernacular romances written for the enjoyment of the aristocratic classes expressed their particular concerns in religion, but no such literature exists for the bourgeoisie of Paris around the year 1200.[117] We are therefore forced to turn our backs to the laity and face the clergy, from whom we hear what they choose to tell us about their parishioners.

CHAPTER FIVE

The Schools

The riot of 1200 illustrates clearly that masters and students of Paris were so numerous and important to the economy that the king submitted to their demands immediately, lest they suspend lectures and migrate from the capital. The Paris schools came into prominence early in the twelfth century at the time when the Capetians chose the city as their chief residence and the bourgeoisie formed the company of water merchants. When Abélard attacked Guillaume de Champeaux at the school of Notre-Dame, this dispute not only kindled excitement but attracted students to the disciplines of dialectics and theology, in which the two masters excelled. Other schools formed on the Left Bank at the abbeys of Sainte-Geneviève and especially at Saint-Victor, which likewise drew students from afar. So successful were these early schools that the scholars revived an ancient legend called the *translatio studii* to compete with comparable scenarios fashioned for the papacy and empire. The papal legitimacy stemmed from the doctrine of apostolic succession, which viewed the pope as the successor to a long line of bishops of Rome who claimed authority from Christ through the first bishop, the Apostle Peter. The contemporary German kings claimed similar authority as successors to the ancient Roman emperors according to the tenets of *translatio imperii.* Echoing the latter, the scholars of France derived their origins from the learning of the ancient east. Alexander Neckham, for example, proposed that Abraham had taught the four liberal arts in Egypt, where Plato found them and transmitted them to the Greeks in Athens, who in turn taught the Romans, who made Italy as renowned for studies as for arms. In Alexander's own day Salerno and Montpellier were celebrated for the study of medicine and Italy for civil law, but Paris was supreme in the liberal arts and sacred Scripture. Even Pierre the Chanter briefly alluded to the theory in his Biblical commentary, noticing that the study of letters came from Athens to Rome and was finally flourishing among the French. So popular was this scholar's legend that the romance writer Chrétien de Troyes adapted it to explain the origins of chivalry as well: accompanying learning, chivalry arose in Greece, proceeded to Rome and finally arrived in France.[1]

Leadership among the Parisian schools nevertheless was retained by the cathedral of Notre-Dame from the days of Abélard and Guillaume through the early thirteenth century. By 1127 the students from out of town had become so numerous that they could no longer be housed in the cloister; in turn, Maurice de Sully forbade canons of the chapter to rent rooms in their houses to scholars.[2] When Pierre Lombard was elected bishop in 1159, after two decades of teaching theology in the cathedral school, the chapter rewarded distinguished scholarship with promotion to the prelacy. Thereafter followed a succession of chancellors all of whom claimed the master's title. Pierre Comestor (1168–1178) was an adherent of the school of Saint-Victor and distinguished for his Biblical scholarship. Pierre de Poitiers, chancellor from 1193 to 1205, had studied speculative theology with Pierre Lombard, and his successor, Prévostin, continued this approach. (1206–1209). Resuming the tradition of Pierre Comestor, Pierre the Chanter pursued Biblical and moral theology at the cathedral simultaneously with the speculative theology of Pierre de Poitiers.

Cathedral schools such as Notre-Dame were the object of educational legislation by Pope Alexander III (1159–1181) that sought to recruit and train a literate, even learned, clergy for western Christendom. His high ideal was expressed in the ancient dictum, "Knowledge is the gift of God; therefore it should not be sold." In a series of decretals culminating in canon 18 of the Lateran council of 1179, Alexander reiterated the principle of free education. All cathedral chapters were ordered to assign one prebend to a master whose sole function was to teach grammar to poor students without charge. Furthermore, the chancellor or schoolmaster (*écolâtre*) of each cathedral was to supervise instruction in the diocese by issuing licenses to teach (*licentia docendi*), which rendered the holder of the license a magister, that is, a teacher. (The title *magister* gave one the right to teach; that of regent master, *magister regens*, signified that the master had a chair and was actually teaching.) Although the chancellor was allowed to judge the qualifications of the applicant, he was strictly forbidden to receive fees for the license, according to the principle of gratuity of education. Despite the lofty goal to further the clergy's education throughout the church, this program, as we shall see, was ill suited to the schools of Paris.[3]

When Guy de Bazoches surveyed the Parisian landscape at the close of the century, he noticed not only the tower of the royal palace overshadowing the Île-de-la-Cité but also the burgeoning schools as they spilled across the Petit-Pont to the Left Bank: "On this royal island dwelt the seven sisters of the liberal arts, here the decretals of the canonists and the laws of the romanists were trumpeted; and theology, the fount of salvation, flowed into the meadows through three streams of history, allegory and morality."[4] Behind these metaphors Guy encapsulated the position of the Parisian schools of his day. The regime at that time was extremely informal. No general statutes have survived before 1215, when Robert de Courson returned to Paris with a papal commission to regulate the activities of the newly emerging university. Our best view of the schools in the intervening period comes from the writings of the masters themselves, in particular the theologians of Pierre the Chanter's school, who were ever sensitive to their milieu. Pierre himself was dead by 1197, but Stephen Langton continued to teach in Paris until 1206 and Robert de Courson until 1212, before he left the French capital on papal business. Masters were licensed by the chancellor of Notre-Dame to teach on the Île-de-la-Cité and at times by the abbot of Sainte-Geneviève for the schools on the Left Bank. Students were simply the boys and men who attended the instruction of the masters. Langton pictured the situation most vividly in a commentary to the Gospels; he likened the schools of Paris to Jesus choosing his disciples. Just as Jesus selected his followers in three stages—acquaintanceship, familiarity and full discipleship—so prospective students reenact Jesus' example. They first seek out the name of a master whose school they wish to attend and hear one or two of his lectures. If they are pleased, they become a member of his family. After proving themselves, they are assigned a place in the class and finally become disciples. In 1215 Robert of Courson decreed that no one could qualify as a student without being attached to a master.[5] Although the bishop claimed general jurisdiction over the clerics of Paris, masters as well had authority to judge their own students in legal matters. The Chanter even suggested that this jurisdiction could extend to other students unless they explicitly submitted to the bishop.[6] Unlike Bologna, where students took the initiative in forming the university, the masters were always dominant at Paris.

Clerical Status

The principal factor that distinguished Paris from Bologna was the clerical status of all masters and students in the former, whereas in Italy the schools contained large numbers of laymen. Because French students enjoyed the privileges of clerical status, they did not need the protections demanded by their Italian counterparts. Whether they were called *scolares* or *discipuli*, Parisian students as well as masters were members of the clergy, that is, *clerici*, who were subject to the exclusive jurisdiction of the church and wore the tonsure (shaving the crown of the head) as proof. Most of them avoided the lower ranks of the clergy (readers, porters, acolytes, etc.) and rarely sought the sacred orders of subdeacon and above that demanded celibate vows. So numerous were these members of schools at Paris that the Chanter designated them as *scolastici* and *clericatus literatura* to distinguished them from strictly ecclesiastical clerics.[7]

From early in the twelfth century, the fame of the Parisian schools attracted scholars from across Europe. Hugo, who opened a school at Saint-Victor, was from Germany; scholars from England and Scotland followed him; at the cathedral Pierre the Lombard came from Italy. Recalling his student days from the time of Pierre the Chanter, Jacques de Vitry designated clerics from England, Île-de-France, Germany, Normandy, Picardy, Burgundy, Brittany, Lombardy, Rome, Sicily, Brabrant and Flanders.[8] In the decades surrounding the year 1200, only about a quarter of the regent masters originated from the Île-de-France or adjacent lands; the remaining three-quarters were drawn from distant lands. By the end of the century, at least a third of all regent masters were English—Langton, Courson and Chobham were a sample from the theologians—with the result that when the university masters of arts grouped themselves into nations in the thirteenth century, the English nation was most prominent.[9] We recall that the students who precipitated the riot of 1200 were Germans lodged in their own hostel. Students naturally followed masters from the county of their origin. This great influx of foreign clerics presented challenges for the local parochial authorities. Under whose jurisdiction were these clerics: their home priests, the Paris masters or the Parisian parishes? To whom should they confess and be absolved? These became questions debated within the Chanter's circle. As a rule Pierre decided that because the clerics were far from home, they were under the jurisdiction of the bishop of Paris or that of a priest whom he designated.[10] By the first decade of the thirteenth century, however, the duties were so burdensome for the bishop that Cardinal Guala and Pope Innocent delegated the abbot of Saint-Victor to take responsibility on the Left Bank. By 1218 the abbot, in turn, assigned the task to a *penitentiarius* at the abbey.[11]

We have seen that by the midtwelfth century all clerics, including masters and students, both domestic and foreign, benefited from two important privileges that protected them from bodily harm. The first was the *privilegium canonis*, which considered their bodies sacrosanct.[12] Any physical violence against a cleric was equated to sacrilege of such severity that it was punished with automatic excommunication that could be absolved only by a penitential visit to the pope. One thought twice before roughing up a cleric. But because injury due to playfulness was equated to violence intended to harm, and because mature priests were not distinguished from mere schoolboys under puberty, the blanket immunity was too broad to be enforced. The canonists began to make distinctions that were quickly adopted by the theologians. Those under the age of puberty, acting in playfulness, and teachers who disciplined students or were acting in self-defense did not fall under the automatic ban; other exceptional cases could be absolved by bishops in lieu of a trip to Rome. Robert of Courson was of the opinion that only those who assaulted clerics with the intention to harm fell under the ban.[13] It was clear that the privilegium canonis had to be adapted to conditions prevailing at Paris, where young clerics were plentiful.

One complaint heard frequently at Paris was about the youthfulness of masters. Evidently the chancellor was not sufficiently rigorous in examining the candidates' qualifications. "Believe only the bearded master" was the Chanter's advice.[14] Robert of Courson's statutes proposed a remedy by stipulating that a master of arts must attain age twenty-one after six years of study, and that theologians must be at least thirty-five after eight years of study. The Chanter recalled the Jewish tradition that prohibited the study of certain difficult and controversial sections of Scripture (such as the beginning of Genesis, the Song of Songs and the vision of Ezekiel) before the age of thirty, and many Biblical commentators noted that Jesus himself was thirty before he began to teach.[15] If masters were young, then students were even younger, thus requiring adjustments to schoolboy behavior when enforcing the privilegium canonis.

The second major protection afforded to clerics was the *privilegium fori*, which furnished immunity from the secular courts. By reason of clerical status, and like all clergy, students were under the exclusive jurisdiction of the bishop's courts or their masters, who heard criminal cases as well. According to canon law, these ecclesiastical courts were restrained by the privilegium canonis from passing any sentence involving the shedding of blood. Clerics who were accused of capital crimes such as murder, rape, armed robbery and arson were therefore immune to the mutilation and death penalty that were the normal punishment of the secular and royal courts.[16]

Although criminous clerics were a problem for any prince who enforced the public peace, it was especially acute at Paris where the clerical population, swelled by the masters and students, reached at least 10 percent. In fact clerical immunities doubtless encouraged riotous behavior among students. Not only in 1200 but also in 1192 a riot had broken out between students and the men of Saint-Germain-des-Prés, where a student was killed.[17] We remember Philip Augustus marveling that the bravery of students exceeded that of knights. Although the latter do not engage in battle without the protection of helmets, the former rush into the melée brandishing knives, with their clean-shaven pates uncovered. Little should the king have wondered, however, because the tonsure, the sign of clerical status, was better protection than armor. Philip may have been inclined to evict troublesome students even before the incident of 1200.[18]

King Henry II of England faced the problem of criminous clerics in the 1160s, when he attempted to restore peace and order to his realm after the anarchy of the preceding reign. In the Constitutions of Clarendon of 1164, he sought to arrive at a solution that would restore peace but respect the rights of the clergy. All clerics accused of major crimes were summoned before the king's court. If they could prove their clerical status, they were transferred to the ecclesiastical courts and tried according to canon law. If they were found guilty, they were degraded, that is, stripped of their clerical status and returned to the king's court to be punished as laymen.

This attempt to mediate between royal and ecclesiastical interests was steadfastly opposed by Thomas Becket, archbishop of Canterbury. Not only did he reject the initial arraignment; he also refused to hand over any degraded cleric to royal justice for punishment, claiming that further penalties amounted to double punishment for the same crime. His Scriptural authority was the apocryphal formula, "God does not judge twice in the same matter." If a degraded cleric committed a second crime, he could of course no longer benefit from clerical immunity. In effect, therefore, every cleric had the right to one major crime without corporal penalty. Despite the extremity of Becket's demands, Henry was forced to accept them after the murder of the archbishop in 1170 at the hands of Henry's knights.

In 1169 Henry had considered submitting his dispute with the archbishop to the French king, the French church or the masters of Paris, but after Becket's death this recourse was no longer an option because the martyred saint had become an instant hero of the Parisian schools.[19] At Notre-Dame the archbishop's martyrdom was celebrated as a feast day (29 December). Not long after Becket's death, Pierre the Chanter debated in public with Master Roger the Norman, dean of Rouen and a Roman lawyer, whether the archbishop was a martyr for the liberties of the church or whether he merited death as a traitor to the kingdom. The question of criminous clerics was discussed in the Chanter's classroom without resolution, but in the *Verbum abbreviatum* Pierre boldly declared that St. Thomas of Canterbury incurred the wrath of the king because he refused to deliver to the royal court a cleric convicted by the church. Since the crime was punished by degradation, Thomas would not turn him over to the executioners according to the principle that God does not punish twice. If, however, the degraded cleric commits a crime afterwards, he merits punishment by the secular arm because he is no longer under ecclesiastical jurisdiction.[20]

Becket's solution to criminous clerics, seconded by the Chanter at Paris, became the principle that Philip Augustus incorporated into his charter of 1200 for the scholars of Paris. The king promised he would not lay hands on a scholar or his chattels without urgent and apparent necessity. If arrest was necessary, the prévôt would deliver the scholar immediately to the ecclesiastical authorities, who would take over. If the arrest occurred at night or while the ecclesiastical courts were unavailable, the scholar would not be imprisoned with common criminals but instead placed under surveillance in a student hostel until the church authorities could take custody. According to the provisions of the privilegium canonis, extreme care was taken to avoid physical injury unless the apprehended person resisted arrest. All complaints of violence were to be investigated. Amidst these details, it is notable that no mention was made of judgment of the accused cleric after the ecclesiastical courts took charge. This judgment became the sole responsibility of the church court according to its own law. As demanded by Becket and seconded by the Chanter, the sole function of the royal prévôt was to apprehend the suspected cleric. Later the king limited the royal agents to arresting clerics only for the major crimes of murder, adultery, rape, housebreaking and assault and battery.[21] Their trial and eventual punishment lay exclusively in the hands of the ecclesiastical authorities. But absolute refusal to deliver degraded clerics into secular hands for punishment was too extreme even for the papacy, which began to worry about clerics convicted of forging papal letters or worse, about clerical heretics. In 1205 Philip Augustus, no longer under the interdict, was in a stronger position to renegotiate the terms and propose what was basically Henry II's compromise at Clarendon. After debate between the clergy and the barons, a compromise was delicately phrased: a convicted cleric should be degraded by the church and afterward should not be released in a church or cemetery but in a place where the king and his justices could seize him and render punishment without incurring the anathema of the church. Although Henry's compromise on criminous clerics was strongly resisted in England, it finally prevailed in France despite the determined opposition of the Parisian supporters of the martyred Becket.

The Economics of Learning

Clerical status not only undergirded the legal rights of masters and students at Paris but also strongly conditioned their economic support. Espousing the ideal of the gratuity of learning, Pope Alexander III's educational program envisaged that each cathedral set aside a benefice or prebend to support a master to teach the elements of grammar freely to poor students. We have seen that the ecclesiastical benefice—that is, an income from church property—was the preferred means for supporting ecclesiastical personnel. One master teaching grammar at Notre-Dame, however, was unrealistic if extended to the schools of Paris, whose teachers numbered in the hundreds. Likely remembering his days in Paris, Innocent III noted that the rule was poorly observed and certainly insufficient in 1215. He proposed that other collegiate churches with adequate income assign a benefice to masters as well, and that archbishops furnish a prebend to support the teaching of theology at their metropolitan sees, but even these measures were insufficient for Paris. Individual endowments at the collegiate churches of Saint-Victor, Sainte-Geneviève and Saint-Germain-l'Auxerrois, for example, would not have satisfied the demand at Paris, and the bishop was not obliged to provide for theology because he was not of archiepiscopal rank.

A more realistic solution was the pragmatic one of papal provisions. By the middle of the twelfth century popes such as Alexander began requisitioning benefices from churches throughout Western Christendom to support clerics with the title of master who taught at schools, particularly at Paris.[22] Soon after becoming pope in 1198, for example, Innocent III demanded a prebend from the chapter of York in England to support Master Pierre de Corbeil, his former teacher in theology at Paris. The prime temptation was, of course, pluralism. Although the papacy, seconded by canonists and theologians, decried the practice, distinguished masters were often rewarded with more than one benefice, among them even the rigorous Pierre the Chanter. Noting possible exceptions to the rule in scholastic fashion, Robert of Courson remarked that when the Chanter left Reims for Paris, the chapter of Reims insisted that he retain his benefice because of his utility to the church. In fact the Chanter would be useful for every church, if it were possible. Pierre's conscience was no doubt troubled because Courson further noted that he, along with Jovinus, the écolâtre of Orléans; Master Pierre de Louveciennes, dean of Saint-Germain-l'Auxerrois; and other God-fearing men worried for the safety of their souls if they died holding more than one benefice. Although the Lateran council of 1215 repeated the prohibition against multiple benefices, it nonetheless allowed papal dispensation for distinguished and learned individuals.[23] Pluralism inevitably encouraged absenteeism as well, a problem afflicting the church at large. How could Pierre de Corbeil and Pierre the Chanter serve their chapters in distant York and Reims? Once again Pope Alexander III and the canonists made an exception for the schools, even to the extent of allowing students as well as to masters to absent themselves from their charges for the sake of study. In 1219 Pope Honorius III allowed clerics holding a prebend to attend the theological schools of Paris for five years.[24] The ecclesiastical benefice remained the preferred economic foundation for learning.

These pragmatic measures, however, remained insufficient to finance the schools at Paris. Early in the twelfth century Abélard confessed that he was not strong enough to dig and too proud to beg. Since he could not work with his hands, he was forced to sell his tongue and to ask fees from his students.[25] Even Alexander III himself was unable to compel the chancellor of Notre Dame to grant licenses without fees. Because of Pierre Comestor's renown, a special exception was made for him in 1174, so long as his fees were moderate. As late as 1212 and 1213, Innocent III still sought to curb the fees of the chancellor, Master Jean de Chandleur.[26] Around the year 1200, Pierre the Chanter and his circle, ever mindful of the principle that knowledge was the gift of God and should not be sold, approached the issues of academic fees directly. Pierre and Stephen Langton wrestled with individual issues in numerous questiones, but it was Robert of Courson who coordinated their arguments and arrived at definite conclusions.[27] Two sets of criteria conditioned their discussion: Did the master possess a benefice? And what subject did he teach? It was generally agreed that masters holding a benefice designated for teaching, as with the écolâtre of Notre Dame, should not charge for their lessons in any subject. If the benefice was for other purposes, the conclusion was debatable. If the master, however, was without benefice, he could receive fees for lessons because of his poverty (governed by the subject he taught; the subjects considered were arts and theology, the two dominant disciplines at Paris). A master of arts who taught the Chaldean alphabet, French or German language, or the liberal arts such as geometry and arithmetic was exercising a mechanical skill like a farmer, artisan and carpenter. Like a farmer who plowed a field, he could contract with his students for fees to remunerate his labor, according to the Scriptural principle that "the laborer is worthy of his hire" (Luke 10:7).[28] Masters of arts could therefore demand fees that were commensurate with their contribution of labor and skill. Theology or the high science of God, however, qualified as knowledge that could not be sold. Theological masters holding a benefice were, of course, denied any fees whatsoever, but those without a benefice could legitimately receive a fee as a gift of gratitude from students after a lesson, but without contractual obligation. Although a poor theologian could not sell the knowledge of God, he was nonetheless permitted to accept sustenance to support his activities, according to the Apostle, who said that "no one wages war at his own expense" (I Cor. 9:7).[29] With these arguments the Chanter's circle justified the system of fees and thereby broadened the economics of learning.

They also transformed the image of teaching. No longer was the master limited to the exalted and sacred priesthood, secure in his ecclesiastical prebend, but he was increasingly viewed as an urban artisan who fashioned intellectual wares in the atelier of his schools and sold them to his students at prices commensurate with his skill and labor. In the distant past, the liberal arts were the exclusive domain of the free Roman citizen or the holy monk, but around the year 1200 at Paris they became mechanical arts that could be bought and sold like the métiers of farmers or artisans.

Equally essential to the schools of Paris was lodging. As early as 1180, Jocius, a rich merchant from London, endowed a room in the Hôtel-Dieu to offer housing free of charge on the Île-de-la-Cité to eighteen poor students who were now excluded from the cloister. This foundation was followed in 1186 by another on the Right Bank at Saint-Thomas-du-Louvre by Robert, count of Dreux. A college of Saint-Honoré was established in 1204–1209. Intended for poor students, these institutions thus initiated the tradition of charitable colleges that accommodated students and proliferated on the Left Bank throughout the thirteenth century and after.[30] The two earliest colleges benefited most likely from royal favor. King Louis VII patronized Jocius, and count Robert was Louis's brother and the uncle of Philip Augustus. As with prebends, however, these colleges were not sufficient for the thousands of students who were at the mercy of rapacious landlords on the Cité or the Left Bank. Langton remarked that hostels along the rue Saint-Jacques that advertised comfortable beds actually furnished heaps of straw. Addressing the problem of high rent, the Chanter was of the opinion that masters could excommunicate students who charged their fellow students exorbitant prices, and in the statutes of 1215 Courson permitted masters and students to enter into agreements controlling the rents of hostels.[31]

Curriculum

We remember that when Guy de Bazoches surveyed the Parisian scene at the end of the twelfth century, he noted that the seven liberal arts, Roman and canon law and theology were taught on the Île-de-la-Cité. Guillaume le Breton found the same curriculum in 1210, with the addition of medicine. As Innocent III mediated between the masters and the chancellor of Notre-Dame in 1213, the masters were distributed among the faculties of theology (*theologia*), canon law (*decreta*), Roman law (*leges*), medicine (*phisica*) and the arts (*artes*).[32] A list of textbooks compiled by Alexander Neckham during the first decade of the century supplied the basic authorities for all these disciplines. By 1215 Robert of Courson's statutes reduced the basic texts to arts and theology, suggesting they had become the primary specialties of the Paris schools.[33]

To survey the curriculum around the year 1200, we shall preface each discipline with a list of prominent masters and the textbooks they taught. The outstanding masters will be furnished by contemporary chroniclers and by the extant treatises of each discipline, the fundamental textbooks by Neckham's list and the statutes of Courson.[34] Although these sources will furnish the curriculum, the Chanter's school supplied the most perceptive commentary, as always sensitive to their milieu.

The Liberal Arts

Masters:
  Alexander Neckham
  Petrus Hispanus
  Mathieu de Vendôme

Textbooks:
  Grammar: Donatus, Priscian
  Logic: Aristotle's *Organon*, Boethius, Porphyry and Cicero
  Rhetoric: Cicero, Quintilian
  Arithmetic: Boethius
  Music: Boethius
  Geometry: Euclid
  Astronomy: Ptolemy

The masters of arts probably numbered at least a hundred around 1200, but very few can be identified by name, and most of their treatises remain anonymous.[35] Petrus Hispanus wrote a commentary on Priscian, and Mathieu de Vendôme taught at Paris, although his best known treatise, the *Ars versificatoria*, was composed at Orléans before he arrived at the French capital.[36] The textbooks identified by Neckham on which the masters lectured consisted of the traditional authorities used in the schools throughout the twelfth century. Donatus and Priscian were the elementary texts for Latin grammar, and Aristotle's *Organon* was the standard work in logic, now complete in a Latin translation that included both the *logica vetus* (*Categoriae, De interpretatione* as well as the *Isagoge* of Porphyry) and the *logica nova* (*Topica, Analytica priora et posteriora* and the *De sophisticis elenchis*). Another scribal hand, most likely that of Alexander himself, added this comment: "Aristotle's *methafisica* and *Liber de generatione et corrupcione* and *Liber de anima* should also be examined." By 1215 Courson reduced the textbooks in the arts faculty to Priscian for grammar and the *logica vetus et nova* for logic, but he also added Aristotle's *ethica* followed by an important stipulation: "the books of Aristotle on *methafisica* and *de naturali philosophia* shall not be the subject of lectures nor his *summae*." Between Neckham's first list and 1215, therefore, Aristotle's important treatises on ethics, metaphysics and natural philosophy became available in Latin and were treated by the masters of arts. Although the ethics appeared to raise few problems, the metaphysics and natural philosophy were formally banned from the curriculum. As we shall see, Courson's statute referred explicitly to the decree of a provincial council in 1210 drafted by Pierre de Corbeil, archbishop of Sens, and Pierre de Nemours, bishop of Paris, which, in condemning the Amaurician heretics of the region, further stipulated "that the books of Aristotle on natural philosophy nor the commentaries on them shall be lectured on at Paris either publicly or privately under penalty of excommunication." (Some observers thought that this restriction lasted only for three years.) The quires of Master David de Dinant, however, that made use of the new Aristotelian treatises were to be burned.[37] Evidently the Greek philosopher's metaphysics and natural philosophy, which were so influential in shaping future scholastic thought, had made their debut at Paris but were flatly rejected by the ecclesiastical authorities. The writings of the Chanter's circle shed no light on this prohibition.

The seven liberal arts introduced the twelfth-century masters to the learning of pagan classical antiquity not only in the form of textbooks but also as literary masterpieces from the classic Roman authors, Vergil, Ovid, Cicero, Seneca and others. From the beginning, Christians had faced the question of what use ancient pagan learning was for their faith. "What does Athens have to do with Jerusalem?" was Tertullian's metaphorical formulation of the issue. The church fathers proposed two extended Scriptural metaphors for resolving the question. Just as the ancient Jews were permitted to despoil the Egyptians of their gold, silver and clothing before departing across the Red Sea (Exodus 12: 35, 36), so Christians can pillage pagan antiquity of its useful learning. Or although pagan letters are always inferior to Christian wisdom, they nonetheless serve as handmaidens to theology, just as the Canaanite women served the children of Israel (Deut. 21: 10–13). Pierre the Chanter referred to these commonplaces throughout his writings, commenting in passing that the arts are the footmen of theology. Recalling the captured Canaanite, Langton likened the Israelite to the theologian, and the captive women to the other faculties. If the theologian perceives an appropriate opinion among the masters of arts, he may adopt it, so long as he shaves the hair and pares the superfluities of the captive.[38]

The liberal discipline that attracted the most attention from the theologians was logic or dialectics. From the time of Abélard dialectics was the rage at Paris, leading to excess in the later theologians' opinion. For example, the study of logical subtleties (*sophistimata logicalia*) trained students to detect logical fallacies by considering frivolous questiones such as the proposition "What you have not lost, you still possess." You have not lost horns; therefore, you must have horns.[39] Aristotle's *De sophisticis elenchis* demonstrated how such arguments were fallacious, but Pierre the Chanter had occasion to cite the horn argument when he decried useless and foolish questions in theology. He maintained that after considering the proposition, no one would be so foolish as to touch his head to see if horns had actually grown. True philosophy deals with realities (*res*), not words.[40] Jacques de Vitry related the *exemplum* of a certain teacher of dialectics at Paris, Master Sella, who while taking a walk in the meadow of Saint-Germain was confronted by the apparition of a deceased student wearing a cloak of parchment that contained all of the *sophistimata* and *curiositates* that the master had taught. Because it weighed more than the tower of the great abbey, the master immediately understood the message and renounced his studies, to become a monk.[41]

Medicine and Law

Medical Masters:
> Gilles de Corbeil

Medical textbooks:
> *Isagoge Johannitii*
> *Tegni* (Hippocrates and Galen)
> *Viaticum*
> *Pantegni*

Roman law textbooks:
> Justinian's *Institutes*, *Codex* and *Digest*

Canon law Masters:
> Sicard of Cremona
> Étienne de Tournai
> Pierre le Breton

Canon law textbooks:
> Burchard of Worms
> Ives de Chartres
> Gratian
> Pope Alexander III, *Decretales*

The teaching of medicine, Roman law and canon law was not nearly as developed at Paris as it was for arts and theology. It is unlikely that more than ten masters taught in each of these disciplines. The only name known in medicine is Master Gilles de Corbeil, who was trained at Salerno, spent time at Montpellier and arrived in Paris before 1193. At Paris he wrote treatises on uroscopy, pulse measurement, diagnosis, symptomatology and pharmacology, as well as a moral invective against the evils of his day, all composed in hexametric verse. For this reason Gilles de Paris, as we have seen, included him in 1200 among the celebrated poets at Paris in the *Karolinus*.[42] The textbooks of the Parisian medical curriculum were the introductory *Isagoge* of Johannitius and the standard authorities of the Salernitan school of medicine, the *Tegni, Viaticum* and *Pantegni*, translated into Latin by Constantinus Africanus, which conveyed to the West the Greek medical learning of Hippocrates and Galen.

When Gerald of Wales resided in Paris from 1176 to 1179, he sought to "erect the walls of Roman and canon law from the foundations of arts and letters." Although Master Roger the Norman (the one who debated the Chanter on Thomas Becket) was present at that time, Roger had previously studied the arts in Paris but learned Roman law at Bologna and may not have taught the subject at the French capital.[43] With the possible exception of Roger, therefore, no teacher of Roman law can be named at Paris around the year 1200, but as with medicine the textbooks for the discipline were standard texts, in this case Justinian's compilation, which was the foundation of Roman law at Bologna.

Roman law, however, was prerequisite for teaching the canon law of the church. After Gerald left Paris in 1179, having lectured there in canon law, a school of canonists flourished in the city into the thirteenth century, as numerous extant canonist treatises attest. Since the canonists, like the masters of arts, were inclined to publish their work anonymously, only a few names can be retrieved. Sicard of Cremona and Étienne de Tournai wrote commentaries on Gratian's *Decretum* as products of their teaching, and Pierre le Breton on the papal decretals in the collection by Bernard of Pavia.[44] The standard textbooks in Neckham's list were Gratian's *Decretum* and the first collections of papal decretals, as well as the earlier compilations of Burchard of Worms and Ives de Chartres.

Despite the attempt to cover the major subjects, specialization was beginning to take hold at Paris, with the liberal arts and theology gaining preeminence over the others, as the statutes of Robert of Courson reflect. When Neckham traced the translatio of learning to the West, he thought of Salerno and Montpellier as the centers of medicine and Italy of Roman law, but the city of Paris was preferred for the arts and Holy Scriptures.

Geoffroy de Vinsauf transposed these commonplaces into verse for Pope Innocent III:

> Salerno heals the sick with power of medicine;
> Bologna arms the naked in court cases with laws;
> Paris dispenses bread and feeds the robust with the arts;
> Orléans raises the tender in the lap of the authors with milk.[45]

Theology

Theological Masters
    Pierre the Chanter
    Robert of Courson
    Stephen Langton
    Thomas of Chobham
    Alain de Lille
    Simon de Tournai
    Master Martin
    Prévostin
    Pierre de Poitiers
    Peter of Capua
    Pierre de Corbeil
    Humbert of Pirovano

Theological Textbooks
    Old and New Testaments

In an entry for the year 1194 the chronicler Otto of Saint-Blaise remarked that three Masters flourished at Paris: Pierre the Chanter, Alain de Lille, and Prévostin; in effect, they represented three schools of theological thought descending from the first half of the century.[46] The Chanter and his students Robert of Courson, Stephen Langton and Thomas of Chobham followed the Biblical and moral emphasis of the school of Saint-Victor through the intermediary of Pierre Comestor at Notre-Dame. Alain de Lille joined by Simon de Tournai and Master Martin were known as *Porretani* or followers of Gilbert de la Porrée. Prévostin along with Pierre de Poitiers and Peter of Capua were the intellectual descendants of Pierre Lombard. Around 1200, no theologian identified himself explicitly with Abélard's school, but the Porretani adopted some of his propositions. The followers of the schools of la Porrée, the Lombard and Abélard were primarily interested in employing reason to understand the central mysteries of the Christian religion (such as the Trinity, Incarnation, Grace and Redemption). If these theologians were thereby preoccupied with the contents of faith, Pierre the Chanter and his school were more concerned with good conduct, growing out of their interest in the sacraments—and especially penance, with its consequences for morality. Although there was overlap, the former were more theoretical and speculative, the latter more practical and casuistic.

More than a score of names of masters teaching theology at Paris can be identified from extant writings or contemporary testimony. (Only a dozen of the most prominent have been listed here.) Evidently the schools of theology were flourishing because Innocent III wrote Bishop Eudes de Sully in 1207 instructing him to limit the masters teaching theology to eight, a number that could be exceeded only in necessity. The pope feared that too many masters would dilute the quality of instruction, but Pope Honorius III admitted that the limitation was no longer respected by 1218.[47] Neckham's list of textbooks for the teaching of theology merely enumerated the individual books of the Old and New Testament, as was appropriate for theologians who described themselves as masters of the sacred page. (The principal textbook omitted was Pierre Lombard's *Four Books of Sentences*, the fundamental text of the speculative theologians.) Courson's statutes ignored the curriculum and turned to the candidates' age and length of study. No one could lecture publicly as a full master before his thirty-fifth year and without eight years of preparation. Those who had studied for five years could give semipublic lectures, provided they did not interfere with the regular masters' hours.

Despite the evident success of theology, the theological masters were nonetheless sensitive to competition from other disciplines. Although the masters of arts could be tolerated as handmaidens to the sacred science, those in medicine and law were considered to be rivals in recruiting students. Because doctors and lawyers were better remunerated and were often promoted to the service of princes and prelates, their subjects were depreciated as "the lucrative sciences" (*lucrative scientie*) in contrast to theology. Pierre the Chanter feared that those who studied law for profit were responsible for the neglect of the liberal arts and theology; students who rushed to Salerno to consult doctors or to pursue human and not the divine law neglected the soul for the body.[48] Addressing students who abandon theology, Langton complained: "You love the rewards of medicine, Roman law, and canon law more than holy scripture." Even the *Bible moralisée* composed for the royal court echoed the cliché; it depicted wicked students who leave the Gospels and divinity to go to Bologna to study the laws and decretals.[49] Robert of Courson judged that those who pursued lucrative studies at Bologna, Salerno and even Paris for worldly promotion were guilty of a kind of simony that included as well the theologian who studied for advancement in the prelacy.[50]

From early in the twelfth century, monks had been prohibited from attending school to study medicine and law. Not only were these subjects incompatible with their chastity and seclusion from the world but the lucrative professions equally violated their vows to poverty. In the council of Paris in 1213, Courson extended these restrictions to the parish clergy as well. Those who were responsible for the care of souls had no need for the secular sciences.[51] The campaign against the lucrative sciences at Paris received further support in the letter *Super speculam* of Pope Honorius III, addressed to the chapter of Notre-Dame and the churches of Paris, in 1219. Although most of the letter was inflated with florid Scriptural metaphors, the pope nonetheless proposed a number of practical measures. The prohibition against monks studying medicine and law and its recent extension to the parish clergy were renewed. To reinforce the theological faculty at Paris, the parish clergy were granted permission to absent themselves for a maximum of five years to study theology at Paris, as has been seen. Of greatest importance, the pope forbade henceforth the teaching of Roman law at the royal capital. Lamenting the competition from the lucrative sciences, the pope also noted that the laity in the French kingdom were not under the jurisdiction of the laws of the Roman emperors.[52] A century later King Philip the Fair claimed that his great-grandfather had, in fact, requested this measure from the pope. It is not unreasonable to conclude that *Super speculam* served a dual purpose: to promote the study of theology at Paris by eliminating a serious competitor, and to abolish the study of a legal system that undergirded the German emperors recently defeated at Bouvines.

Pedagogy

By the end of the twelfth century, the masters of the schools had assembled a common pedagogy that was applicable to all disciplines. Instruction began with the standard textbooks for each subject: Donatus and Priscian for grammar, Aristotle's *Organon* for logic, Justinian's *Corpus juris civilis* for Roman law, Gratian's *Decretum* and the early collection of papal decretals for canon law and the Scriptures for theology. Since these textbooks were authoritative, they were to be thoroughly mastered by students. As authorities, they served as the *auctor*, or plaintiff, in Roman law who brought charges and set the trial or discussion in motion, but they did not always determine the final decision or conclusion, because authorities—it was frequently affirmed—had noses of wax that could be deflected in different directions. Although the pedagogy was uniform throughout the schools, it achieved its clearest articulation among the theologians. The architectural metaphor of the Chanter's formulation became classic by the end of the century:

> The training of Holy Scripture consists of three exercises: reading (*lectio*), disputing (*disputatio*), and preaching (*predicatio*) against which prolixity is the enemy, the mother of oblivion, and the stepmother of memory. First, reading is laid down like the basement and foundation for what follows, so that from this source all support is derived by the other two exercises. Secondly, the structure or walls of disputation are put in place for, as Gregory says, nothing is fully understood or faithfully preached unless first chewed or ground by the tooth of disputation. Thirdly, the roof of preaching is erected. . . . One should preach after, not before, the reading of Holy Scripture and the investigation of doubtful matters. The Christian religion truly consists of faith and good conduct of which reading and disputation pertain to faith and preaching to conduct. After the roof of preaching has been put into place so that we and our neighbors are protected from the heat, rain, hail and wind of vice, the consistory of the palace of the High King will be completed in which he distinguishes laws and right.[53]

The theological orientation is clear from the emphasis on faith, good works and preaching, but the first two functions of reading and disputing remained basic to the other disciplines as well.

Reading

In the context of the schools, to "read" (*legere*) a text was to expound it publicly before an audience, or in other words, to lecture on it. By the time of Courson's statutes, these lectures could be "ordinary" (*ordinarie*), that is, at hours reserved for the masters (usually in the morning), or cursively (*ad cursum*), more rapidly by less qualified teachers, often in the afternoon. When a master read or lectured, he usually began by offering an introduction (*accessum ad auctores*) in which he identified the author, the title, the author's intention, the circumstances for writing, the disposition and number of the chapters, the utility of the work, its place within the discipline and external material that would further an understanding of the text. Then the master proceeded to read and reread the text word by word, sentence by sentence to the class. The first reading was literal (*ad litteram*) to correct textual errors and to clarify the grammar. (Remember that the instruction is in Latin, a foreign language to all members of the class.) Another gave the sense (*sensus*) of the text, and a final probed the author's deeper meaning (*sententie*). These exercises were performed orally before a student audience, but the final goal was to produce a written commentary or gloss to the text. The schools produced hundreds of such commentaries to the basic texts of each discipline: Aristotle, Gratian, Justinian and the Scriptures. Although it was possible to compose these commentaries privately, most commonly they originated from the notes (*reportationes*) taken by a student in the class that were later reviewed and corrected by the master. They could be written as glosses around the margins with a system of references to the text at the center of the page, or they could be transcribed consecutively across the page with the relevant portions of the text underlined, usually in red. By this intensive oral activity on a written text, the masters sought to impart the full meaning of the authoritative textbooks of each discipline.

When the theological masters lectured on a book of Scripture, they followed a procedure that went back to the fathers of the early church. At the end of the twelfth century, the theologians benefited from standard glosses that selected, excerpted and made available this wealth of patristic commentary. The theologians at Laon had prepared a short version, called the *glossa ordinaria*, which Gilbert de la Porrée enlarged for the *media glossa* and Pierre Lombard still further as the *magna glossa*. In making frequent use of these glosses, the Chanter and his school also applied the exegetical techniques of the school of Saint-Victor. Hugo, the founder of the school, also employed the popular architectural metaphor: Scripture should be read at three levels. One lays the foundations with the literal sense, which establishes the grammatical and historical meaning as the original authors intended. Only after the literal is securely in place can one pass to the metaphorical senses, that is, to erect the walls of allegory that teach Christian doctrine (particularly Christology) and raise the roof of tropology that instructs good conduct. Or, to change the metaphor, Guy de Bazoches envisaged them as the three streams that irrigated the meadow of theology. From decades of lecturing at Paris, Pierre the Chanter was the first theologian to offer a commentary to all the books of the Old and New Testament according to the literal, allegorical and tropological senses.[54] He was followed by Langton, who glossed all the Scriptures not just once but occasionally twice or even three times. Together their classrooms produced scores of manuscripts of Biblical commentary recorded by their students as *reportationes*.

As a congenital critic, Pierre nonetheless harbored reservations about the praxis of lecturing. His treatise the *Verbum abbreviatum* drew its title from the Apostle Paul (Rom. 9:28): "An abbreviated word the Lord shall make upon the earth." Pierre continued: "If Christ the Word, the unencompassable son of God, whom the whole world cannot contain, consented to be confined to the virgin's womb, how much more should the word of the sacred page be shortened which he bequeathed to us as an earnest and pledge of his love."[55] Thereafter followed two chapters arguing "against the superfluity and prolixity of glosses." Mixing and heaping up a veritable mountain of Scriptural, patristic and classical (from Ovid and Seneca, for example) passages on this theme, the Chanter seems to be unaware of his own prolixity, but occasionally he gave practical advice. He warned, for example, that Bibles burdened with excessive glosses are like those who prefer sumptuously illuminated codices to plain but well-annotated books, as Ovid remarked: "We are won over by the dress, all is concealed by gems and gold; a woman is the least part of herself." By preferring ponderous books, moreover, we lose time in copying, reading, correcting and even carrying them about.[56]

A further complaint about Scriptural commentaries was the tendency toward excessive allegory. Pierre reported that at Reims a learned Jew once reproached a Christian master for allegorizing the New Testament. Although the Hebrew Scriptures could be treated in that way, why the Gospels? The Jew interpreted application of allegory to the New Testament as an attempt to subvert the Gospel's clear meaning, for which reason he personally rejected Christianity.[57] The Chanter, we remember, approved of the Hebrew tradition that forbade young men under thirty to comment on the beginning of Genesis, the beginning and the end of Ezekiel and the Song of Songs, passages that encouraged allegory and dug pitfalls for the immature interpreter.[58] Moreover, he felt that allegorical interpretation of Biblical numbers, genealogies and measurement of the tabernacle or temple was of little value to the theological student. In these criticisms he appears to have targeted the work of Richard of Saint-Victor and his own colleague at Notre-Dame, the Chancellor Pierre de Poitiers, who wrote commentaries on the doubtful books and were particularly interested in genealogies and the dimensions of the Mosaic tabernacle.[59] Although the Chanter may have slipped into prolixity in his *Verbum abbreviatum,* his Biblical commentaries nonetheless followed his own advice. Making use of the short glossa ordinaria, his exposition by and large moved briskly through the text. Although he did not totally neglect allegorical readings, he preferred the literal and tropological senses, which conformed to his commitment to morality.

Disputing

"Nothing is fully understood," Pope Gregory the Great had maintained, "unless [it was] first chewed . . . by the tooth of disputation." The walls of the Chanter's house of learning consisted of disputation, or questioning, as it was also called. Nearly synonymous, the two terms covered a broad range of meaning. Consisting of discussion, dialogue, confrontation of theses, comparison of texts or even "altercation," they could be applied to any subject. They were an intellectual method as well as a pedagogical procedure. After treating reading, the Chanter added, if a question arises in the text it should be noted and deferred until the hour of disputation.[60] Neckham and Langton reported similar procedures; Simon of Tournai's disputations were organized according to days. By the end of the century, it is clear that questioning and disputing were separated from lecturing and reserved for special hours.

The authoritative texts read in lectio frequently had a habit of being unclear, inconsistent, or in conflict with one another. Questio was the technique devised to resolve problems and harmonize conclusions in all disciplines. Early in the century, for example, Abélard compiled his *Sic et non* in which he posed more than a hundred questions current in theology, to which he marshaled authoritative texts from the Scriptures and church fathers both for and against each proposition, thus generating the title (*Yes and No*). In like fashion Gratian collected the conflicting sources of canon law and attempted to reconcile them in a textbook titled *The Concordance of Discordant Canons,* otherwise known as the *Decretum.* Although not as frequent, the procedure could be applied to Roman law and medicine as well. In the process of reconciling the conflicting texts, the scholars often resorted to use logic or dialectics as formulated by Aristotle's *Organon.* This posed few problems for secular subjects, but it raised a fundamental question for the theologians: what role did reason (*ratio*) play in understanding the divine mysteries of revelation?

Faith seeking understanding, or the penetration of reason into the domain of belief, became a major preoccupation of the twelfth century. Abélard and

Gilbert de la Porrée applied dialectics to understand better the mystery of the Trinity, against which Bernard, the influential abbot of Clairvaux, objected vociferously. By the end of the century, Gauthier de Saint-Victor penned a polemic, *Against the Four Labyrinths of France*, that accused Abélard, Gilbert de la Porrée, Pierre Lombard and Pierre de Poitiers, the major theologians at Paris, of desecrating theology with their dialectics.

Sensitive to controversy, Pierre the Chanter devoted three chapters of his *Verbum abbreviatum* to the procedure of questioning-disputing, which implicated the role of reason in theology. He opened his discussion by making preliminary distinctions:

> Having laid the foundations of reading, we should proceed now to raising the walls of disputation. In theological disputations certain questions are futile and useless. Since they deal neither with faith or morals, they can be eliminated immediately. Others are useful but clear and they can be omitted. Certain are useful and troublesome (*scrupulose*) and these can be discussed with modesty and without wrangling. Others can be left to the woodpeckers and frogs of the sophists lest one grasp for clouds and emptiness. Those that edify without contention should be pursued because their goal is faith and morals.[61]

Since the foolish and vain questions were easily disposed of, Pierre passed to the serious and rash (*temerarias*) questions that bred error and subverted the soul. Bernard of Clairvaux proposed that certain areas of faith, such as the Trinity and the Incarnation, were beyond the realm of reason and therefore not appropriate for disputation. More recently, Étienne de Tournai feared that the ineffable mysteries of God, the Incarnation and the Eucharist, were being exposed irreverently to public debate at Paris.[62] Just as Moses encircled Mount Sinai with boundaries to prevent beasts from treading on holy ground, the Chanter likewise maintained that the Holy Scriptures were protected against rash queries involving the sacraments, Christ's humanity and the paternity and names of God. Such questions spawned heresies and divided theologians.

Unlike secular philosophers, who split between realists and nominalists, the theologians should live in unity.[63] Commenting further on the Biblical passage "Thou shall not plant a grove of trees near the altar of the Lord," he interpreted the altar as the mystery of the Passion or Incarnation, and the grove of trees as philosophy, which should not dispute these mysteries with secular wisdom.[64] In like manner, Langton chastened theologians for unclothing God's secrets by disputing the Trinity and the divine properties, which offered little edification for the soul.[65] Despite attempts to protect these mysteries from the scrutiny of dialectics and disputation, the proscribed subjects were in fact treated regularly in the questiones of Pierre de Poitiers, Prévostin, Master Martin and even Langton himself. Because Pierre the Chanter's *Summa* was principally concerned with the sacraments, he also treated the sacramental mysteries in his questiones but avoided the other subjects that preoccupied the contemporary theologians. Since the section devoted to faith was omitted altogether in Robert of Courson's *Summa*, he thereby avoided crossing the forbidden boundaries.

In the third chapter devoted to disputations, Pierre the Chanter offered positive advice. Theologians should fashion their discussions not as "altercations" but as *collationes* or the common pursuit of truth. Refraining from histrionics, they should proceed with due deliberation. The example found in Roman law should be emulated, requiring a strict procedure of examining witnesses, producing lawyers, according delays and testing accusers before a final sentence was pronounced. In like manner, Aristotle was reputed to have requested a delay until the following day even when examining a simple proposition.[66]

Careful to avoid abuse, the Chanter did not seek thereby to eliminate disputation from the classroom pedagogy. His school produced at least a dozen manuscripts containing hundreds of questions organized around the sacraments. At the outset individual questions were arranged according to a discernable plan, were polished in form and usually came to a definite conclusion, but after the sacrament of penance was reached the organization broke down. The structure became sketchy and conclusions were often omitted, suggesting that the compilers did not have time to revise. In principle each individual item consists of an opening question to which authorities and arguments pro and con are cited and a resolution offered. Precisely how the questions were generated in the classroom does not become immediately apparent from the written evidence, but most probably they were the result of collaboration between the master and his students. The informal questions at the end of the collection occasionally reveal the master's presence in the third person (*magister dixit*) as well as other masters, sometimes named. These written records in fact bear the marks of reportationes, or inscription of the student collaborators' notes. Robert of Courson's *Summa* offered a final and polished edition of the questions debated in the Chanter's school, and Langton's questiones, resulting from years of teaching at Paris, bear the same characteristics as the Chanter's; his were likewise revised in a final version by a student, Geoffroy de Poitiers.

Aristotle's *Organon* furnished the rules of logic that governed the theologians' pedagogy of questioning and disputing. We have seen that it was duly inscribed in Neckham's list of textbooks for the masters of arts at Paris. The Greek philosopher's works on ethics, metaphysics and natural science were likewise translated into Latin at Toledo and Venice during the second half of the century. Neckham appended some of these treatises to his list during the first decade of the thirteenth century. At the same time, the chronicler Guillaume le Breton noted that certain treatises of Aristotle, particularly the metaphysics, had been translated into Latin at Constantinople and were taught at Paris before the provincial council banned them in 1210.[67] Except in a handful of anonymous and pseudonymous writings, these new works of Aristotle have left little trace. The theologians descended from the schools of the Porretani, and the Lombard appeared to have ignored them; the Chanter's school, ever respectful of the boundaries of sacred science, made no mention of them whatsoever. Even Courson, who repeated the prohibition in his statutes of 1215, was totally silent in his *Summa*. This silence remained until the third decade of the thirteenth century, when they were finally acknowledged by the new generation of theologians, Guillaume d'Auxerre, Philippe the Chancellor and Guillaume d'Auvergne.

Preaching

"Thirdly, the roof of preaching is raised. . . . One should preach after, not before, the reading of Holy Scripture and the investigation of doubtful matters." The crowning stage of Pierre the Chanter's theological pedagogy prepared students for preaching to the laity, which was required by Bishops Maurice and Eudes de Sully for the diocese of Paris, as was seen in the previous chapter. The Chanter left no securely identified sermons behind, but Langton was survived by hundreds.[68] According to the threefold program, therefore, Langton was the exemplary product of the Chanter's theological pedagogy. All composed in Latin, many of the sermons were directed to clerical audiences. Another of the Chanter's students, Thomas of Chobham, likewise preached at Paris. Although three of his sermons were delivered in Latin at the parish church of Saint-Jacques on the Right Bank, most of his preaching took place before the monks of Saint-Germain-des-Prés and the regular canons of Saint-Victor on the Left.[69] Preaching also marked an important step in the theologian's career.

After finishing his studies, a new master of theology mounted his professorial chair (cathedra) and began his lectures with an inaugural sermon called an *inceptio*, in honor of Holy Scripture. The two earliest of these sermons to have survived at Paris were delivered by Langton and Thomas of Chobham. Langton's homily dates before 1187, when he began to teach at Paris; it bears the rubric "The lectio of Master Stephen Langton which he delivered at his inception." Chobham's may stem from his first residence at Paris as a master, between 1189 and 1193, or more likely either in 1208–1213 or 1222–1228. It opens, "Here begins the lectio of Master Thomas of Chobham when he began to teach theology at Paris." Entitled *lectiones* as well, the two sermons appear at first sight to be lectures on the Bible.

Taking as his text "And the people took their dough before it was leavened, their kneading troughs being bound up in their clothes upon their shoulders" (Ex. 12:34), Langton offered an elaborate moral exposition of the Hebrew exodus from Egypt. Egypt stands for the world, the desert for life's pilgrimage, and the promised land for eternal rest. The daily manna is Holy Scripture, which is broken in reading, ground with the pistil of disputation and baked in the oven of meditation. After proceeding at length in this fashion, Stephen concluded with a personal affirmation: "What am I, who have neither eminence of life nor of knowledge, to say to these matters and yet I ascend the professorial chair? Relying on the inexhaustible goodness of divine grace and not on human presumption, I transform my tongue and mind in obedience to my Redeemer and commit myself and my resolution to his grace."

For his inceptio, which is much shorter, Thomas chose the text "When Jacob awoke from his sleep he said, 'Truly God is in this place and I knew it not.' And being afraid he said, 'How terrible is this place. It is none other than the house of God and the gate of heaven'" (Gen. 28: 16–17). Meditating on Jacob's dream, Thomas developed six stages relevant to a theologian. After distinguishing four kinds of sleep, Thomas followed with numerous Scriptural metaphors that he applied to the tasks of theology and the Holy Scriptures. Within the plethora of his remarks, he inveighed against superfluity and subtlety in glossing the Scripture, thus reproducing passages taken directly from Pierre the Chanter's *Verbum abbreviatum*. Apparently running out of time, he postponed to another occasion the last points (on the gate of heaven and the house of God) and concluded quickly with a benediction. Although both sermons were called lectiones, they were not, in the final analysis, Biblical commentaries that followed the order of Scripture but true sermons that developed their arguments homiletically, relying on collections of Biblical distinctions, like the Chanter's *Summa Abel,* to furnish appropriate passages.

The Schools and Society

The schools' primary task was to produce masters qualified to teach the disciplines of arts, medicine, law and theology. Around 1200 no more than a quarter of the regent masters (actually teaching) at Paris came from the Île-de-France or its environs; the vast majority were recruited from distant lands, with at least a third originating from England. Those whose social origins were noted encompassed the social scale; about half were from the landed aristocracy, a quarter from "lowly origins" (of whom most were illegitimate, that is, sons of priests) and a mere handful from the class of barons or above.[70] Regent masters were, of course, not the only masters in town, but they were most closely associated with the schools and constitute those for whom we have the best evidence.

If recruitment indicates the schools' intake, the output consisted of the opportunities available for employing masters outside the schools. Since all Parisian masters were clerics, the church was inevitably the largest employer. As might be expected, at least 40 percent of all regent masters later became prelates (archbishops, bishops, abbots, etc.), 35 percent dignitaries of collegiate chapters (dean, chanter, archdeacon, chancellor, and so on) and the rest monks, canons and other ecclesiastics. Those who became chancellors remained at that post (the five master chancellors at Paris, for example), suggesting that it was the preferred teaching post. Because of abundance, statistics are most reliable for the theologians. Of the twenty-four documented regent masters of theology at Paris, eleven (46 percent) became prelates (of whom four cardinals) and seven (30 percent) chapter dignitaries.[71] The cardinals included Stephen Langton, Robert of Courson, Peter of Capua and Humbert of Pirovano; among the archbishops were Langton, Pierre de Corbeil and Anders Sunesen. In the early twelfth century, prominent Parisian theologians such as Guillaume de Champeaux, Gilbert de la Porrée and Pierre Lombard were rewarded with bishoprics. Because high preferment had become an established tradition among the theologians at Paris, their complaint that the law and medicine were the lucrative sciences might appear less than sincere, but doubtless they were thinking of the lawyers' and doctors' ability to charge high fees. Robert of Courson, one of the fortunate theologians himself, candidly averred that theology could be studied for advancement to the prelacy, not for God's sake.[72]

To measure the penetration of masters into society at large, we benefit from one peculiar foible of the profession itself: a master would rarely allow his name to be recorded without his academic title, except, of course, if he enjoyed a more honorific dignity such as bishop, abbot or dean. In a satirical poem describing an ass named Burnel, who left the study of arts and theology at Paris to proceed to Bologna in pursuit of the degree of magister, the learned beast brashly proclaimed that "if anyone should say Burnel, but perchance leave "Master" off, he shall be my public foe."[73] We cannot tell where masters received their degree or what subjects they studied, but we can count on them to display their title. In legal documents, as well as in other sources, the degree was rarely omitted.[74] As the production of masters increased throughout the twelfth century, these men appear more frequently in the sources, particularly in ecclesiastical documents. Bishops in France who claimed the degree increased from 3 percent under King Louis VII to 15 percent under Philip Augustus, at a time when 29 percent of the English sees elected masters as bishops. Around 1200 the entourages of the chapters of Paris and Laon contained about 20 percent of their personnel claiming the degree, whereas in England the saintly Hugh of Avalon, bishop of Lincoln, recruited an entourage containing 42 percent masters, a figure that was not untypical for the kingdom (London, 47 percent, York 46 percent). The entourage of the archbishop of Canterbury consisted of as many as 63 percent masters around 1200. A new ecclesiastical post that required a master's degree, as we have seen, was the officialis or chief legal officer of the bishop. As appeals to the papal curia grew during the pontificate of Innocent III, increasingly teams of judge-delegates were composed of three persons: a prelate, a lesser dignity (dean or archdeacon) and a cleric whose only distinction was his master's degree.

Not only were masters finding greater employment in the church but kings were likewise taking advantage of their expertise. No master surfaces in the Capetian entourage until the reign of Louis VII, when two or three appear, but Philip Augustus enjoyed the service of at least a dozen who journeyed on diplomatic missions, especially to Rome to deal with the king's matrimonial problem.[75] The English kings' employment was even greater. Henry II, Richard and John were rarely without the permanent company of a half dozen masters, particularly in the chancery. At least three of John's fifteen active itinerant justices carried the title, which cannot be matched by Philip Augustus's baillis, who were exclusively laymen. The sole surviving financial account of the Capetians in 1202–1203 yields the names of two masters; the English pipe roll for the same year has twenty-two. One striking conclusion may be drawn from comparing the ecclesiastical and royal administrations of France with those of England. If the celebrated schools of France produced more masters than elsewhere, the prelates and kings of England offered twice as many opportunities for employment as the French. This conclusion is further corroborated by the preponderance (at least a third) of English students and masters at Paris, which apparently served as the chief training school for the English kingdom. This high employment of masters may be the result of the administrative precocity of both the English church and the royal government.[76] The administration of Kings Richard and John required more highly trained personnel than did the Capetians, whose government did not catch up until the midthirteenth century.

It is easier to trace penetration of the Parisian masters into society at large than to respond to the ultimate question of *cui bono*. Of course, medical doctors may have contributed to the public health and the canon lawyers to efficient administration of the church. The Roman lawyers, soon to be extinct at Paris, had no official function in the lands of northern France, where their law was excluded, but they helped to perfect the formation of the church lawyers who drew heavily on Roman jurisprudence. The masters of arts contributed to the level of literacy in an illiterate society that was becoming increasingly dependent on written documents. Not only by teaching Latin grammar but also by instructing logic and rhetoric, they trained men to think rationally and systematically, thereby improving the writing of clerics and literate laymen. The chief function of the masters of theology, to be sure, was to define, articulate and impart the tenets of the Christian faith that were so highly valued in contemporary society, but the followers of Pierre the Chanter at Paris sought to orient this contribution in a particular sense. As specialists in the curative powers of the sacrament of penance, it was their task to diagnose the multifarious ills of sin, devise remedies for healing them, instruct confessors on how to apply these remedies and convince a sick and sinful world to accept them. In short, they saw themselves as the conscience and reformers of their age.

The Reform of Society

As practitioners of the medicine of penance, the theologians of the Chanter's circle sought to perfect their skills as confessors. Diagnosing the ills of society, they were trained to pay attention to particular circumstances, which in turn made them sensitive and acute observers of their surroundings. Not only were they contemporary witnesses, however, but as doctors of the soul they were also reformers.

Reform for them was to return to an earlier and purer epoch. As with later reformers of the sixteenth century, these masters of the sacred page located this period in the primitive church and the Gospels. To recover this era involved pruning intervening tradition. Pierre devoted a long chapter in the *Verbum abbreviatum* to defining four kinds of onerous traditions: those of diabolical origin and contrary to the law of God, those that are licit and useful but nonetheless obscure God's law, honest traditions that on account of their multitude impede the law and finally new traditions that because of their multitude likewise obscure the law. To illustrate his argument, Pierre cited the example of a certain Ives de Chartres, who made an impassioned plea at the Lateran Council of 1179 to avoid enacting any more papal decretals that give cause only for the wrangling of scholars in the schools and of lawyers in the courts. Rather, the council should simply command obedience to the Gospels, which have been honored in the breach.[77] Ives's plea, in fact, echoed the inaugural sermon at the council actually delivered by the canonist Rufinus, bishop of Assisi. Evoking the theme of the recovery of the Book of Law during the restoration of the Temple under King Josiah (II Chron. 34), Rufinus advocated a return to the now-lost law of God.[78] The Chanter identified particular traditions ranging from monastic customs, liturgical usage and excessive allegorization to social issues involving marriage customs and ordeals. These were the traditions that should be pared away to return to the verbum abbreviatum, the simple, abbreviated word of God.

The chief instrument for bringing about reform was the general council. Pierre most likely attended the last Lateran council of 1179, which he vividly evoked in his writings. Not only did he call for a council throughout his Biblical commentaries, but his student Robert of Courson remembered that his master was prominently in favor of convoking a general council to return the church to its primitive state in regard to the clergy's celibacy. Courson himself proposed a council to encourage all men to work physically and spiritually for their bread as a part of his campaign against usury.

It is no surprise therefore that when Lothario di Segni, their most illustrious student at Paris, mounted St. Peter's throne in 1198 as Innocent III, one of his urgent items of business was to call a general council at Rome to reform the church. More than a decade and half was spent making preparations. By 1213 Courson was appointed cardinal and papal legate to travel throughout France, holding local councils and preparing legislation for the forthcoming meeting at Rome. Langton, likewise elevated to cardinal, returned to England as archbishop to hold councils and issue synodical statutes for the diocese of Canterbury. When the great council finally convened at the Lateran palace on 1 November 1215, it drew 412 bishops (a record), plus twice the number of abbots and many royalty and powerful laymen from across Western Christendom. By the time it closed on 30 November, it had drafted seventy-one statutes of reform.[79]

The statutes of the Lateran council opened with a definition of the articles of faith, a *symbolum*, the first of its kind since the ancient ecumenical councils. This formulation drew on a century of theological discussion in the Paris schools in which a technical vocabulary for expressing the mysteries of the faith was forged by speculative theologians such as Pierre Lombard, whose *Quator libri sententiarum* was explicitly acknowledged in the council's statutes. The creedal statement also defined the seven sacraments of the church on which the Chanter's school had labored, including the crucial term *transsubstantiatis*, which encapsulated the mystery of the Eucharist. Equally important, canon 21 formulated the administration of confession that implemented the long discussions of the Chanter's school on penance. In addition to these weighty matters of dogmatic theology, the council was also concerned with the details of moral discipline that preoccupied the Parisian masters.

We have noted that as the Chanter and his followers observed contemporary society, they habitually proposed reforms. Some were taken up in papal decretals; others were treated in the Lateran Council's legislation. Some were adopted, others rejected or ignored. To cite a sample of the many that were accepted and that we have already considered: institution of diocesan preachers and of written synodical statutes, regulation of relics, hiring literate laymen in secular chanceries and curtailing monastic exemptions. Becket's solution for criminous clerics and the reduction of celibacy for the clergy was rejected. Most sought to reform the church and the clergy, but three in particular were equally important to lay society. They were marriage law, capital punishment and ordeals.

Philip Augustus's recent attempt to separate himself from Queen Inge-borg, which resulted in the interdict of 1200, merely highlighted a funda-mental problem that was endemic to contemporary marriage practice: the conflict between aristocratic endogamy and ecclesiastical exogamy. On the one hand, aristocrats at all levels preferred marriage with a close relative to keep their landed wealth and political power within the family. More wide-spread, lower-class men and women were endogamous because they were virtually immobile in their rural parishes. On the other hand, churchmen since ancient times had spun a vast web of restrictions to impede marriages that were within the bonds of consanguinity and affinity. According to the traditional system, no partner could marry within the seventh degree of consanguinity and a complex scheme of affinity. In other words, if couples had common ancestors within seven generations or by a common marriage, their union was "impeded," but it becomes immediately evident that "un-impeded" marriages were thereby extremely scarce. Whatever the rationale for extending exogamy, it was difficult to enforce at its outer limits. What became equally apparent, however, was that because an impeded marriage could be legally dissolved, the system of impediments worked against an-other ecclesiastical ideal, the indissolubility of marriage. This was the first justification (albeit fraudulent) that Philip Augustus's lawyers raised against Ingeborg—claiming rightfully, however, that separations had been recently granted to King John of England, the Emperor Frederick Barbarossa of Germany and above all to his father, the pious Louis VII in the case of his first wife, Eleanor of Aquitaine. Pierre the Chanter, who had served on the papal commission investigating Philip's marriage, recognized that what was permitted to royalty was also widely available to the aristocracy. Citing a personal experience, he remembered that a knight about to take a wife had confessed, "She has a large dowry and is related to me in the third kind of affinity. If she doesn't please me, I can procure a separation."[80]

The papal solution to the dilemma was pragmatic. Since Alexander III, the popes were accustomed to grant dispensations in individual cases that allowed an impeded marriage to be celebrated but that by the same logic permitted dissolution of the impeded marriage simply by petitioning for removal of the dispensation. This solution produced arbitrary decisions and endless days in court. Again, the Chanter illustrated the problem with a per-sonal reminiscence. Two of his relatives, married and related within the fifth and sixth degrees, came for his advice, knowing that their marriage was im-peded. Pierre sent them to the pope, who referred them to the archbishop of Sens, and then to Maurice de Sully, bishop of Paris, who finally confirmed the marriage. Such procedure, however, was open to abuse. Langton reported that in England, whenever the king wished to arrange alliances between his barons by marriage, he was always able to procure the necessary dispensations from the papal court. In an extended discussion, Robert of Courson blamed the destructive wars between France and England on papal compliance with the consanguineous marriage between Henry II and Eleanor of Aquitaine.[81]

Viewing the issue as a variable and pernicious tradition, Pierre the Chanter proposed a return to Scripture. "The Lord has given," he wrote in his *Verbum abbreviatum*, "certain and inviolable laws of matrimony that exclude twelve persons from marriage (Lev. 18: 6–18 and 20: 11–21), to which we have added as exceptions the fifth, sixth and seventh degrees [of consanguinity]. . . . And to these we have joined second and third kinds of affinity." On Scriptural authority, therefore, consanguinity should be limited to the fourth degree and to the first kind of affinity. Echoing the Chanter's complaints against the variability of human law and tradition, canon 50 of the Lateran council likewise reduced the impediments of consanguinity to the fourth degree and of affinity to the first kind. The inspiration for the reform is clear. Not only was Innocent III a student at Paris during the Chanter's day, but a certain Master Lothario (Innocent's baptismal name) was cited in the Chanter's questiones as posing a similar question for his teacher to solve.[82] The council's decree, to be sure, did not resolve all problems involving impediments and divorce, but it reduced the volume of cases that obstructed the church courts and enriched the lawyers.

The remaining social issues—capital punishment and ordeals—were equally lay concerns, but the Chanter and his school approached them from the perspective of clerical involvement in the shedding of blood. We have seen that as an exalted and sacred personage the cleric was obliged to abstain from pollution, not only sexual but also of blood, to the extent that a cleric could not participate in a court trial that ended in mutilation or death. If, however, clerics were prohibited from deciding whether a specific individual accused of homicide merited the death penalty in a classroom or in a courtroom, scholars were not prevented from discussing in theological disputations whether death was a fit penalty for a particular crime because their debate did not directly result in shedding blood.[83] A case in point was the hanging of thieves. Throughout France and England, hanging was the customary and appropriate punishment for theft. A simple and efficient solution, it involved

little of the expense and inconvenience of imprisonment. Gallows for hanging thieves were prominently displayed to publicize a lord's rights over justice,
such as the abbot's gallows before the gate of Saint-Germain-des-Prés or those
of the bishop on the hill at Saint-Cloud. As Biblical scholars, however, the
Chanter's circle uncovered a discrepancy between this custom and Scripture.
How can it be explained that in the Old Testament adultery is punished with
death, but not theft, while today we hang the thief and not the adulterer?
Neither Roman law nor Scripture sanctions hanging thieves, but the law of
God imposes fines. Testifying that his master used to debate this question
with deep feeling, Robert of Courson expanded the Chanter's arguments.
Crimes against human sanctity merit severer correction than those against
personal property. Why are we more concerned over the loss of an old hat
than the abuse of wives and children? Thieves who steal because of hunger
are punished more harshly than inveterate corrupters of youths and virgins.
Robert concluded by advising a prelate to instruct his prévôt to execute only
those customary penalties that can be found in the Old and New Testaments.
Incorrigible robbers should be imprisoned, not hanged. Thomas of Chobham observed that these punishments had been enacted to serve as deterrents
in regions where theft and robbery were rampant.[84]

Although the hanging of thieves was treated in the Bible, Pierre had a contemporary issue in mind. If God gave the land, air and water for the common enjoyment of mankind, he continued, how could princes prevent their
subjects from hunting, fowling and fishing? Does not a prince sin mortally
who mutilates men for hunting beasts common to all?[85] Here the Chanter
was thinking of the forest laws of France and England, which imposed harsh
penalties for poaching on the hunting rights of lords. In England the royal
forest laws were infamous for their barbaric punishments of death, blind-
ing and emasculation. Thomas of Chobham applied his master's question
directly to the justices of the royal forest in the island kingdom. If the beasts
and fowl belong by natural right to all, the officers who kill and mutilate
in executing the forest law are guilty of homicide in the confessional.[86] The
forest laws were notoriously unpopular in England, perhaps for the reason
that they outraged the clergy by recognizing no exception for clerical status.
When the English barons met King John at Runymede in 1215 in the presence of Archbishop Stephen Langton, they included abolition of the forest
penalties in their preliminary draft of the Magna Carta. This provision was
dropped in the final version, but it resurfaced in the Forest Charter of 1217,
when the young King Henry III promised that henceforth none should for-

feit life or limb for the king's venison. Although a direct influence of the Parisian masters may not be apparent on this issue of baronial reform, the Chanter's sensibilities nonetheless agreed with this English opinion.

Of all the reforms that Pierre the Chanter proposed in his classroom, abolition of ordeals touched him the closest.[87] Originating from ancient Germanic legal practices, these "foreign judgments" (*judicia peregrina*), as they were called, consisted basically of two kinds by the late twelfth century: unilateral hot-iron, hot-water and cold-water trials, submitted to one person, and the bilateral or judicial duel undertaken by two. They were also called "judgments of God" (*judicia dei*) because they required direct divine intervention through the clergy's mediation to arrive at a decision. Unknown to Roman law, they were accepted by the papacy and the canon lawyers only with ambivalence, usually when all other means of proof were unavailable. Even Innocent III, on becoming pope, accepted a proof by the hot iron in a case of canonization. At Paris the canonist Étienne de Tournai, when he was abbot of Sainte-Geneviève, participated in a judicial duel with the inhabitants of Rosny-sous-Vincennes when one was ordered in the royal court in 1179.[88] We remember too that in 1200 water judgment was proposed to Thomas, the royal prévôt of Paris, to purge himself of accusations raised by students.

Such equivocation, however, was not shared by Pierre the Chanter. No one in the late twelfth century was more preoccupied with the problem than he. It was a theme that reoccurred throughout his Biblical lectures and questiones and to which he devoted a lengthy and passionate chapter in his *Verbum abbreviatum*, burgeoning with contrary arguments and examples.[89] He even traveled to Rome to present his case personally before the cardinals. His panoply of arguments against ordeals can be reduced to three. First and foremost, by requiring God to intervene in judicial judgments at the will of humans, ordeals constitute a pernicious tradition that violates the Biblical commandment of the Old and New Testaments: "Thou shall not tempt the Lord thy God" (Deut. 6:16 and Matt. 4:7). Second, experience shows that ordeals often do not work. To counteract the saints' lives, which inserted successful ordeals among their miracles, Pierre took malicious delight in collecting stories that showed how they failed to uncover the truth. For example, when Pope Alexander III lost a precious vessel, he forced a suspect to submit to the hot iron. The accused failed the test and did restitution, but the pope was more misfortunate when the stolen article was found in the hands of the true thief. Or more seriously: of two English pilgrims who departed to Jerusalem, one returned without the other, was accused of assassinating his companion, was put to the ordeal and was hanged, to the consternation of many—and especially of his companion who showed up later.[90] Everyone knew that ordeals, moreover, could be manipulated. Decisions in the hot-iron trial, for example, depended on the calluses on hands. Candidates for the cold-water trial could be pretested for their propensity to sink. Finally, the clergy's participation offered both a third argument and a line of attack. Because clerics were forbidden to participate in the shedding of blood, they could not attend judicial duels where injury was inevitable, nor other trials where mutilation or execution might result from the decision. Since the clergy's participation was essential to the functioning of the ordeal—priests must bless the elements, offer prayers, lend relics or books—the most effective means for abolishing these practices was to forbid clerical presence. By disconnecting the clergy the Chanter hoped to deal a mortal blow. His personal stance was militant: "Even if the universal church under penalty of anathema commanded me as a priest to bewitch the iron or bless the water, I would quicker undergo the perpetual penalty than perform the deed."[91]

Perplexed by possible exceptions, Robert of Courson was not able to maintain the unequivocal position of his master, but a more influential student, Pope Innocent III, was finally convinced. Canon 18 of the Lateran Council formally forbade clerics from consecrating the hot and cold water or the hot iron of the unilateral ordeals and renewed the censures of former councils against bilateral judicial duels as well.[92] By placing this prohibition in a canon excluding clergy from participating in affairs resulting in the shedding of blood, the pope likewise adopted the Chanter's strategy. The Lateran prohibition had the greatest effect on the unilateral ordeal, where the clergy's presence was most essential. These customary practices were quickly eliminated from English and Danish royal law but disappeared elsewhere more slowly. Trial by battle was more difficult to extirpate, but the decree of 1215 laid an ax to the root. Looking over the last half-century, the English historian Mathew Paris listed abolition of the water and iron proofs as one of the significant events of his time.[93]

From Schools to the University

In those days [1210] the study of letters flourished in Paris. We read that there was never in Athens and Egypt or any other place in the world such a multitude of scholars as those who dwelt at Paris for the sake of learning.

This came about not only because of the admirable pleasantness of the place and the superabundance of all goods, but also because of the freedom and special rights of defense with which King Philip and his father [Louis VII] before him endowed the scholars. And so, although in that noble city one found copious and excellent teaching about not only the trivium and quadrivium, but also about questions of canon and Roman law, and about how the body is healed and health preserved, nevertheless they were taught Scripture and theological questions with more ardent zeal.[94]

This passage of Guillaume le Breton was the first sustained notice a royal chronicler devoted to the schools of Paris. By alluding to the traditional myth of the translatio studii, by stressing the city's material advantages and the king's contribution to the scholars' freedom and by enumerating the subjects taught, Guillaume added up the achievements of the past two decades, but except for fleeting recognition in a following passage concerning the heretic Amaury de Bène, Guillaume ignored an important transformation that was then taking place. This was the emergence of the university at Paris. The charter of liberties that Philip Augustus granted to the Parisian scholars in 1200 breathed not a word about a university. An equal silence was maintained by Pierre the Chanter, Stephen Langton and Robert of Courson, who actively taught and acutely observed their surroundings during the period. By 1215, however, Courson's statutes, which meticulously regulated studies and discipline at Paris, finally pronounced the word *universitas* but felt no need to define it.

As the university took form during the succeeding decades of the thirteenth century, it acquired the defining characteristics of a corporation or a guild that shared the common terminology of *universitas, societas, consortium* and *communitas*.[95] Conditioned by the schools of the previous century, it was a corporation of masters, not of students. A corporation was a group of people who took a common oath to admit to and expel from membership, to enforce its will on the membership through statutes and regulations, to elect officers and to act as a single person through representatives or procurators. If the terminology and the functions were ignored by the chroniclers, the theological masters and the prescriptive documents, they begin to appear in other sources. In 1208–1209, for example, Innocent III intervened in a dispute between the masters and a certain Master G. who had been expelled for refusing to take an oath. The masters of theology, canon law and arts elected a committee of eight to draw up regulations about studies, dress and funerals to which they had required their colleagues to take an oath of obedience. In seeking to reinstate the expelled master, the pope recognized the legitimacy of the masters' actions and bestowed on them the defining terms of societas, consortium and *universitas magistrorum*. While arguing their case before the pope, the masters dispatched a procurator to represent them. Innocent explicitly confirmed this essential function to "your university" in 1210–1212.[96] The chief obstacle to the masters forming a corporation was, however, the chancellor of Notre-Dame, who we recall claimed the exclusive right to grant the license (licentia) that was prerequisite to teaching at Paris. Jean de Chandleur, the current chancellor (1209–1214/1215), opposed the masters by insisting that each candidate swear an oath of obedience before receiving his license and by persisting in the inveterate habit of charging fees. A commission of arbitrators representing the chancellor and the masters arrived at an agreement in August 1213. The chancellor was obliged to abandon the oath and fees, but most important, a procedure was instituted for issuing licenses. In the future the chancellor could no longer refuse to license a candidate who had been deemed suitable by the majority of the regent masters in each of the disciplines of theology, canon law, Roman law and medicine. In the subjects of arts, a committee of six (three named by the masters, three by the chancellor) approved the candidate, but again the chancellor could not reject their decision.[97] The chancellor's absolute monopoly over the license to teach was finally broken. In its place was instituted the masters' votes in each of the disciplines, followed by the candidates' reception in the ceremony of the inceptio, or the inaugural sermon, as we have seen among the theologians.

By 1215 at the latest, therefore, the masters at Paris had defined the characteristics of a corporation—oath, membership, regulations and procurators—and could thereby call themselves a true "university of masters and scholars at Paris," as the terminology was finally enunciated in 1221.[98] It cannot be determined for how long the growth germinated before it broke to the surface and was momentarily acknowledged in Courson's statutes of 1215. A division among a lower faculty of arts and three higher faculties of theology, canon law and medicine did not come until later, but the teaching of individual subjects had been noticed for decades. The subdivision of the arts faculty into nations (French, Norman, Picard and English) was not adumbrated until 1219, although the preponderance of foreigners and the prominence of the English were evident since the previous century.[99] Full papal confirmation of the university's constitution, including its right to suspend lectures, finally arrived in 1231 in the celebrated bull *Parens scientiarum Parisius*, of Pope Gregory IX.[100]

In 1219, moreover, Dominic of Caleruega dispatched to Paris eight brothers of his newly found order, the Dominicans, "to study, preach and establish a convent." After residing briefly near the Hôtel-Dieu on the Île-de-la-Cité, they founded a convent on the rue Saint-Jacques on the Left Bank four years later, housing at least 120 friars. The same year as Dominic, Francis of Assisi sent his "minor brothers" or Franciscans to Paris, where they first settled at Saint-Denis before establishing themselves at the Corde-liers by 1230 on the lands of Saint-German-des-Prés, also on the Left Bank. The emerging corporation of masters by 1215, the abrupt appearance of the mendicant orders by 1217 and the eventual papal permission to teach pub-licly the metaphysics and natural science of Aristotle by 1231 (despite the prohibition of these texts in 1210) constituted three formative elements in the development of the university of Paris and scholastic thought in the thirteenth century. The mendicants arrived from the outside, but the cor-poration of masters and the reception of the new Aristotle gestated progres-sively and internally, although with little publicity, at Paris during the years surrounding 1200.

CHAPTER SIX

Delight and Pain

The year 1200 interposed a brief moment of sunshine into the political climate of northern France. The clouds of war and violence began to recede when Philip Augustus obtained peace treaties with his chief opponents. Baudouin, count of Hainaut and Flanders, came to terms at Péronne in January 1200, and Renaud, count of Boulogne, in August of the following year. Most important, King Richard's unexpected death in 1199 allowed the French king to strike an agreement with Richard's successor, King John of England, in the treaty of Le Goulet in May 1200. This clearing of the skies allows the opportunity to taste some of the joys that Parisians experienced before new clouds of discord, violence and war gathered on the horizon. The renewed call for crusades, both overseas and to the south, and the mounting menace of heresy—not to speak of the military attacks against the Anglo-Normans that have already been considered—brought renewed distress to the inhabitants of the royal city, which is the subject of the second half of this chapter.

Royal Festivities

As for celebrations, however, the year 1200 itself was not memorable for Parisians. The papal interdict not only silenced the city's bells from January until September but also canceled the great ecclesiastical festivities of Easter, Pentecost and the Virgin's Ascension as well. The chanting of the laudes regie at Easter was thereby omitted. No marriages were celebrated at Paris; that of Prince Louis and Blanche of Castile was performed in the small village of Port-Mort near Les Andelys, outside of the diocese of Paris. The chroniclers suggest that King John, having signed the treaty of Le Goulet in May, preferred to delay his visit to the Capetian capital until the following year. When he did appear in June–July 1201, he stopped first at Saint-Denis, where the monks greeted him with solemn processions and hymns of praise; he then descended upon the capital, where the clerics and bourgeoisie received him with reverence and dancing. Philip Augustus lodged him at the royal palace on the Île-de-la-Cité, plied him with wine and showered him with gifts of gold, silver, vestments and horses. Moving on to the royal palace at Fontainebleau, John and his entourage had further opportunity to taste the royal wine, but the French domestics were amused that the king and his men consumed the poorer wines, leaving the wines of quality untasted.[1]

John's visit received a few lines from Rigord, but the royal chroniclers normally paid little attention to festivities at Paris, seeming to prefer catastrophes like the periodic floods with their attendant penitential processions. Royal births were naturally an excellent excuse for rejoicing, but at Philip's birth in 1165 Rigord ignored the pealing of bells and the torches and bonfires in the squares that put the capital ablaze and so impressed the young Gerald of Wales, who was pursuing his studies there at the time.[2] At Prince Louis's birth in 1187, however, Rigord did note the weeklong celebration accompanied by singing and torches illuminating the night.[3] Royal marriages, a further cause for celebration, were limited to the coronation and anointing of Philip's first wife, Isabelle de Hainaut, in 1180. Since the ceremonies took place at Saint-Denis, Rigord paid particular attention to the events unfolding at the abbey, including the nuptial blessing offered by the archbishop of Sens and the crowds that assembled from the surrounding suburbs and villages.[4] The subsequent marriages to Ingeborg of Denmark and Agnès de Méran were too problematic to elicit public rejoicing.

The first truly festive occasion of Philip's reign did not occur until Pentecost of 1209. It was Prince Louis's knighting, delayed until he was twenty-two years of age, taking place not at Paris but at Compiègne to the north of the capital. Although Guillaume le Breton's account was brief, he did not spare the superlatives:

> Louis, the firstborn son of King Philip, put on the belt of knighthood from the hand of his father with such solemnity and in the presence of the assembly of magnates of the realm and of the multitude of men and accompanied with such a generous abundance of food and gifts (*largiflua victualium et donorum abundantia*) as was never seen or read of before that day.[5]

An anonymous vernacular chronicler observed that Robert and Pierre, the two sons of the count of Dreux and royal cousins, were also knighted, to which a later English writer added that in all one hundred knights received their belts. The occasion was certainly unprecedented because at Pentecost in 1203 the king knighted only three young noblemen. As might be expected of one writing for the French aristocracy, the anonymous chronicler was particularly interested in what took place at the table. Guy de Thouars, count of Brittany, served the first two courses at the high table; Robert, count of Dreux, the next; Renaud, count of Boulogne, the remaining; Pierre, count of Auxerre, carved the meat before Prince Louis, the honored guest.[6] The final and climatic celebration of the reign came five years later, in July 1214, after the victory of Bouvines. When the triumphal royal cortege reached the capital, bringing the counts of Flanders and Boulogne in chains, Paris exploded with a week's revelry that rivaled Prince Louis's birth. Crowds of bourgeoisie and scholars sang songs and hymns. Since the days were not sufficient, the nights were brightened with torches as if it were day; the scholars were tireless in singing and dancing.[7]

In 1209 Prince Louis swore to his father at Compiègne that he would not attend tournaments except as a spectator, presumably to protect the royal succession from the fate of Geoffroy, count of Brittany, who apparently was a victim of the sport. To reduce temptation, Louis further promised not to bear arms but to come only in a hauberk and a helmet.[8] His father likewise was never recorded as participating in this most popular of aristocratic entertainments. The king was too young to have participated in the tournament at Châtillon-sur-Marne that took place near Reims in November 1179 just after the coronation.[9] No tournament, moreover, was noted at Paris or even in the Île-de-France. Of the thirteen recorded for the years 1168 to 1184 by the chronicler of the count of Hainaut, Philip's father-in-law, and of the eighteen recorded by the *Histoire de Guillaume le Maréchal* for roughly the same period, most took place in the Rhineland, Champagne or Normandy, but a number skirted the borders of the Île-de-France, at Gournay to the north, Anet to the west, Epernon and Maintenon to the southwest. The closest, however, was at Lagny-sur-Marne to the east.[10] This exclusion of tournaments from the Paris region is mute testimony to the Capetians' deep aversion to the sport.

It is likely that Philip's attitude was reinforced by the loss of a dear friend, Count Geoffroy in 1186, but the incident remains clouded with ambiguity. The well-informed English chroniclers Benedict of Peterborough and Roger de Hoveden state clearly that he died of wounds inflicted in an undesignated tournament. Much later Guillaume le Breton suggested enigmatically that he died at the Champeaux in Paris.[11] The only incontrovertible element in the affair, however, is that Philip buried him with grief and ceremony at Notre-Dame and endowed chaplains to sing masses for his soul. Since canon law forbade burial in consecrated ground of those killed in tournaments, the funeral at Notre-Dame would have been possible only if Geoffrey had repented of his action before death. This was Pierre the Chanter's and Thomas of Chobham's interpretation of the prohibition.[12] Gerald of Wales, who tells the poignant story that the king's sorrow was so great he had to be restrained from leaping into the grave, averred that the count died of a fever. Rigord supplied the longest (but also the vaguest) account. He reported that Geoffroy came to Paris and fell sick. King Philip summoned the doctors of the city to save him. When their efforts failed, he was buried ceremoniously at Notre-Dame.[13] If the count had actually fallen in a tournament, then observers favorable to the Capetians such as Gerald and Rigord, might have preferred to overlook the fact. On close reading, however, their accounts are not irreconcilable with the English versions. In all likelihood the count was wounded on the tourney field, but died repentant at Paris from trauma and fevers attending his wounds.

Aristocratic Festivities

Because churchmen were hostile to tournaments, clerics writing in Latin, like Rigord, preferred to ignore these aristocratic sports. Even Gislebert de

Mons, the official historiographer of Count Baudouin V of Hainaut, limited himself to divulging the place, date and cost of his patron's thirteen tourneys but omitted other details. Only the unique *Histoire de Guillaume le Maréchal*, composed in French for a baronial patron, and the literary romances also written in the vernacular for the amusement of noble audiences depicted these aristocratic exercises in full detail and brilliant colors. Like Chrétien de Troyes before him, Jean Renart, for example, felt obliged to include a full account of fictional tournaments in his romances, but Jean situated them in actual places such as Saint-Trond near Liège and peopled them with historical personages with whom their audiences could readily identify.[14]

Since the normal habitat for the aristocracy, both great and small, was the countryside, Paris was not their principal address. Knightly families such as the Poissys and Montreuils held property in the city, and others such as the great seneschal Thibaut, count of Blois; the royal knight and counselor Barthélemy de Roie; and the bailli Pierre du Thillay rented or owned houses in Paris to accommodate their duties at the royal capital. It was the authors of romance, however, who painted the most vivid tableau of the festivities and pleasures of the aristocratic court, subjects that scarcely engaged the clerical historian. Compare, for example, Guillaume le Breton's terse account of Prince Louis's knighting at Compiègne with the recitation of a fictive dubbing of the chivalric hero Guillaume, a future count of Normandy,that Jean Renart sent to the count of Hainaut. In this romance the count of Toulouse announces that he will make Guillaume a knight as soon as possible and summons to his court all of the young men in the land who wished to be dubbed in his company:

> Why should I prolong the matter? Jean Renart interjects. In two weeks Guillaume was dubbed a knight. The Count [of Saint-Gilles] gladly created him and thirty others. . . . Why should I recount the joy, the festivities, and the honor? Since the great city of Troy was burned down, never were there so many high ladies and worthy ladies assembled. . . . The belle Aelis [Guillaume's future wife] offered riches of great value . . . jewels, belts, rings, and clasps. . . . Guillaume enriched his friends even more. . . . By gifts of furs, he enlisted into his household . . . those who became knights because of his honor and nobility [*Escoufle* vv. 7900–7924].

This abbreviated excerpt sparkles with details, in contrast to Guillaume le Breton's superlative but laconic Latin "abundance of gifts" (*donorum abundantia*).

Jean Renart spiced his romances with a profusion of tastes, smells, sights, and sounds of festive pleasure. Let us again contrast Guillaume le Breton's "generosity of food" (largiflua victualium) with Jean's description of an aristocratic table:

> Excellent food was served in brand-new dishes, along with clear, cold Moselle wine. There were lots of pastries filled with tender goat meat and plenty of larded venison and good creamy cheese from the Clermont valley [*Roman de la rose* vv. 367–74].

That was only lunch; now for dinner:

> To count the dishes isn't easy, there were so many: boar and bear and venison, cranes, wild geese, and roasted peacock. The servants did no dishonor to whom they brought a ragout of vegetables and lamb (which was in season since it was May), and fat beef and forced-fed goslings. Everyone had the choice of red and white wines. . . . [*Roman de la rose* vv. 5449–58]

Equally requisite to a festive occasion was the participants' clothing, a subject passed in silence by the clerical chroniclers. As the heroine Lienor prepares for her triumphal entry into Mainz to plead her case, Jean Renart's attention is devoted to her clothing:

> Her own clothing was a pure marvel made from blue silk with an ermine lining. Never was there fur so white nor fine nor well sewn. Over a white chemise decorated with flowers, she wore a tunic of green silk that was completely lined with fur, body and sleeves. . . . To embellish the beauty of her neck, she placed a clasp on her chemise that was a masterpiece of craftsmanship and gold. This permitted an opening of a finger's width through which one could perceive her breasts whiter than the snow on branches. . . . On her head was placed a wimple and a belt around her waist fitted with a golden buckle worth more than twenty-five livres [*Roman de la rose* vv. 4350–84].

Male finery received comparable notice. To prepare for meeting the emperor, for example, Guillaume de Dole, Lienor's brother, selected a robe of *escarlate* (scarlet) lined with ermine, which was immediately recognized as the latest French fashion.[15]

Sparse information has survived as to how the Parisian bourgeoisie clothed themselves in the year 1200, what they placed on their tables or how they celebrated their festivities. If they were well off, we surmise that they imitated the fashions of their aristocratic betters, a suspicion that is reinforced by a vernacular sermon attributed to Bishop Maurice de Sully.

Preaching to a Parisian audience on the Sunday after Easter, he quoted from
a courtly lyric to warn of the Devil's snares:

> When [the Devil] sees the weather turn warm,
> and the days turn fair,
> the food become more tasty,
> people don fine robes,
> the frivolous turn eagerly to games,
> the women begin to dance,
> and the young men turn to love,
> all of these elements conspire to deceive people.[16]

In this short verse Maurice totaled up the components of courtly festivity—spring days, sumptuous food, elegant clothing, amusements, dancing
and thoughts of love—all features he knew his Parisian audience would recognize immediately.

Jongleurs

At the aristocratic court no festivity was possible without entertainers called
jongleurs. The bourgeoisie at Paris were equally served by such entertainers
because they inhabited a street on the Right Bank under the jurisdiction of
Notre-Dame that bore the name rue des Jongleurs.[17] Like the festivities over
which he was in charge, the jongleur (*joculator*) was a gray, furtive shadow
in the Latin chroniclers' pages. In the vernacular literature, however, his
figure springs to life. Jean Renart's *Roman de la rose*, for example, pictures
jongleurs everywhere—at tournaments, marriages, coronations, any occasion calling for celebration:

> then entered the minstrels.
> this one played one piece, that one another,
> one recited the story of Perceval
> another of Roncevaux,
> circulating through the rows of barons [vv. 1745–49]

The titles attributed to these entertainers were diverse: *jougleour, villieors,*
but the preferred term was *menesterel.* From these crowds Jean singles out
one in particular, with the eponymous name Juglet:

> he was intelligent and of great renown,
> having heard and learned
> many songs and many a fine story [vv. 640–41].

Juglet is identified as a fiddler (*vïeleor*), but at his introduction he recounts a *lai* about a valiant knight from Champagne who loves a lady on the marches of Perthois (vv. 657–74), which was actually a story that Jean Renart had composed under the title of the *Lai de l'ombre*. Doubling as a storyteller and musician, Jouglet was rewarded with quantities of robes and clothing from his patrons.

Jongleurs also attracted the attention of Pierre the Chanter and his circle. As in the vernacular literature, diverse terms identified them: jongleurs (joculatores), actors (*histriones*), mimes (*mimi*), buffoons (*scurri*), as well as acrobats, jugglers and bear trainers. The Chanter associated them with other dubious professions such as gamblers, magicians, participants in tournaments and especially prostitutes, who were burdened with the status of *infamia*, which prevented them from suing in ecclesiastical courts, entering holy orders or receiving the Eucharist. Like prostitutes, these entertainers put their bodies to shameful use. One canonist, for example, defined actors (*ystriones*) as storytellers (*ystoriones*) who transformed their faces and clothing to tell a story corporally.[18] This shared corporality between prostitutes and entertainers rendered them anathema. Entertainers, moreover, were the chief rivals of the clerical preachers who strove to compete for the crowd's attention on the church's high holidays.

Adopting the well-circulated aphorism of the Church Father Jerome that "to give to actors was to sacrifice to demons," the Chanter and his colleagues sought to attack the economic foundations of the entertainment profession. Thomas of Chobham remarked dryly that actors would be forced to abandon their profession if they received no contributions.[19] Among the contemporary princely courts—Champenois, Flemish and Angevin—that of the Capetians was the only one to follow the Chanter's program. Rigord noted that the courts of kings and princes were crowded with actors who solicited gold, silver, horses and garments through their jongleuresque words. In a week an entertainer could gain robes worth twenty to thirty marks of silver, enough to nourish as many poor souls for a year. In contrast Philip, the most Christian king of France, inspired by the Holy Ghost and remembering the words of holy men that to give to actors was to sacrifice to demons, donated his garments to the naked and poor, thus setting an example for his princes. The royal financial accounts of 1202–1203 that contained gifts of robes to new knights, however, were silent about donations not only to jongleurs but also to the poor.[20] The king's example, was resisted by contemporary princes as well as by the prelates of the church. According to the Chanter, one entertainer boasted he could count on the donations of churchmen and townsmen as if they were fixed rents. Citing three cases, he claimed that he expected one hundred livres annually from the French prelates alone. The theologians maintained that actors, like prostitutes, should be refused admittance both to the Eucharist and to the prelates' tables—a measure that was adopted by the councils of Paris and Rouen convoked by Robert of Courson and by Pope Innocent III at the Lateran council.[21]

The popularity and ubiquity of these entertainers at the courts of both princes and prelates may have encouraged the theologians to reconsider their strictures. Employing the techniques of the classroom, Pierre and his colleagues sharpened definitions and introduced distinctions. The Chanter and Thomas of Chobham separated actors who persisted in bodily wantonness from those who refrained. The Chanter envisaged a kind of jongleur who could be tolerated if he sang of deeds (*de gestis rebus*) for the recreation or information of his audience, or if, as Thomas specified, he glorified the deeds of princes (*gesta principum*) or the lives of saints (*vitas sanctorum*) for the solace of humans in sickness or distress. Clearly the theologians were thinking of the chansons de geste and saints' lives that jongleurs had long included in their repertories. Pierre noted that jongleurs often selected songs to suit the mood of their audience. If the themes of Landri or Antioch were displeasing, they switched to Alexander or Apollinus, or finally to the ever-popular Charlemagne.[22]

Not only edifying stories but, most important, music likewise served to exonerate the profession of jongleur. Pierre the Chanter concurred with current canonist opinion that songs accompanied by instruments, or instrumental music alone, could be performed without guilt. Thomas of Chobham specifically exonerated the jongleur who accompanied his chansons de geste and saints' lives with instruments for the solace of his audience. To exemplify this rehabilitation, both Pierre and Thomas related an encounter between a jongleur and Pope Alexander III. With his fiddle slung from his neck, the performer requested the pope's permission to pursue his profession. After hesitation, the pope conceded that it was legitimate as long it was conducted without lechery or turpitude. Around the year 1200, therefore, Jean Renart's fictional Juglet and the flesh-and-blood jongleurs at Paris could gain their livelihood honorably by reciting edifying stories, singing recreational songs and playing on their fiddles and other instruments.

Profane Lyrics and Music

By employing music to exonerate professional entertainers, Pierre the Chanter and Thomas of Chobham were sensitive to a new cultural phenomenon, the flourishing of musical activity in both secular and in religious realms. The last quarter of the twelfth century witnessed not only the continuation of the vernacular chansons de geste and the appearance of courtly romances but also a new corpus of courtly lyric, short verses composed to music. Just as Maurice de Sully employed one such lyric to make a homiletic point, other preachers substituted vernacular verses well known to their audiences in the place of Scriptural texts to provide themes for their sermons. The popular rondeau "*Bele Aelis*," for example, to which one sang and danced, became the text for a sermon on the Virgin Mary that has survived in at least seven manuscripts, one of which was attributed to Stephen Langton. Another sermon took the popular song "*Sur la rive de la mer*" as its text.[23]

Since the early twelfth century, the chansons de geste had been sung in the courts of high barons, and since the last quarter of the century trouvères had composed courtly lyrics to music. The contemporary vernacular romances, although composed in verse, were recited in public without music when they were not read silently in private. About the same time that the Chanter and Chobham were valorizing music, Jean Renart announced a startling innovation for romance. Opening his *Roman de la rose*, he proposed:

> For just as one places red dye
> in cloth in order to gain praise and renown,
> thus he [Jean] has added poems and melodies
> to his *Roman de la rose*.
> It is such a novelty
> and the interspersed embroidery of beautiful verse
> is so different from other works
> that villains will not be able to understand it [vv. 8–15].

The novelty was twofold. In the first place the lyric poetry was meant to be sung:

> He who turned this story into romance
> [or: translated this story into vernacular],
> in which he noted beautiful songs
> to be remembered. . . . [vv. 1–3]

The phrase "noted beautiful songs" can suggest different meanings: "to take note of," "to perform music on an instrument," "to sing," or even "to have musical notes transcribed." The unique manuscript of the *Rose* contains no musical notation, but it was composed in a format that resembled song books (*chansonniers*) that did include notation.[24] Jean nonetheless may have intended his romance to be performed as a modern operetta because he prescribes that his was to be sung and read (*i chante et li. . . . chanter et lire l'orront*; vv. 19, 22), unlike former romances. The music would have been monophonic, as in contemporary lyrical songs, the equivalent of the clergy's plainchant.

The second innovation was to include forty-eight lyrics within his romance, making it the first and largest anthology of its kind. Jean even boasted that the words of the songs fitted the story so well that one could imagine he had composed the songs himself (vv. 26–29), but such was not the case. Encompassing the entire spectrum of secular music at the time, Jean's anthology copied many pieces that were known elsewhere or whose composers can be identified. Twenty-two of them were rondeaux or refrains suitable for dancing, including at least six versions of the "Bele Aelis" that was cited in the sermons. In addition there were five *chansons de toile*, two *pastourelles* and most important sixteen *grands chants courtois*. Throughout the romance Jean offered vivid scenes of musical performance. Major and minor characters sing their lyrics with or without instrumental accompaniment. Fiddles, flutes and other instruments supply music for the dancers on festive celebrations. In the revelries before the tournament at Saint-Trond, for example, the fiddles and flutes played so loudly that they drowned out God's thunder (vv. 2348–51).

As Jean boasted, the songs were chosen to fit the situations demanded by the characters of the narrative. Thus the heroes, heroines and supporting cast, including the jongleur Juglet, intone the grands chants courtois that articulate the feelings of delight and pain required by the love situations of the narrative. Of the sixteen grands chants selected, only six of the authors were named, but some of the remaining were so well known that the audience could have identified them without difficulty. The repertory of the southern troubadours was represented by Jaufré Rudel and Bernart de Ventadorn; the northern trouvères included the Châtelain de Coucy and lesser composers; but the best known, represented by three grands chants, was Gace Brulé, certainly the most popular trouvère of his time. After Juglet has depicted the belle Lienor with such allure that Emperor Conrad has fallen in love with her verbal portrait, the two men sing a stanza in honor of Monseigneur Gace:

> When the flower and gladiolus and greenery wither away,
> when the birds dare not utter a sound
> (because of the cold they all withdraw with fear
> until the warm season, when they return to singing),
> I shall sing, for I cannot forget
> the good love which God grant me to enjoy!
> For all of my thoughts are of her and come from her [vv. 846–52].

Furnishing the earliest transcription of this poem, Jean Renart included only the first stanza. Later chansonniers supplied the remaining stanzas and some eighty additional poems of Gace together with their music.[25] Like his fellow trouvères, Gace found it imperative to love and sing at the same time (*amer m'estuet. . . . chanter m'estuet*), thus affirming that desire and creativity were inseparable. If love results in an inevitable alternation between joy and suffering, pain nonetheless predominates. Unlike in the joyous rondeaux, the seasons of spring and summer bring no relief, yet love is necessary to survive the winter, even if it is unrequited. Highly formalized and endlessly repetitive, Gace Brulé's verses were extremely popular among aristocratic circles. He was the Cole Porter of his day. Almost totally reticent about himself, he was no doubt of the knightly class. He made oblique references to Thibaut, count of Troyes; and Geoffroy, count of Brittany, but his most prestigious patron remained unnamed. The first register of Philip Augustus's chancery, however, reveals that between 1205 and 1212 Gace's name was added to the prévôté of Mantes as the recipient of a fief-rente worth 24 livres, to be paid annually on All Saints' Day.[26] This patronage included him within the circle of the royal court, despite the king's better publicized aversion to entertainers. Jean Renart claimed that the aristocratic grand chants would be unappreciated by the peasant (*villain*), but the king's favor may have reinforced Gace's popularity not only among the aristocracy but among the bourgeoisie of Paris as well.

The Language of the Laity

Up to this point, our principal witnesses to Parisian pleasures have expressed themselves in the vernacular. Around 1200 the inhabitants of the royal capital spoke the French dialect current in the Île-de-France that has been called Francien by modern philologists and that differed from other forms of regional French such as Picard, Champenois or Anglo-Norman. When the trouvère Conan de Béthune, for example, arrived at the royal court early in Philip Augustus's reign, the king and royal family ridiculed him for his Picard dialect.[27] Apart from the French sermons that the bourgeoisie heard from preachers, however, the townspeople left no vernacular writing to which we might listen for the language in which they conversed. Although the authors of contemporary *fabliaux* in the vernacular set their stories among peasants and small village burghers, they were not from the royal capital but chiefly from Picardy. The language of the Parisian bourgeoisie, however, was the same as the Francien spoken in the royal court or by the aristocracy of the Île-de-France. The Francien of Jean Renart's *Roman de la rose*, therefore, was appropriate for his addressee Milon de Nanteuil, who was both prévôt of the chapter of Reims and a local prévôt (of Rosnay-en-Brie) of the chapter of Notre-Dame.

Since the aristocratic romances were closely synchronized to oral performance, they reverberate with sound. Although no one but jongleurs likely spoke in octosyllabic verse with rhymed couplets (the poetic form of contemporary romance and fabliaux), the romance nonetheless makes it possible to eavesdrop on the conversations of the laity. Whenever we tune in to them in the *Roman de la rose*, we are struck by the torrent of oaths that the speakers employ in ordinary parlance. Not only the simple "adieu," but "by God," "in God's name," "if God pleases," "God grant you," "thank God," "God help me," increasing to "by the five wounds of God" and "since God was born without sin." Saints were likewise recruited, to fill in the rhymes and help with meter—St. Paul, St. George, Lady St. Mary—and simply to keep the torrent flowing.

This penchant for interlarding one's conversation with expostulations of the divine would appear to contravene the Second Commandment (Exod. 20:7, "You shall not take the name of the Lord your God in vain"). It is not clear whether Jean Renart would have considered this a problem, but the theologians classified these locutions as oaths (*juramenta*), that is, assertion of a certain proposition through the witness of a sacred thing. Pierre the Chanter devoted a chapter of his *Verbum abbreviatum* "against those prone to swearing." When Jesus admonished his followers in the Sermon on the Mount "not to swear at all, but let your words be 'yes, yes' and 'no, no'" (Matt. 5 33–34), how can we, Pierre queried, square this injunction in a world where oaths are rampant? Pierre contrasted the Jewish sobriety of tongue fostered by the Second Commandment with the frequency of oaths in the contemporary church. When one utters oaths for frivolous reasons and without necessity—for example, swearing "by God" idly or in jest—this is a venial sin, but if it becomes habitual, it could become mortal.[28] In applying the Second Commandment to ordinary speech, Robert of Courson agreed that such oaths were normally venial, and if uttered under provocation they could be excused. Thomas of Chobham, however, emphasized that if idle oaths were habitual they were always venial sins, if not mortal.[29] Since these frivolous oaths bordered on blasphemy, the theologians found them difficult to identify because the multifarious species of "bad swearing" had long defied canon lawyers to define and evaluate them.[30]

In contrast to idle and frivolous swearing were oaths stigmatized as "ignominious" and always a mortal sin. The Chanter signaled those that were uttered knowingly on the eyes, tongue or blood of God. Chobham alluded to members of Christ that should not be named; mincing no words, Courson identified them as the genitals of Christ and his mother, and proposed deposition if the offender was a cleric and excommunication if a layman.[31] Contemporaries would have instantly recognized that the most notorious offenders were the Angevin kings of England, who took delight in swearing on the members of God, in contrast to Philip Augustus, whose oaths rarely exceeded the "lance of St. James."[32] Pierre the Chanter remembered that King Philip had once cleared his palace of those who swore ignominious oaths on God and the saints. The wealthy offenders were fined 5 sous, to be donated to the lepers, and the poor were dunked in the river fully clothed. Other princes adopted similar penalties. This exemplum in which the king was identified by name merely recalled a celebrated story of the royal historian Rigord. When a knight who was gambling in the king's presence let slip an inadvertent oath, he was immediately ordered to be thrown into the river, and Philip published an edict that forbade blasphemous swearing on the head, stomach or any other part of God. This decree, now lost, was the first Capetian legislation to eradicate blasphemy that Philip's grandson Louis IX took up with zeal.[33] It was predictably a hard battle. In 1213 Pope Innocent III complained to the archbishop of Reims that men were still not afraid to swear by the feet, hands and more secret members of Christ and his saints and urged the bishops to apply the ecclesiastical sanctions they had neglected.[34] Like the aristocracy in Jean Renart's *Roman de la rose*, the bourgeoisie of Paris surely indulged in idle swearing, if they did not dare the more dangerous oaths. We may surmise that it relieved psychic tension if not providing pleasure.

Christmas Festivities at Notre-Dame

When the lugubrious interdict was lifted in September 1200, Parisians could resume their accustomed routines, thus sparing the joyous festivities of the Christmas season. At Notre-Dame the most active period of the liturgical calendar unfolded at Christmas, a season that was busier than Easter.[35] In addition to the great annual feast of the Nativity (25 December), the high status of duplex feast was assigned to Reception of the Relics (4 December), St. Nicholas (6 December), and then in rapid succession after Christmas St. Stephen (26 December), St. John the Apostle (27 December), the Holy Innocents (28 December), and finally the Circumcision (1 January).[36] As duplex feasts, these occasions called for liturgical music beyond traditional plainchant and posed a challenge for Masters Leoninus, Perotinus and their colleagues at Notre-Dame to compose ambitious polyphonic pieces in two to four voices. Each of these feast days, moreover, was assigned to its own order of the clergy: St. John to the priests, St. Stephen to the deacons (because the martyr was a deacon), Circumcision to the subdeacons and the Holy Innocents to the choirboys (appropriately they were the youngest). On the feast of St. Nicholas, the younger clergy elected a boy bishop who presided over the following feast days.

Although the liturgy for the Christmas week itself was long established at Notre-Dame,[37] special efforts were made to embellish the feast of the Circumcision with polyphony. Perotinus composed a beautiful conductus, *Salvatoris hodie*, in three voices,[38] and another conductus in two voices that captured the exuberance of New Year:

> On this healthful day
> the new year urges with applause
> a renewal, and renewed,
> to lead in a circle of dance.
> Reborn, the year causes
> joy to abound,
> in this, in this,
> in this,
> in this year.
> Let voice resounding
> tune lips
> without delay,
> in this, in this,
> in this,
> in this,
> in this, in this, in this year.[39]

Because youthful clerics were in charge, the boundaries of decorum were tested. At the feast of the Circumcision the staff of the Chanter—indeed of the eminent Pierre the Chanter—was confided to a subdeacon who led processions to and from his house before and after the services. A donkey, standing in for the beast that bore Mary to Bethlehem, was paraded in the procession while the choir sang the conductus *Orientis partibus*, also in polyphony for three voices with a vernacular refrain that sounded like the donkey's braying:

> From orient lands
> an ass came,
> handsome and strong,
> an excellent beast of burden.
> Hey, ho, hey, Sir Ass, and hey![40]

In this anomalous spirit of the occasion Pierre de Roissy penned a bizarre chapter in his *Manuale de mysteriis ecclesie* titled "Why we do adore the cross but not the donkey" (since both bore the Savior!).[41] The young clerics could not resist the temptation to revert to the New Year revelries of Janus from pagan times. Parody and outrageous behavior in word, music, dance, costume and drink abounded. By the end of the century, the feast day earned the titles Feasts of the Staff, of the Ass and, most appropriately, Feast of Fools.

By 1198 the excesses could no longer be tolerated. Master Pierre of Capua, papal legate to France, complained to the bishop of the enormities. Not merely were polluted words uttered; blood was shed at the noble church of Paris in the capital and the celebrated city of the kingdom. Freshly elected to the see, Bishop Eudes nonetheless responded in moderation. The ringing of bells was restricted, and the worst abuses of verse, masks and special lights in the extraliturgical processions were abolished. The main liturgy, however, was merely reformed. The subdeacon-lord retained his staff, but authority was restored to the chanter over the choir. Two, three and four voice pieces were prescribed for specific parts of the service, thus preserving the polyphonic innovations.[42] Pierre the Chanter died the year before the Bishop Eudes's reforms, but it was his staff that was traditionally turned over to the presiding subdeacon. Although Pierre took little interest in liturgy, he was nonetheless responsible for the discipline of the choir. He observed that during the Feasts of Fools, St. Nicholas, the Holy Innocents and the miracle plays, the edge rather than the flat of a sword was sometimes used, and blood was inadvertently shed in the church. Priests were occasionally struck by inflated bladders in games played by the young clergy.[43] Christmastide was a joyous time for the lower clergy of Notre-Dame, allowing them to vent their ebullient energies. Unlike the moderate Bishop Eudes, the more severe Robert of Courson as papal legate sought to dissuade clerical attendance altogether at such ceremonies, but with little success.[44] The Feast of Fools outlasted the Middle Ages.

The Joys of Marriage

In effect, the interdict of 1200 punished Parisians for the personal disaster of the king's wedding night on 14–15 August 1193, when Philip contracted an inexplicable revulsion for his new bride, the princess Ingeborg of Denmark.[45] The inhabitants of the royal city, however, may not have been aware that by 1200 he had found marital bliss with a new wife (or concubine), Agnès de Méran, who delivered him a daughter, Marie, in 1198 and now a son, Philippe, in 1200. If Gace Brulé and his fellow trouvères and troubadours insisted that love's sufferings outweighed its pleasures, it was mainly because the objects of their desire were inaccessible women, usually married to someone else. With great ingenuity the belle Lienor, Jean Renart's heroine, however, finally succeeded in joining herself in marriage to the Emperor Conrad. Their wedding night Jean described in direct contrast to Philip Augustus's experience with Ingeborg:

> I have not told you
> of the happiness the king had that night.
> All of the pleasure a man can know
> in embracing his beloved
> in a bed the whole night;
> one can be sure that he knew it.
> Even when Tristan loved Iseut the most,
> and was able to be wholly at ease
> in embracing and kissing her
> with the surplus that follows,
> or Lanval or twenty other lovers like him,
> then you will truly know
> that one cannot compare
> their happiness to this one very easily. [*Roman de la rose* vv. 5501–15].

As a sacrament, marriage was entirely within the jurisdiction of churchmen. Pope Innocent III, for example, sanctioned the king and his lands to force him to submit his marriage to the Church's judgment. Since all aspects were included, ecclesiastical authority did not neglect the sexual side, which was permitted only within the boundary of matrimony and chiefly for engendering progeny. For this reason, the earliest marriage rites devised by churchmen were those of blessing the nuptial chamber and bed. In Jean Renart's *Escoufle*, for example, Count Richard and the lady of Genoa are led to bed; the bishop blesses it with the sign of the cross and sprinkles it with incense before they enter the covers. When the count performs his marital duty and gives his spouse pleasure, they appropriately conceive a son Guillaume, who becomes the hero of the romance (vv. 1738–53).

The masters of medicine in the schools of Paris who followed the ancient Salernitan tradition treated the sexual act from all standpoints—psychological as well as physiological—including even the influence of food and drink and of the yearly seasons. When they examined anatomy, for example, they held that the male body was normative for the female; even in respect to the genitals the feminine was homologous to the masculine. The uterus responded to the male scrotum, the vagina to the penis. A woman was merely a man turned outside in. Following the ancient Greek medical doctrine of the two seeds initiated by Hippocrates and Galen, moreover, they maintained that both sexes were equipped with testicles, which produced sperm or seed, and both required pleasure to ejaculate.[46] Because the doctors emphasized that conception could not occur without simultaneous pleasure and ejaculation to mix the seeds, they paid particular attention to how a couple could come to a climax at the same time. If the two partners played their roles simultaneously so that they neither anticipated nor delayed the culmination (*celebratio*), they would produce such pleasure that they would conceive and be encouraged to repeat the act often.[47]

The theologian Pierre the Chanter fully accepted the two-seed theory of the Salernitan tradition current at Paris. For him conception occurred when the seed of a man and women were united in the uterus. Breaking with phallic metaphors of the Old Testament and Augustine, which represented sexuality as a man's single finger or his hand sewing seed on the ground, Pierre envisaged it as the fingers of both partners each touching the other.[48] Ecclesiastical law reinforced this duality and complementarity. A true marriage was formed by the free and mutual consent of a man and a woman expressed with words in the present tense (*verba de presenti*). Once contracted it was subjected to the Pauline doctrine of the marital debt (I Cor. VII). A husband returns his debt (that is, sexual relations) to his wife, and conversely the wife to her husband. The obligation is absolutely reciprocal because the wife disposes not of her own body but of her husband, and the husband's belongs entirely to his wife. The Chanter's comment was, "Both are equal here despite the domination of the husband over the wife."[49] In other words, despite male superiority being normal in social, economic and other relations, the husband and wife were totally equal in bed. Both medical and theological authority reinforced reciprocal pleasure and simultaneous climax. The reciprocity in sex advocated in the Latin schools of Paris found echoes in contemporary vernacular literature. The fabliaux, which portrayed life in the countryside and in the small villages, abounded with prodigious sexual energy, but it would be difficult to distinguish who was having more fun, men or women.[50] Even in aristocratic romances, where sexuality was less explicit, reciprocity remained imperative. Romances such as Jean Renart's *Escoufle* that explored the nascent sexuality of young couples such as Guillaume and Aelis trace their mutual development into mature, loving marriage. In Jean's *Roman de la rose* the heroine Lienor refuses to accept calumny passively but exerts all of her ingenuity to reclaim what she believes to be her right: to become the emperor's spouse. At the glorious dénouement of the romance, the lovers intone not a doleful and unrequited grand chant courtois but a simple, jubilant rondeau sung as a duet:

> What do you ask,
> when you have me?
> What do you ask;
> am I not yours?
> I ask nothing,
> if I have your love [*Roman de la rose* vv. 5106–11].

Our modern sensibilities—seeing nothing exceptional here—will prevent us from appreciating the importance of the situation, if we are not aware of what followed shortly. Around 1200 the masters of arts at Paris began reading Aristotle's newly translated natural works, in which they found the one-seed theory in contradiction to the Hippocratic-Galenic two-seed model. Following the Greek philosopher, Master David de Dinant, whose writings, we have seen, were condemned at Paris in 1210, proposed that only the male emits sperm, that only the male truly engenders, that the female merely nourishes the fetus with menstrual blood, that without her own seed the woman has no need for pleasure in order to conceive, and that reciprocity in sexual desire is therefore optional. Quoting Aristotle's notorious epigram, David maintained: "The woman is essentially an imperfect male, just as is a boy."[51] In effect, therefore, Aristotle's authority reinforced the Old Testament and Augustinian metaphors of the phallic finger and the male who sews his seed with his phallic hand on the female soil. As the scholastics developed these ideas within an Aristotelian framework at the university of Paris in the thirteenth century, the male became the efficient cause contributing form, the female the material cause contributing only matter; the male was active, the female passive. This scientific rationale established the prevailing paradigm of gender relations for male dominance and female submission into the early modern period. Despite the scientific shortcomings of the Salernitan two-seed theory, it and the theological doctrine of sexual reciprocity made the period around 1200 the last privileged epoch of gender reciprocity for centuries to come.[52]

The Art of Love

Pierre the Chanter took notice of the two-seed theory of the Salernitans with its consequences for married love, but he was also aware of a much more controversial idea that was current in the schools.[53] This was the "art of love" (*ars amandi*), which encompassed the whole spectrum of love, including its most illicit aspects. Among Pierre's *Nachlässe* was a questio titled "On the Art of Love" (*De arte amandi*) that was not incorporated into the major manuscripts and consequently not included in the published edition. Ovid, the ancient Roman poet, was the acknowledged master and authority on this subject. Around 1200 his erotic works, "Art of Love" (*Ars amatoria*) and "Remedy of love" (*Remedia amoris*), were listed by Alexander Neckham on the curriculum for the masters of arts at Paris,[54] and they were the specialty of the schools in the Loire valley as well. We shall see that the Amalrician heretics affirmed that Ovid spoke with authority equal to that of Augustine. The first treatise addressed the questions of how to find, seduce and keep a woman; the second addressed how to get rid of her. In exquisite verse he produced an urbane manual of seduction that afforded little respect for the conventions of matrimony.

Since love was an "art," it could by definition be taught, but the pertinent question in the clerical schools was "Why?" The masters at Orléans explained that its purpose was to teach boys and girls the precepts of love and render them expert, but this seemed incongruous for schools devoted to young men who sought careers in the church that foreswore them to future celibacy.

Formulating pros and cons in scholastic fashion, the Chanter's questio faced the dilemma squarely. On the positive side he postulated that all knowledge comes from God. The art of love is knowledge, so it is good and its use is good, because nothing but good comes from God. The act of love itself comes from God and is good, both in marriage and in coupling with prostitutes. On the negative side, if love is good in itself, it can nonetheless be put to bad use, just as poison is good in itself but can be used harmfully. Does he who teaches it commit a mortal sin? If he teaches it to corrupt women, it is mortal sin, but in the final analysis a master teaches it not for use but to serve as a caution (*ad cautelem*).[55] In other words, by learning the art of love one avoids its pitfalls.

These rapid and sketchy arguments that quote Ovid's *Ars amatoria* and come to an abrupt conclusion demonstrate that the questio was unfinished, thereby suggesting why it was not included in the major collections; but the underlying thesis can be fitted into a contemporary context. One commentary explained that Ovid realized his young friends were perverting his precepts to assail married women and virgins, so he wrote the "Remedy" to correct their excesses. Most important, however, the motive of "caution" was one of the rationalizations André the Chaplain employed to justify his treatise "On Love" (*De amore*). This enigmatic figure, who was probably a cleric in the court of Philip Augustus in the 1180s, wrote a Latin treatise for a certain friend Gautier in which he approached the subject in scholastic fashion. Encyclopedic, complex and madly contradictory, his treatise sought to analyze and synthesize a variety of sources, including, of course, Ovid. Vaunting the qualities of clerics, he proposed that they were better lovers than laymen because their learning made them more prudent and cautious. To his friend Gautier, André advised that if Gautier mastered André's doctrine of love, he himself would become more cautious in practice. In the violent palinode of the last book, André promised that those who knowingly resist temptation have greater merit in God's sight than those who lack experience.[56] However we may trust the sincerity of these two clerics' argument, the Chanter—the austere moral theologian—nonetheless demonstrates his willingness to recognize and consider seriously the rationale of profane love that was so vigorously proposed by the ancient Ovid and his twelfth century spokesman, André the Chaplain. In raising this question, Pierre once again exhibits his acute sensitivity to the profane interests and delights of the laity.

The Renewal of the Crusade

In 1200 Philip Augustus was prepared to declare war against King John as soon as an opportunity presented itself, but other clouds threatening the tranquility of the Parisian scene gathered from afar. When Innocent III mounted the papal throne in January 1198, high among his priorities was renewal of the campaign to free the Holy Land from the Saracens. The inability of Philip Augustus and Richard to retake Jerusalem and the holy sites in the Third Crusade remained an egregious scandal. Once again the pope intended to mobilize all the resources of the Western kingdoms to bring the task to completion. By February he revealed his intentions to the Latin Patriarch of Jerusalem; by August he announced his program to the prelates of France.[57]

If Pierre the Chanter's testimony is representative, the Saracens and the Holy Land remained remote to the concerns of contemporary Parisians. The main questions that surfaced in his classroom involved Christians who lived in the Holy Land under Saracen rule. Should a bishop remain with his flock, or attempt to flee? If a Christian foreswore escape by an oath, was he thereby held to his word if the opportunity presented itself? Should Christians genuflect to Muslim idols? What was their moral responsibility if they were forced to manufacture arms for the Saracen armies? The Christian merchants from Marseilles who supplied arms to Alexandria were cited as an example.[58] Pierre also shared with his contemporaries an admiration for Saladin, the Saracen leader which he illustrated by an exemplum. After the Muslim general captured Acre, he was curious about the eating and drinking habits of the Christians who remained in the city. When he was told that on days before feasts they were content with two or three dishes of meat and six wines, but on feast days they demanded more plentiful and sumptuous food and varied drink, he concluded they should forfeit their rights to the country because of their gluttony. He therefore ordered the casks of the city to be emptied, in fear that his own soldiers, who were unaccustomed to such abundance, would become inebriated. Pierre concluded that, to the shame of Christians, Muslims were always dry and sober.[59]

The Holy Land, however, was not to remain remote for long. On accession to the papacy, Innocent III immediately commissioned the Chanter's charismatic student Foulques de Neuilly to preach the crusade with papal authority. In 1199, when the preacher arrived at a tournament at Écry on the confines of Champagne, he found scores of knights who presented an ideal audience for his mission. Apparently his homiletics were irresistible because Geoffroy de Villehardouin, the chronicler of the Fourth Crusade, reported the names of nearly a hundred participants who took the cross then or shortly after. Among them were the youthful but powerful Counts Thibaut of Champagne and Louis of Blois, and subsequently Baudouin of Hainaut and Flanders. With likely exaggeration, an English chronicler declared that Foulques had persuaded two hundred thousand people to take the cross and raised impressive sums for the campaign, which were deposited with the Cistercians.[60] Needless to say, Philip Augustus was not tempted to join the venture. He harbored unpleasant memories of the competition with Richard on the last crusade, and he had more important business against King John. For this reason, he was not opposed to the departure of Counts Thibaut, Louis and especially Baudouin, who might have resisted his ambitions. For their part, the Paris theologians were remarkably uninterested in issues involving the crusades. Perhaps tellingly, the only question Robert of Courson raised about the crusade was that of dispensing the vow to take the cross.[61]

As is well known, the crusaders, despite the auspicious fanfare, never saw the Holy Land but ended their adventure with the capture of Constantinople, detoured by the machinations of the Venetians. Baudouin, count of Hainaut and Flanders, was chosen emperor of the new Latin kingdom before he disappeared in a military expedition against the Bulgarians in 1205. In that year the inhabitants of Paris received direct word from the pope about Constantinople. The prelates of France were requested to send Cistercians, Cluniacs and regular canons to assist in establishing true religion among the Greeks, and the masters and scholars of Paris were invited to reform learning in the eastern city by contributing to its literary disciplines,[62] but undoubtedly the Parisian masters were too preoccupied with the new university in the French capital to accept assignment overseas. Nor was Philip Augustus tempted by the offer to be made emperor of Constantinople by Margaritus, "king of the pirates," when the latter visited Paris in 1200.[63]

Repression of Heresy

Of immediate concern to Parisians were the menacing clouds of heresy that accumulated on the horizon within France. Scattered groups of heretics had been reported with increasing frequency since the eleventh century. Particularly noteworthy were four heretics called the Paterini at Arras, who were discovered in 1182, convicted, and condemned to the stake and whose property was confiscated by the combined efforts of Guillaume, archbishop of Reims, and Philippe, count of Flanders, both prominent in the youthful king's government.[64] Since churchmen were forbidden by canon law to participate in blood judgments, coercion of heresy was accomplished by a procedure known as the *traditio curie*, by which the churchmen handed the convicted heretic over to the prince for corporal punishment. At the Lateran councils of 1139 and 1179, the papacy did not hesitate to enlist the cooperation of the secular power to punish such persons, who were hopelessly incorrigible to spiritual sanctions.[65] The crucial question was what form the punishment was to take. Since the late Roman Empire, heresy was equated with treason and punishable by death. King Robert the Pious had applied the sanction in the eleventh century, and the authorities repeated it recently at Arras, but churchmen remained ambivalent about this ultimate recourse. Augustine had two minds on the subject, as reflected in Gratian's *Decretum*. Although certain canonists accepted the solution, others such as Rufinus and Huguccio were less certain.

Pierre the Chanter joined the ranks of the latter and cited Scriptural authority for not killing heretics. For example, the Apostle Paul advised Titus (3:10) to issue two warnings to heretics, not to kill them or hand them over. Just as David refrained from killing the concubines whom his rebellious son Absolon had defiled (I Sam. 16:22 and 20:3) but isolated them for life, so his example should be followed in treating heretics whom the devil has defiled.[66] As in other matters, Pierre's preferred solution was not capital punishment but life imprisonment, to quarantine the contagion just as was decreed at Reims in 1148 when Archbishop Samson imprisoned the Breton heresiarch Eon de Stella for life.[67] Only if the heretic opposed the church with physical force should he be punished with death, an opinion that was seconded by Thomas of Chobham for England.[68]

An incident that illustrated the danger of applying the death penalty to heresy came to the Chanter's attention from the campaign of Archbishop Guillaume and Count Philippe at Arras in 1182. Pierre noted that unscrupulous clergy and agents of the prince used their arbitrary powers to extort from and blackmail orthodox women who resisted their lecherous advances; they were thereby threatened with being enrolled on the lists of condemned persons. Many innocent people perished along with the guilty. The English chronicler Ralph of Coggeshall included a story recounted by Master Gervase of Tillbury, who was in fact a cleric of Archbishop Guillaume at the time of the prosecution at Arras. As Ralph tells it, Gervase pictured himself in the act of seducing a young woman when he discovered that she was a heretic because she protested that if she lost her chastity she would be condemned forever to perdition. (The Paterini, like the Cathars, as shall be seen, believed that marriage and sexuality were irredeemably evil.) To bring the story to a close, when neither Gervase nor the archbishop's clerics could convince the girl of her error, she was led away to the stake. Even if the victim was a heretic, the Chanter's warnings about the potential abuse of capital punishment was vindicated. For this reason he expressed his preference that the guilty— Jews, pagans and heretics alike—should be spared the death penalty, if only to save one innocent soul.[69]

As heretics continued to proliferate in France, particularly in the south, where they were called Cathars, and later Albigensians, the papacy began to adopt more stringent measures. In 1189 Pope Lucius III formulated specific procedures in the decretal *Ad abolendam* by which both laymen and clerics who were judged incurably heretical by ecclesiastical tribunals were handed over to the secular power to receive their just punishment (*animadversione debita*). Innocent III reinforced these provisions in his decretal *Vergentis* (1199) by adding the Roman law equation of heresy to treason. The nature of the punishment was left to the discretion of the prince, whether it was a fine, confiscation, exile or death. As an ecclesiastical personage, the pope or clerical judge was not at liberty to specify the death penalty, but by leaving the sanction open the pope allowed recourse to capital punishment for heresy, for which secular law furnished ample precedent. By including heretical clerics, Pope Lucius circumvented the inconvenient principle, inherited from Archbishop Thomas Becket,that limited punishment of heretical clerics to degradation in the first instance since subsequent death would amount to double punishment.[70]

The full consequences of the papal decretal were seen by Parisians in 1201, when a notorious case was brought to their city for judgment. In the Auxerrois to the southeast of Paris, which was particularly troubled by heresy, Evrard de Châteauneuf, an influential knight who enjoyed the favor of Hervé, count of Nevers, was accused of Bogomil beliefs (a dualist heresy) by Hugues de Noyers, the zealous bishop of Auxerre. The trial was conducted at Paris under the presidency of Octavian, the papal legate, who assembled archbishops and bishops from the realm, and included the masters of Paris. After public accusations were presented by the bishop and supported by testimony from irrefutable witnesses, Évard was convicted and condemned to death by fire, which was carried out by the count in Auxerre.[71] Doubtless among the Parisian masters who participated in the trial was Robert of Courson, who referred to the case and reported on the discussion of the death penalty that went behind the facts narrated by the chroniclers. In an elaborate questio that wrestled with the complexities of churchmen's involvement in blood judgments, Robert rehearsed the arguments in Evrard's case. After his condemnation, the ecclesiastics turned him over to the secular court and asked the prince to decide on the punishment in accordance with the decretal *Ad abolendam*, but the prince countered: "It is you who know the law of God and what penalties should be assigned according to quality of the crime and the authority of the fathers." To this the churchmen replied: "No, it is not our concern to define for you the method of punishment in such matters because you have your own codices in which the various penalties are written by the emperors, just as we have our Old and New Testaments that prohibit us from killing." Robert himself, however, was not satisfied with the reply; when you say to the prince you have your codex, you are saying to him, in effect, to kill the defendant because nothing else can be found in the codex. In the end, however, the prince had the final word: "I am prepared," he declared, "to hang, burn or set free this malefactor however you instruct me, but I am not able to incarcerate him for a long time because such would require prisons for three to four thousand malefactors."[72] Thus Évard de Châteauneuf was consigned to flames at Auxerre, but of equal importance an answer from a prince was addressed to Pierre the Chanter's solution of incarceration rather than capital punishment to repress heresy. Here was revealed the major deficiency of contemporary prisons: they were too small and costly to be employed against widespread crime. As always, death was cheaper and appeared more efficient.

Heresy at Paris

Évard de Châteauneuf was a layman who was brought to Paris in 1201 from the Auxerrois to be tried and convicted of heresy by a council of bishops and masters of the schools. Not long afterward, the royal city began to produce its own crop of heretics who were not only clergymen but, equally important, masters from the faculties of arts and theology.[73] The first to surface was Master Amaury de Bène (near Chartres) who, as one chronicler reported, was on friendly terms with Prince Louis. Amaury had long been a regent master of arts before he began his theological studies, but he acquired his own method of learning and teaching that resulted in doctrines peculiar to himself. Since these were contradictory to catholic belief, he was forced to go to Rome and submit to an interview with Pope Innocent, who listened to his defense and to the contrary arguments from the Parisian masters. After receiving an unfavorable ruling, Amaury returned to Paris and confessed his errors to the university, but in his heart he never changed his mind. The experience was so humiliating that he took sick and died around 1206 and was buried near Saint-Martin-des-Champs.

Amaury's ideas nonetheless proliferated at Paris among a band of followers who caught the attention of Bishop Pierre de Nemours. The bishop and Brother Guérin, the king's principal clerical counselor, commissioned a certain Master Raoul de Namur to infiltrate the group. Dissimulating sympathy, he participated in their activities, traveled with them widely and was able to learn of their doctrines. After making a preliminary report to (Jean) the abbot of Saint-Victor; Master Robert (of Flameborough); Brother Thomas (of Marlborough?); and three regent masters of theology (Richard Poore, the dean of Salisbury; Master Robert of Courson; and Master Stephen Langton?), he drew up a list of the accused and a schedule of their articles of faith, which became the basis for prosecuting the heresy.

In 1210 Bishop Pierre summoned fourteen by name to a provincial council at Paris headed by Master Pierre de Corbeil, archbishop of Sens and a former theological master at Paris. (One of the accused lived within the city; the others resided in the diocese.) Of the fourteen, only one was a layman— Guillaume de Arria, a goldsmith, who exercised charismatic leadership over the group through prophetic gifts. The remaining ecclesiastics consisted of at least six and perhaps as many as fourteen priests, two deacons and three subdeacons. At least three claimed a master's degree. Two of them, Masters Guillaume de Poitiers and Guérin, like Amaury de Bène, had taught the arts at Paris before studying theology. The outstanding characteristic of the group, however, was that eight had studied theology at Paris, one for ten years and another a long time, and one (Master Guérin) had been a student of Master Stephen Langton. Two of the group averred to be in their sixties. Unlike earlier heretical communities, these followers of Amaury de Bène were not illiterate laymen but clerical elite, high within the ecclesiastical orders and benefiting from advanced education, particularly theology. It is clear that the theological faculty of Paris harbored the heterodox among its students.

The surviving fragment of the official decision and the major accounts of the event come to near agreement over the identity of the accused and the judicial procedures to which they were subjected. Two surviving fragments of their articles of faith and the contemporary accounts, however, are less coherent about their actual beliefs. (This is normally the case when orthodox opponents report the tenets of heterodox faith.) It appears that Master Amaury and his followers held to a pervasive pantheism that was vaguely defined. God was both one and everywhere, so that little distinction was made between the divine being and the created world. Special emphasis was placed on the operation of the Holy Spirit, following the threefold schema of Joachim of Fiore: the age of the Father, ruled by Mosaic law; that of the Son, governed by the sacraments; and the present age of the Holy Spirit, which will continue to the end of time. (Pierre the Chanter had already acknowledged and rejected Joachim's escatological scheme in his Biblical commentary.[74]) The third person of the Trinity is everywhere and incarnate in everyone. Since the Holy Spirit now reigns, the sacraments have been abolished, including baptism and the Eucharist. In a pantheistic universe transubstantiation of the Host cannot take place because the bread, like the world, is part of the Holy Spirit before and after consecration. For similar reasons, it is useless to venerate the saints. Antinomianism was another consequence of the present age of the Holy Spirit. Filled with the Spirit, the believer is controlled by divine love (*caritas*) and cannot commit sin, even the sins of fornication and adultery. Particular applications of the doctrine of a pervasive Holy Spirit included the statement that God spoke through Ovid as he did through Augustine, a dictum that held subversive implications in the superiority of theology over the arts. Another was the boast of one adherent that he was impervious to fire and torture, a claim that was unfortunately put to the test. Finally, the Amauricians issued short prophetic pronouncements with rash political overtones. God would speak through seven men, of whom Guillaume the Goldsmith was one. Four plagues would arrive in five years. In the first the poor people would die of hunger, in the second the nobility would die by the sword, in the third the houses of the townsmen would disappear in an earthquake and in the final the prelates would perish in fire. Evidently the Amauricians had modified the traditional scheme of the three orders (peasants, knights and clergy) by adding a third class, the bourgeoisie, which acknowledged their Parisian origins. Each order therefore disappears in a fate adapted to its function. More subversive was the claim that the pope was the antichrist and Rome was Babylon, but the most self-serving was the prophecy that all kingdoms will be subjected to the French king, and that Prince Louis, who will live in the age of the Holy Spirit, will not die.

Figure 30. Heretics put to the stake by the king, *Bible moralisée*, fol. 30va, Austrian National Library, Vienna, Picture Archiv+Signature.

Because priests were numerous among the accused, a provincial council consisting of the archbishop and at least six bishops was required to render a judgment, and newly devised inquisitorial procedures were followed. After the articles of faith were read, the defendants responded with confession or refusal to recant. Thus convicted, they were degraded of their ecclesiastical status in the presence of the clergy at the church of Saint-Honoré outside the western walls of the Right Bank on 14 November, and ten of them were handed immediately to the secular court. Philip Augustus, however, was not in town. When he returned, they were led to the field of Champeaux outside the northern walls and put to the flames on 20 November. The last of the group was apprehended later and burned at Amiens.

Despite Prince Louis's earlier friendship with Master Amaury and despite the prophecies favorable to the Capetian, the king and his chief agent, Brother Guérin, cooperated fully with the ecclesiastical authorities to extirpate the heresy in the royal capital. Following the procedures outlined in the papal decretals *Ad abolendam* and *Vergentis*, Philip found an opportunity to apply the solution of the accords of 1205–1206, whereby degraded clerics were handed over immediately to the royal authority for due punishment. Thomas Becket's protection against double punishment granted to the scholars in 1200 was no longer available to the Amauricians in 1210. Four of the accused, however, were sentenced to life imprisonment. This small number testified to the argument, voiced by the count of Nevers, that imprisonment was impractical on a large scale.

After the Amauricians were exterminated, the memory of Amaury de Bène, their founder, remained to be dealt with. The council took the unusual step of excommunicating him posthumously throughout the churches of the province, and exhuming his bones from consecrated ground and scattering them over a field. Robert of Courson discussed the legitimacy of this procedure.[75] Although the dead in principle were not to be excommunicated, an exception could be made in heinous cases of heresy to act as a deterrent to others. Even the supreme pontiff of the church was unable to forget the affair. Reacting as a former master of the theological schools of Paris, Pope Innocent revived the anathema in the opening chapter of the Lateran Council of 1215: "We reprove and condemn the most perverse doctrine of the wicked Amaury, whose mind had been so blinded by the father of lies that his doctrine may be judged to be more insane than heretical."[76] To prevent contamination of the laity, the provincial council ordered that formulations of the Apostles' Creed and the Lord's Prayer and theological books in the French vernacular should be handed over to the diocesan bishops for inspection.

The Albigensian Crusade

Crusades against the infidel beyond the borders of the kingdom had been in operation for well over a century; now the ultimate sanction was applied against heretics at Paris by both ecclesiastical and royal authorities. Simultaneously another heretical movement,that of the Cathars, so threatened the entire Languedoc in the south of France that it called for combining the two procedures. When the preaching of the Cistercians failed to contain the contagion, Pope Innocent sent papal legates to southern France and enlisted the support of Philip Augustus. The brutal assassination on 14 January 1208 of the papal legate, Pierre de Castelnau—who had recently excommunicated Raymond VI, count of Toulouse, for complicity—became the spark that ignited a new crusade. Again the French king found excuses for not participating, but the pope appealed to the French barons and knights in March. By 1209 an army from the northern regions assembled at Lyon for a march into the south. Thus began the Albigensian crusade, which was eventually to enlist Philip's son Louis first as prince and then as king, and to engulf the

Figure 31. Crusaders battle the Albigensians, *Bible moralisée*, fol. 40vd, Austrian National Library, Vienna, Picture Archiv+Signature.

southern provinces in a maelstrom of heresy hunting, warfare and devastation for more than two decades.

Numerous lords and knights joined the expedition from the Île-de-France, including most notably Simon de Montfort, who eventually took command of the forces. Because of the king's reluctance to become involved, the royal city was spared from the direct effects of the conflict, but Parisians could not ignore the threatening clouds in the south. While debating the question of clerics involved in bloodshed and application of the papal decretal *Ad abolendam*, Robert of Courson reported hearing of the new order, from Pope Innocent to King Philip, to move against the Albigensians with force.[77] A continuation of Bishop Eudes de Sully's synodical statutes urged parishioners to arm themselves against the Albigensian heretics and profit from crusading indulgences. The manuscript of the synodical statutes that enjoined the clergy to say prayers for the king and for Lord Louis included also the lands of Jerusalem and Constantinople and added a prayer for divine help in converting the Albigensians.[78] In their orisons under the vaults of Notre-Dame, Parisians took cognizance of the three distant conflicts at Jerusalem, Constantinople and the south.

Raising the Roof

In the year 1200 construction of Notre-Dame was half completed. The choir was finished; the walls of the nave and most of its vaulting were in place; the foundations for the west front were laid, and the portals were under way. At that point Parisians could appreciate its capacious dimensions and the beauty of its sculpture and glass, and imagine Bishop Maurice de Sully's final vision for his cathedral. At the same time, the walls of the Right Bank were nearing completion and the trajectory of those on the Left Bank had been laid out so that Parisians could again take measure of the full circuit.

To evoke the significance of Paris in 1200, I shall make use of the architectural analogy that was so dear to the theologians. In terms that became commonplace in their lectures, the foundations were laid, the walls were raised and all that was missing was the roof, but enough could be seen to know how the final structure would look. "To protect the building against heat, rain, hail and wind," as Pierre the Chanter phrased it, the roof was the finishing touch. During the thirteenth century this was the task of Louis IX and Philip (IV) the Fair, whose achievements are better known.

At Notre-Dame the roof was extended to protect the vaults of the nave. The west front was raised beyond the gallery of the kings to the rose window, the arcade and finally the two western towers. By the end of the century, Jean de Chelles and Pierre de Montreuil added façades and roses to the north and southern transepts, thus producing the cathedral we admire today. In the city itself, the walls on the Left Bank were brought quickly to completion, and the round tower of the Louvre was surrounded with a rectangular wall furnished with turrets. Monumental construction continued on the western end of the Île-de-la-Cité. Louis IX built the Sainte-Chapelle to serve as an exquisite reliquary for his newly acquired treasures, accompanied by a smaller chapel to house the archives. The royal palace was enlarged with the Gallerie de Merciers and the Sale sur l'Eau, to which Philip the Fair made further additions at the end of the century in the present Consergerie. Princes and barons, among them Alphonse de Poitiers and the counts of Artois and Flanders, began constructing sumptuous palaces to accommodate their sojourns in the royal capital. Louis added to the hospitals of the city the Quinze-vingts to provide for three hundred blind people, and the Water Merchants found housing at the Parloir aux Bourgeois on the Place de Grève. Among the échevins of the bourgeois population, the names of Sarrazin, Barbette, Pisdoë, Popin and Arrode remained prominent. (This is to be expected because these established families have been used to identify the important bourgeoisie of the preceding epoch.) As Louis placed restrictions on the money lending of the Jews, they increasingly found competitors from the Lombards newly arrived from Italy. To further commercial interests, however, the king himself minted a stable coinage; added a heavier silver coin, the *gros*; and revived gold coinage in the *écu*, although the latter's significance was only symbolic. Returning from his first crusade to Egypt, which failed spectacularly in its objectives, Louis sought to expiate his guilt by making reforms in government. Changes were imposed on the finances of the bailli-prévôt of Paris—among them, placing the official on salary—and the new incumbent, Étienne Boileau, drew up a *Livre de métiers* that recorded the regulations of the trades of the city. Most important, "the whole city was filled up with houses right up to the walls," as the chronicler Guillaume le Breton had predicted: the inhabitants multiplied from about 50,000 in 1200 to 200,000 by the beginning of the next century.

At Paris the judicial functions of royal government began to exploit the bureaucratic organization already established in the financial organs. Taking the name of parlement, the king's court was housed in the royal palace with a fixed schedule, a permanent body of trained personnel and careful records. At the Temple, the bureau of accounts further refined its techniques by producing a triennial budget as well as the regular accounts of prévôts and baillis; by the end of the century it was called the *chambre des comptes* and incorporated further specialization. In the provinces Philip Augustus's conquests were finally conceded by the son of King John, Henry III, in the treaty of Paris of 1259. Under Louis IX, Mâcon was added to the royal domain in Burgundy and two new *sénéchaussées* created in the south, Beaucaire-Nîmes and Carcassonne-Béziers, from the incursions of the crusaders against the Albigensians. Philip the Fair profited from family succession and marriages to add the great fiefs of Poitou, Toulouse and Champagne to the royal domain. Louis placed the prévôts under the supervision of baillis, and he instituted reforms among the latter to regulate their conduct; they were in turn supervised by new officials called *enquêteurs*, who traveled through the royal domain to report to the king in writing. The Norman exchequer was retained at Caen and served as the administrative center of the duchy; similar institutions were instituted elsewhere, for example at the *grands jours de Troyes* in Champagne. Philip the Fair nationalized these local assemblies in the *états généraux* by the end of the century. Both Louis and Philip the Fair were powerful and effective monarchs who added to the renown of Capetian France. Although of differing personality, Louis retained warm memories of his grandfather, Philip Augustus, and cited him as a model for his own governance; but the combined effect of Louis's deep piety and his unrestrained generosity put a severe strain on the resources he had inherited from his predecessors. The American medievalist Charles Homer Haskins used to affirm to his classroom that St. Louis was a luxury that France could afford only because of Philip Augustus. Despite Philip the Fair's evident governmental abilities, he was faced with challenges from the English, Flemish and papacy that seriously threatened the Capetian monarchy.

The great innovation in the ecclesiastical life of Paris after 1200 was the arrival of the mendicant orders in 1217. Established at the convents of Saint-Jacques and the Cordeliers on the Left Bank respectively, the Dominicans and Franciscans offered new models of preaching, learning and poverty for the clergy. Their ultimate goal was to preach the Gospel to the laity of cities such as Paris, in the streets and the squares—wherever they could be heard. They believed their preaching would be more effective if strengthened by Scriptural learning, so they immediately sought out the university and enrolled in theology. Equally important, they were convinced that their preaching would be accepted by the laity if it were backed by a holy life (in their case, one of absolute personal poverty).

These features of their program—preaching, learning and exemplary living—had been adumbrated by Pierre the Chanter at Notre-Dame before their arrival. Although dead for two decades, it would little exaggeration to suggest that the Chanter played the role of John the Baptist to the new mendicant clergy.

The university that had been germinating around the year 1200 surfaced in the documentation of the next decades. In 1229 another Lenten riot, replicating that of 1200, erupted, but this time the masters and scholars made good on their threat to go out on strike, and they suspended their lectures and disputations for nearly two years. When calm was restored in 1231, Pope Gregory IX confirmed the salient features of the university in the bull *Parens scientiarum*. Integration of the mendicants into the university produced still another riot and strike in 1251–1252, but the friars, benefiting from papal support, were ultimately accepted by the masters. The Franciscans Alexander of Hales and Bonaventure and the Dominicans Albert the Great and Thomas Aquinas rose to prominence in the theological faculty by the second half of the century, thus initiating high scholasticism that made Paris renowned throughout western Europe. Their thinking was stimulated and nourished by Aristotle's treatises on metaphysics and natural philosophy newly surfacing in the arts faculty in 1210 and fully inscribed in the curriculum by 1250, but their learning rested on the foundations of lecturing, disputing and preaching that the masters had perfected around 1200.

Except for the first decade of the reign of Louis IX, when the barons sought to test a youthful king and a mother regent, peace was never seriously threatened in France until the end of the century when England, Flanders and the papacy began to contest Philip the Fair's aggrandizements. During the middle years of the thirteenth century, reinforced by a puissant and exemplary monarch, French culture expanded throughout and dominated western Europe. French became the *lingua franca* from the Scottish borders to the eastern limits of the Levant. French vernacular romances, culminating in the *Roman de la rose* of Guillaume de Lorris and Jean de Meun, were translated or imitated throughout the Western world. French cuisine and styles of clothing became the rage of the upper classes. Gothic architecture, or the opus francigenum, crossed borders and set the model for constructing new churches. Until the seventeenth century, never was French culture so influential.

Like the year 1200, however, each moment of history can claim its own novelties, import and interest. Whatever its specific achievements, I trust that the foregoing sketch of thirteenth-century France, although rapid and frequently rehearsed, will nonetheless demonstrate how much the reigns of Louis IX and Philip the Fair owed to the achievements that were already in place in Paris around 1200. Philip Augustus and his contemporaries had laid the foundations and erected the walls that supported the crowning roof of the remaining decades. The myopia of later inhabitants of the royal capital may have given them occasion to demur at this optimistic picture, but with deeper perspective their successors of the Valois period, battered by the misfortunes of dynastic dissolution, the intrusion of the English and their allies and decimating warfare, plus the horrors of the Black Death, felt justified in seeing the thirteenth century as the happy times of the good king St. Louis (IX). This was the roof of the building solidly erected by the Parisians of 1200.

Selected Bibliography

Short Titles of Selected Sources

Actes
> *Recueil des actes de Philippe Auguste*, 5 vols. ed. Henri-François Delaborde, Charles Petit-Dutaillis, Jacques Boussard and Michel Nortier (Paris, 1916–2004).

Archives de l'Hôtel-Dieu
> *Archives de l'Hôtel-Dieu de Paris*, ed. Léon Brièl (Paris, 1894.)

Audouin, *Essai sur l'armée*
> Édouard Audouin, *Essai sur l'armée royale au temps de Philippe Auguste* (Paris, 1913).

Baldwin, *Aristocratic Life*
> Baldwin, John W., *Aristocratic Life in Medieval France: The Romances of Jean Renart and Gerbert de Montreuil, 1190–1230* (Baltimore, 2000).

———, "Étienne de Gallardon and the Making of the Cartulary of Bourges"
> "Étienne de Gallardon and the Making of the Cartulary of Bourges," *Viator*, 31 (2000), 121–46.

———, Government
> *The Government of Philip Augustus: Foundations of French Royal Power* (Berkeley, 1986).

———, "Jongleur"
> "The Image of the Jongleur in Northern France Around 1200," *Speculum*, 72 (1997), 635–63.

———, *Language*
> *The Language of Sex: Five Voices from Northern France Around 1200* (Chicago, 1994).

———, *Masters*
> *Masters, Princes and Merchants: The Social Views of Peter the Chanter and His Circle*, 2 vols. (Princeton, 1970).

———, "Masters at Paris"
> "Masters at Paris from 1179 to 1215: A Social Perspective," *Renaissance and Renewal in the Twelfth Century*, ed. Robert L. Benson and Giles Constable (Cambridge, Mass., 1982), 138–72.

————, *Medieval Theories of the Just Price*
Medieval Theories of the Just Price: Romanists, Canonists and Theologians in the Twelfth and Thirteenth Centuries, Transactions of the American Philosophical Society, New Series 49 (4) (1959).

————, "Ordeals"
"The Intellectual Preparation for the Canon of 1215 Against Ordeals," *Speculum*, 36 (1961), 613–36.

————, "Paris et Rome"
"Paris et Rome en 1215: Les reformes du IVe Concile de Latran," *Journal des savants* (1997), 99–124.

————, "Penetration"
"*Studium and Regnum*: The Penetration of University Personnel in French and English Administration at the Turn of the Twelfth and Thirteenth Centuries," *Revue des études Islamiques*, 46 (1976), 199–215.

————, "Philippe Auguste, Pierre le Chantre et Étienne de Gallardon"
"Philippe Auguste, Pierre le Chantre et Étienne de Gallardon: La conjuncture de *regnum, studium*, et *cancellaria* au tournant du 12ème au 13ème siècle," *Comptes rendus de l'Académie des Inscriptions et Belles Lettres* (2000), 437–57.

————, "Tibi et regno tuo"
"*Tibi et regno tuo specialiter nos teneri fatemur*: Innocent III, Philip Augustus and France," *Innocenzo III: Urbs et orbis*, ed. Andrea Sommerlechner, 2 vols. (Rome, 2003), 2, 985–1007.

————, "Vie sexuelle de Philippe Auguste"
"La vie sexuelle de Philippe Auguste," *Mariage et sexualité au moyen âge: Accorde ou crise?* ed. Michel Rouche, Culture et civilisations médiévales (Paris, 2000), 217–29.

Benedict of Peterborough, *Gesta regis*
Benedict of Peterborough, *The Chronicles of the Reigns of Henry II and Richard*, 2 vols., ed. William Stubbs (London, 1867).

Bériou, *L'avènement*
Nicole Bériou, *L'avènement de la parole: La prédication à Paris au XIIIe siècle*, 2 vols. Collection des études Augustiniennes. Série moyen âge et temps modernes 31, 32 (Paris, 1998).

Boileau
Le Livre des métiers d'Étienne Boileau, ed. R. de Lepinasse and F. Bonnardot (Paris, 1879).

Bove, *Dominer la ville*
Boris Bove, *Dominer la ville. Prévôts des marchandes et échevins parisiens de 1260 à 1350* (Paris, 2004).

Buc, "L'ambiguïté du livre"
Philippe Buc, *L'ambiguïté du livre: Prince, pouvoir, et peuple dans les commentaries de la Bible au moyen âge*, Théologie historique 95 (Paris, 1994).

Budget
  Le Premier budget de la monarchie française: Le Compte général de 1202–03, ed. Ferdinand Lot and Robert Fawtier, Bibliothèque de l'École des Hautes Études, Sciences historiques et philologiques 25 (Paris, 1932).

Caesarius of Heisterbach, *Dialogus*
  Caesarii Heisterbacensis monachi ordinis Cisterciensis Dialogus miraculorum, 2 vols., ed. Joseph Strange (Cologne, 1851).

Cartulaire de Notre-Dame
  Cartulaire de l'église de Notre-Dame de Paris, 4 vols., ed. Benjamin Guérard (Paris, 1850).

Chanter, Pierre the, *De oratione*
  Pierre the Chanter, *De oratione et speciebus illius,* ed. Richard C. Trexler, *The Christian at Prayer: An Illustrated Prayer Manual Attributed to Peter the Chanter (d. 1197),* Medieval and Renaissance Texts and Studies 44 (Binghamton, N.Y., 1987).

————, *Summa de sacramentis*
  Summa de sacramentis et animae consiliis, 4 vols., ed. Jean-Albert Dugauquier, Analecta mediaevalia Namurcensia 4, 7, 16, 21 (Louvain, 1954–1967).

————, *Verbum abbreviatum,* PL
  Verbum abbreviatum in PL 205: 21–554.

————, *Verbum abbreviatum,* ed. Boutry
  Petri Cantoris Parisiensis Verbum adbreuiatum: Textus conflatus, ed. Monique Boutry, Corpus christianorum: Continuatio mediaevalis 196 (Turnhout, 2004).

Chartes de Saint-Magloire
  Chartes et documents de l'abbaye de Saint-Magloire, 3 vols., ed. Anne Terroine, Lucie Fossier, Yvonne de Montenon (Paris, 1966–98).

Chobham, *Summa confessorum*
  Thomas de Chobham, *Summa confessorum,* ed. F. Broomfield, Analecta mediaevalia Namurcensia 25 (Louvain, 1968).

Chronique des rois de France
  Anonyme de Béthune, *Chronique des rois de France,* ed. Léopold Delisle, RHF 24, 750–75.

Coggeshall
  Radulphi de Coggeshall Chronicon Anglicanum, ed. J Stevenson (London, 1875).

Courson, *Summa,* ed. Kennedy
  V. L. Kennedy, "Robert Courson on Penance," *Mediaeval Studies,* 7 (1945), 291–336.

Courson, *Summa,* ed. Lefèvre,
  Georges Lefèvre, "Le traité 'De Usura' de Robert de Courçon," *Travaux et Mémoires de l'Université de Lille* 10, 30, (1902).

Courson, *Summa,* fol.
  Robert de Courson, *Summa,* Ms. Paris, BnF Lat. 14524.

CUP
  Chartularium universitatis Parisiensis, 4 vols., ed. Heinrich Denifle and Émile Châtelain (Paris, 1889).

David de Dinant, *Quaternuli*
  Davidis de Dinanto quaternulorum fragmenta, ed. Marian Kurdzialek (Warsaw, 1963).

Delisle, *Catalogue*
  Léopold Delisle, *Catalogue des actes de Philippe Auguste* (Paris, 1856).

Diceto, *Ymagines*
  Ralph de Diceto, *Opera historica*, 2 vols. ed. William Stubbs, 2 vols. (London, 1876).

Erlande-Brandenburg, *Notre-Dame*
  Alain Erlande-Brandenburg, with Caroline Rose, *Notre-Dame de Paris* (Paris, 1991).

Flameborough, ed. Firth
  Robert of Flameborough, *Liber poenitentialis*, ed. J. J. Francis Firth, Pontifical Institute of Medieval Studies, Studies and Texts 18 (Toronto, 1971).

France de Philippe Auguste
  La France de Philippe Auguste: Le Temps des mutations, ed. Robert-Henri Bautier, Colloques internationaux du Centre National de la Recherche Scientifique 602 (Paris, 1982).

Friedmann, *Paris, ses rues*
  Adrien Friedmann, *Paris, ses rues, ses paroisses du moyen âge à la Révolution* (Paris, 1959).

Gerald of Wales, *De principis instructione*
  Giraldi Cambrensis opera, 8 vols., ed. G. F. Warner (London, 1891), 8, 3–329.

————, *De rebus a se gestis*
  Giraldi Cambrensis opera, 8 vols., ed. J. S. Brewer (London, 1861), 1, 3–122.

————, *Gemma ecclesiastica*
  Giraldi Cambrensis opera, 8 vols., ed. J. S. Brewer (London, 1862), 2, 3–364.

Gislebert de Mons, *Chronique*
  Gislebert de Mons, *Chronique*, ed. Léon Vanderkindere (Brussels, 1904).

Guillaume le Breton, *Gesta,* I
  Oeuvres de Rigord et Guillaume le Breton, 2 vols., ed. Henri-François Delaborde (Paris, 1882), 1, 168–327.

————, *Philippidos,* II
  Oeuvres de Rigord et Guillaume le Breton, 2 vols., ed. Henri-François Delaborde (Paris, 1885), 2.

Histoire de Guillaume le Maréchal
  Histoire de Guillaume le Maréchal, 3 vols., ed. Paul Meyer, Société de l'histoire de France (Paris 1891–1901), 255, 268, 304.

Histoire des ducs de Normandie
Anonyme de Béthune, *Histoire des ducs de Normandie et des rois d'Angleterre*, ed. F. Michel (Paris, 1840).

Innocent III, *Regesta*, PL 214–17.

Jacques de Vitry, *Historia occidentalis*
The Historia occidentalis of Jacques de Vitry, ed. John Frederick Hinnebusch, Spicilegium Friburgense (Fribourg, Switz. 1972), 17.

Jean Renart, *Escoufle*
Jean Renart, *Escoufle: Roman d'aventure*, ed. Franklin Sweetser (Geneva, 1974).

———, *Roman de la rose*
Jean Renart, *La roman de la rose ou Guillaume de Dole*, ed. Félix Lecoy (Paris, 1979).

Jordan, *French Monarchy and the Jews*
William Chester Jordan, *French Monarchy and the Jews from Philip Augustus to the Last Capetians* (Philadelphia, 1989).

Lasteyrie
Robert de Lasteyrie, *Cartulaire général de Paris* (Paris, 1887).

Lombard-Jourdan, *Aux origines*
Anne Lombard-Jourdan, *Aux origines de Paris: La genèse de la rive droite jusqu'en 1223* (Paris, 1985).

Manhes-Deremble, *Vitraux narratifs . . . de Chartres*
Colette Manhes-Deremble, *Les vitraux narratifs de la cathédral de Chartres. Étude iconographique*, Corpus vitrearum, France, Études 2 (Paris, 1993).

Mansi
Sacrorum conciliorum nova et amplissima collectio, 31 vols., ed. J. D. Mansi (Florence and Venice).

Mathew Paris, *Chronica majora*
Mathew of Paris, *Chronica majora*, 7 vols., ed. H. Luard (London, 1872–1883).

MGH SS
Monumenta Germaniae historica, Scriptores.

Mortet, "Maurice de Sully"
Victor Mortet, "Maurice de Sully, évêque de Paris (1160–1196): Étude sur l'administration épiscopale pendant la seconde moitié du XIIème siècle," *Mémoires de la Société de l'histoire de Paris* 16 (1889), 105–318.

Nortier and Baldwin, "Contributions"
Michel Nortier et John W. Baldwin, "Contributions à l'étude des finances de Philippe Auguste," *Bibliothèque de l'École des Chartes* 138 (1980), 5–33.

Notre-Dame, ed. Anderson
Notre-Dame and Related Conductus: Opera omnia, 10 vols., ed. Gordon A. Anderson (Henryville, Pa., Ottawa, and Binningen, Switz., 1979–1981).

Obituaires de Sens
Obituaires de la province de Sens, 4 vols., ed. Auguste Molinier, Obituaires RHF 1.

Pierre de Roissy, *Manuale*, ed. D'Alverny
Marie-Thérèse D'Alverny, "Les Mystères de l'église d'après Pierre de Roissy," *Mélanges offerts à René Crozet*, ed. Pierre Galais and Yves-Jean Riou (Poitiers, 1966), 1085–1104.

———, *Manuale*, fol.
Ms. Paris, BnF nouv. acq. lat. 232.

PL
Patrologiae cursus completus. . . . series latina, 221 vol. J. P. Migne (Paris, 1857–1903).

Prose Salernitan Questions
The Prose Salernitan Questions, ed. Brian Lawn, Auctores Britannici Medii Aevi 5 (Oxford, 1979).

Recueil de Saint-German-des-Prés
Recueil des chartes de l'abbaye de Saint-Germain-des-Prés, 2 vols., ed. René Poupardin, Société de l'histoire de Paris et de l'Île-de-France (Paris, 1909, 1930).

Recueil de Saint-Martin-des-Champs
Recueil de chartes et documents de Saint-Martin-des-Champs, 4 vols., ed. J. Depoin, Archives de la France monastique, 13, 16, 18, 20 (Paris, 1912–1921).

Recueil des jugements
Recueil des jugements de l'échiquier de Normandie au XIIIème siècle (1207–1270), ed. Léopold Delisle (Paris, 1864).

Registres
Les Registres de Philippe Auguste, ed. John W. Baldwin, Françoise Gasparri, Michel Nortier and Elisabeth Lalou, RHF, Documents financières et administratifs 7 (Paris, 1997).

RHF
Recueil des historiens de la France, 24 vols. (Paris, 1734–1904).

Rigord
Oeuvres de Rigord et Guillaume le Breton, 2 vols., ed. Henri-François Delaborde (Paris, 1882, 1885), I, 1–167.

Robert d'Auxerre, *Chronicon*
Roberti canonici S. Mariani Autissiodorensis chronicon, ed. O. Holder-Egger, MGH SS 17, 216–87.

Robson, *Maurice de Sully*
C. A. Robson, *Maurice of Sully and the Medieval Vernacular Homily* (Oxford, 1952).

Roger de Hoveden, *Chronica*
Chronica magistri Rogeri de Hovedene, 4 vols., ed. William Stubbs (London, 1868–1871).

Roux, *Paris au moyen âge*
Simone Roux, *Paris au moyen âge* (Paris, 2003).

Statuts synodaux, ed. Pontal
  Les Statuts synodaux français du XIIIème siècle. Les Statuts de Paris et les synodes de l'ouest (XIIIème siècle), ed. Odette Pontal, Collection de documents inédits sur l'histoire de France, Section de philologie et d'histoire jusqu'à 1610, série in 8°, 9 (Paris, 1971).

Teulet
  Layettes du Trésor des Chartes, 5 vols., ed. Alexandre Teulet (Paris, 1863), 1.

Wright, *Music and Ceremony*
  Craig Wright, *Music and Ceremony at Notre-Dame of Paris, 500–1550* (Cambridge, 1989).

X:
  Decretales of Gregory IX, in *Corpus iuris canonici*, 2 vols., ed. E. Friedberg (Leipzig, 1881), 2.

Zink, *La prédication*
  Michel Zink, *La prédication en langue romane avant 1300*, Nouvelle bibliothèque du moyen âge 4 (Paris, 1982).

Selected Manuscripts

London, BL cod Addit. 19767
Paris, AN L 547, no. 1
———. BnF lat. 1112
———. BnF lat. 2294
———. BnF lat. 14524
———. BnF nouv. acq. lat. 232
Vienna, Bibl. Nat. 2254.

Notes

Notes to Prologue

1. Rigord 147.
2. Rigord 148.
3. *Actes* 2, no. 621.
4. *Actes* 2, no. 633.
5. Roger de Hoveden, *Chronica* 4, 120.
6. *Actes* 1, no. 644.
7. M. L. Colker, "The 'Karolinus' of Egidius Parisiensis," *Traditio* 29 (1973), 199–325; Andrew W Lewis, "Dynastic Structures and Capetian Throne-Right: The View of Giles de Paris," *Traditio* 33 (1977), 225–52.
8. They are found in the sources listed in abbreviation.
9. Fuller discussion of the Chanter's circle can be found in Baldwin, *Masters* 1, 17–46. On Pierre de Roissy see now Manhes-Deremble, *Les vitraux narratifs . . . de Chartres* 21–26, who emphasizes his relations with Chartres but acknowledges his Parisian connections.
10. The nature of their testimony is treated in Chapter Five.
11. In the romances *Escoufle* (1200–1202) and *Roman de la rose* (c. 1209) Jean Renart demonstrated an acute sensitivity to the contemporary world in which he lived by employing numerous *effets de réel* that illuminate the historical context. The *Escoufle* was addressed to Baudouin, count of Flanders and of Hainaut (1194–1205) and the *Roman de la rose* to Milon de Nanteuil, prévôt of the chapter of Reims (1207–1217), both of whom were associated with the Anglo-Norman, Flemish, Guelf party that opposed Philip Augustus in the northeast of the kingdom (Baldwin, *Aristocratic Life* 31–49). Despite Milon's Guelf proclivities, however, he was also prévôt of Rosnay-en-Brie near Melun (*Cartulaire de Notre-Dame* 2, 221, 265, 270, 275) near Melun. Although Rosnay was in the direction of Champagne, the prévôté belonged to the chapter of Notre-Dame of Paris and made Milon a member of their chapter. This membership gave him, and through him Jean Renart, a connection to Paris. (This relationship was unknown to me in *Aristocratic Life*.)

Notes to Chapter One

1. Recently Gaëtan Desmarais, *La morphogenèse de Paris: Des origines à la Révolution* (Paris, 1995), has returned to the origins of the city, but his discussion is more concerned with applying postmodern theory than with resolving historical and geographical questions.

2. Roger Dion, "Le site de Paris dans ses rapports avec le développement de la ville," in *Paris croissance d'une capitale*, ed. Guy Michaud (Paris, 1961).

3. Diceto, *Ymagines* 2 142; Rigord 164, 165; Guillaume le Breton, *Gesta* 1, 225.

4. *CUP* 1, 55, 56.

5. On the royal palace, see Jean Guérout, "Le Palais de la Cité à Paris des origines à 1417: Essai topographique et archéologique," *Mémoires des sociétés historiques et archéologiques de Paris et de l'Île-de-France*, 1 (1949), 57–212.

6. *CUP* 1, 55–56.

7. Lombard-Jourdan, *Aux origines*, is the authoritative study of the Right Bank.

8. Rigord 53, 54.

9. Lombard-Jourdan, *Aux origines* 78.

10. *Actes* 1, no. 31.

11. Rigord 33, 34, 70.

12. *Budget* CLVI(1), CLXXXII(1), CCI(2), CCII(1).

13. Marcel Aubert, *Notre-Dame de Paris: Sa place dans l'architecture du XIIe au XIVe siècle* (Paris, 1929); Caroline Bruzelius, "The Construction of Notre-Dame in Paris," *Art Bulletin* 64 (1987): 540–569; Erlande-Brandenburg, *Notre-Dame*; and Stephen Murray, "Notre-Dame of Paris and the Anticipation of Gothic," *Art Bulletin* 80 (1998), 229–253.

14. For the chronology see Dany Sandron, "Observations sur la structure et la sculpture des portails de la façade," *Monumental* 2000, 10; "La galerie des rois de Notre-Dame de Paris," *Commission du vieux Paris, Procès verbal* (2002) no. 5, 10–13.

15. Murray, "Notre-Dame," *Art Bulletin* 80 (1998), 246–248.

16. Chanter, *Verbum abbreviatum* PL 258A, 257B; Baldwin, *Masters* 1, 66–69.

17. Pierre de Roissy, *Manuale* ed. D'Alverny 1096.

18. *Actes* 1, no. 346.

19. Louis Halphen, *Paris sous les premiers Capétiens (987–1223): Étude de topographie historique* (Paris, 1909); *L'enceinte et le Louvre de Philippe Auguste*, Action artistique de la Ville de Paris (Paris, 1988); *Les enceintes de Paris*, ed. Béatrice de Andia (Paris, 2001).

20. Rigord 105.

21. Baldwin, *Government* 298–300. Michel Fleury, "Le Louvre de Philippe Auguste," in *L'enceinte et le Louvre* 137–73.

22. *Actes* 2, no. 834 and 3, no. 1109.

23. *Registres* 249.

24. Alexandre Grady, "Les enceintes d'abbayes," in *Les enceintes de Paris* 90–91.

25. *Actes* 3, no. 1102; In 1217–1218 Philip confided the upkeep of the gate of Saint-Honoré, formerly belonging to Master Raymond, to his sergeant Foulques de Compiègne. *Actes* 4, 1478.

26. Guillaume le Breton, *Gesta* I, 240–41.

27. Alain Erlande-Brandebourg, "L'architecture militaire au temps de Philippe Auguste: Une nouvelle conception de la défense," *La France de Philippe Auguste* 595–603; Baldwin, *Government* 377–87.

28. Charles Coulson, "Fortress-Policy in Capetian Tradition and Angevin Practice: Aspects of the Conquest of Normandy by Philip II," *Anglo-Norman Studies* 6 (1983), 24–30.

29. Guillaume le Breton, *Gesta* I, 241.

30. Robert-Henri Bautier, "Quand et comment Paris devint capitale," *Bulletin de la Société d'Histoire de Paris et d'Île-de-France* 105 (1978), 34; Roux, *Paris au moyen âge* 20.

31. Chanter, *Summa de sacramentis* 3 (2a) 255; Guillaume le Breton, *Gesta* I, 240, 241; *Actes* 3, no. 1109.

32. Ph. Dollinger, "Le chiffre de la population de Paris au XIVe siècle: 210,000 ou 80,000?" *Revue historique* 216 (1956), 35–44; Robert Cazelles, *Paris, de la fin du règne de Philippe Auguste à la mort de Charles V,* Nouvelle histoire de Paris, IV (Paris, 1972), 131–40; Bove, *Dominer la ville* II.

33. Statistics from F. L. Ganshof, *Étude sur le développement des villes entre Loire et Rhin au moyen âge* (Paris, Bruxelles, 1943), 58–59 and Carlrichard Brühl, *Palatium und civitas: Studien zur Profantopographie spätantiker civitates von 3. bis zum 13. Jahrhundert* (Cologne, 1975), I, 19, 149, 165, 194; and 2, 258.

34. *Actes* I, no. 426. Guillaume le Breton, *Gesta* I, 241.

35. Friedmann, *Paris, ses rues* 114–19, 190–97, 277–93; Lombard-Jourdan, *Aux origines* 100. See pp. 164–65, 178–79.

36. Biller, *The Measure of Multitude: Population in Medieval Thought* (Oxford, 2000), 68.

37. Rigord 70.

38. *Recueil de Saint-Martin-des-Champs* 3, 370–71.

39. Rigord 128–32, 139–41. Wheat sold at 16 sous/setier and barley from 10 to 14 sous/setier, in contrast to the prices of 6 and 3 sous respectively found in the *Budget* of 1202–1203, CLXI(1) and CLXXXII(2).

40. François-Olivier Touati, *Archives de la lèpre. Atlas de lèproseries entre Loire et Marne au moyen âge,* Mémoires et documents d'histoire médiévale et philologie 7 (Paris, 1996), 45, 52, 307ff; Lombard Jourdan, *Aux origines* 100–102.

41. Sharon Farmer, *Surviving Poverty in Medieval Paris: Gender, Ideology and Daily Life of the Poor* (Ithaca, New York, 2002), 84.

42. Innocent III, *Regesta* PL 215: 1382; *Actes* 4, no. 1796; Baldwin, *Government* 463, n.53.

43. Jacques de Vitry, *Historia occidentalis* 91.

44. Chanter, *Summa de sacramentis* 3 (2a) 171–74; Chobham, *Summa confessorum* 296, 346–53; Baldwin, *Masters* I, 133–37; *Langages* 132–42.

45. Farmer, *Surviving Poverty* 147; J. M. Reitzel, "The Medieval Houses of Bons-Enfants," *Viator* II (1980): 199.

46. Constance Berman, "Cistercian Nuns and the Development of the Order: The Abbey at Saint-Antoine-des-Champs Outside of Paris," *The Joy of Learning and*

the Love of God: Studies in Honor of Jean Leclercq, ed. E. Rozanne Elder (Kalamazoo, Mich., 1995), 123.

47. Jacques de Vitry, *Historia occidentalis* 94–101; Rigord 132, 139–40; Otto of Saint-Blaise, *Chronicon* (1198), in MGH, SS, 20: 230; Innocent III, *Regesta* PL 214: 102.

48. Courson, *Summa* in Baldwin, *Masters* 2, 94–95, nn. 141, 145; Mansi 21, 854.

49. Ms. Paris, AN L 547, no. 1.

50. Lasteyrie nos. 254, 289, 480; *Actes* I, nos. 256, 366, 370, 371, 426, 448, 2 nos. 640, 670, 3, nos. 1108, 1385, 4, no. 1625. See also A. Vidier, "Les origines de la municipalité parisienne," *Mémoires de la Société de l'histoire de Paris et d'Île-de-France* 49 (1927), 250–91; Joseph de Corcia, *"Bourg, Bourgeois, Bourgeois de Paris* from the Eleventh to the Eighteenth Century," *Journal of Modern History* 59 (1978), 207–33. The status of *burgensi regni nostri* was explicitly regulated by Philip IV on 27 May 1287. Bove, *Dominer la ville* 545, 546.

51. Joseph Morsel, "Comment peut-on être Parisien? Contribution à l'histoire de la genèse de la communauté Parisienne au XIIIe siècle," *Religion et société urbaine au moyen âge: Études offertes à Jean-Louis Biget* (Paris, 2000), 370–74 argues from *Actes* 2, no. 644 that the royal charter regulating the dispute between students and the prévôt of Paris of 1200 suppresses the *nostri* and thereby marks the emergence of self-consciousness of "being Parisian bourgeoisie." It is difficult to imagine that royal charters were necessarily sensitive to bourgeois consciousness. The absence of *nostri* may simply indicate that the king was distancing himself from the prévôt and the bourgeoisie in this dispute.

52. Rigord 100, 103,104; The names were identified by Delisle, *Catalogue* p. lxiii.

53. *Actes* I, nos. 366, 370, 371, 375, 381, 382, 390–93.

54. Chanter, *Summa de sacramentis* 3 (2a), 62. Since the clerics came from churches at Bologna, Salerno, and Montpellier, they appear to be masters. *Summa de sacramentis* 3 (2b), 770. "Item de confraternitatibus dubitatur utrum labem simonie committat qui admittitur ad eas sub certa pactione aliter non admittendus. Puta laici instituunt confraternitates suas ad consilium questuariorum sacerdotum qui hujusmodi omni adinveniunt scilicet ut nullus admittatur sine certa summa pecunie. Tu ergo si intras percepturus interventu pecunie orationes et exequias in morte et ita non gratis accepturus es illa que spiritualia sunt. Ergo simoniam committis cum non intres per hostium." Courson, *Summa* 9, 8, fol. 45ra.

55. A.J.V. Le Roux de Lincy, "Recherches sur la grand confrèrie Notre-Dame aux prêtres et bourgeois de la ville de Paris," *Mémoires sur les antiquités nationales par la Société royale des antiquaires de France* 17 (1844), 200–318; H. Omont, "Documents nouveaux sur la grande confrérie Notre-Dame aux prêtres et bourgeois de Paris," *Mémoires de la Société de l'histoire de Paris et Île-de-France* 32 (1905), 1–88.

56. Bove, *Dominer la ville* 183–87, 209–13, 334–43.

57. Bove, *Dominer la ville* 452, 471 480, 485, 493.

58. Lasteyrie no. 536; *Recueil de Saint-Germain-des-Prés* I, no. 222, 2, no. 318; *Actes* I, no. 321, 2, no. 587, 5, no. 1840; *Chartes de Saint-Magloire* I, no. 54; Christian Gut, "Les actes de Maurice de Sully relatifs aux possessions parisiennes de Saint-

Victor (1180–96)," *Huitième centenaire de Notre-Dame de Paris* (Paris, 1967), 42; Halphen, *Paris* 74; Lombard-Jourdan, *Aux origines* 172 and n. 748.

59. Lasteyrie no. 578; *Archives de l'Hôtel-Dieu* 53, 74, 77; *Obituaires de Sens* 1 (1), III, 460, 2, 800, 803.

60. *Obituaires de Sens* 2, 794, 830; E. Richemond, *Recherches généalogique sur la famille des seigneurs de Nemours du XII au XIV siècle* (Fontainebleau, 1907), 2, p. xxiv; *Chartes de Saint-Magloire* 1, no. 67.

61. *Archives de l'Hôtel-Dieu* 50, 52, 56, 59, 60, 70; *Recueil de Saint-Germain-des-Prés* 2, no. 389.

62. *Archives de l'Hôtel-Dieu* 61; *Actes* 4, no. 1469.

63. Lombard-Jourdan, *Aux origines* 104.

64. Bove, *Dominer la ville* 119, 136, 397, 565.

65. Bove, *Dominer la ville* 158, 156.

66. Roux, *Paris au moyen âge* 102, 103; Bove, *Dominer la ville* 380–390.

67. Chanter *Verbum abbreviatum* ed. Boutry, 764. PL 331C. The proverb was still being quoted in the fourteenth century in the *Mesnagier*. Roux, *Paris au moyen âge* 233.

68. *Actes* 2, no. 321; *Recueil de Saint-Martin-des-Champs* 4, 92–93, 184–86; Bove, *Dominer la ville* 221–23, 574–78.

69. *Actes* 1, nos. 173, 306–08, 392, 2, no. 587, 4, no. 1424–27; Le Roux de Lincy, "Recherches sur la grand confrèrie" 250. See Baldwin, *Government* 482, n. 16.

70. Henri Stein, "Testament d'un chambellan de Philippe Auguste (1205)," *Bulletin de la Société de l'histoire de Paris et de l'Île-de-France* 30 (1930), 156–57. His most important legacy was to give to the monastery of Saussaye rents from his house under the royal hall on the Cité. For his career as chamberlain, see Baldwin, *Government* 484, n. 60.

71. A. Vidier, "Les origines" 278.

72. Michel Nortier (*Actes* 5, pp. 221–33) has assembled all the evidence for "corps de métiers" from Boileau and later sources for the reign of Philip Augustus.

73. *Registres* 176.

74. The complex jurisdiction may be deduced from Boileau 7, 13, 14, *Actes* 3, no. 1091, and A. Dutilleux, "Abbaye de Joyenval au diocèse de Chartres," *Mémoires de la Société historique et archéologique de Pontoise et du Vexin* 13 (1890), 78, 79. Joyenval later sold it to the nuns of Longchamps. Jules Tardif, *Monuments historiques (Carton des rois)* (Paris, 1866), no. 850.

75. *Actes* 3, no. 1238. On the butchers see Lombard-Jourdan, *Aux origines* 94–96.

76. Lasteyrie nos. 240, 255, 266, 380; *Actes* 3, no. 1121.

77. *Actes* 1, no. 74.

78. Boileau 212, 213; *Actes* 3, no. 1068, 4, no. 1469.

79. *Actes* 4, no. 1568.

80. *Actes* 1, no. 426.

81. *Actes* 1, no. 251, IV, no. 1625. For the operation of the *crierie* see Boileau 21–24.

82. Lombard-Jourdan, *Aux origines* 93, 96.

83. Chanter, *Summa de sacramentis* 3 (2a), 244–45. For a mention of the post at Bourges, see *Actes* 3, no. 1105. Boileau notes the practice later in the century, 32, 217.

84. The section on the book industry draws from François Avril, "A quand remontent les premiers ateliers d'elumineurs laïcs à Paris?" *Les dossiers de archéologie* 16 (1976), 36–44; Richard H. Rouse and Mary A. Rouse, *Illiterati et uxorati: Manuscripts and Their Makers: Commercial Book Producers in Medieval Paris 1200–1500* (London, 2000) 1, 20–40; Christopher de Hamel, *The Book: A History of the Bible* (London, 2001), 114–38.

85. Baldwin, *Masters* 2, 120, n. 34.

86. Alfred Hessel and Walther Bulst, "Kardinal Guala Bichieri und seine Bibliothek," *Historische Vierteljahrschrift* 27 (1937) 781, 782.

87. Lombard-Jourdan, *Aux origines* 98–100 has presented the relevant charter and topographical data for the trades.

88. *Actes* 1, nos. 94, 95. *Ordonnances des rois de France* 3, 528.

89. Boileau 66, 103.

90. Baldwin, *Masters* 1, 58; 2, 44, n. 105; Chobham, *Summa confessorum* 290–91.

91. Boileau 83, 149, 198.

92. Boileau 164.

93. Roux, *Paris au moyen âge* 49, 50, 164.

94. *Actes* 1, no. 74, 2, no. 670. Boileau 4, 255.

95. Boileau 13.

96. Boileau 44, 66, 103.

97. *Actes* 1, nos. 135, 448, 3, no. 1107.

98. Jean Renart, *Roman de la rose* vv. 611–17.

99. Chanter, *Summa de sacramentis,* text in Baldwin, *Masters* 2, 211, n. 103. The Chanter was concerned not only with stolen goods but also with revealing their defects to potential buyers.

100. *Actes* 2, no. 610; *Registres* 558; Courson, *Summa* in Baldwin, *Masters* 2, 174, n. 93.

101. Lasteyrie nos. 192, 480.

102. *Actes* 2, no. 850.

103. *Actes* 1, no. 206. In 1200 Philip forced the count of Auxerre to return to the former tolls on salt charged to the bourgeoisie of Paris. *Actes* 2, no. 640. In 1209–1210 he resolved a dispute between the merchants of Paris and Rouen over salt measure at the Port de Paris. Teulet 1, no. 913.

104. *Actes* 3, nos. 1316, 1385. In 1213 the king settled a dispute between the monks of Saint-Denis and the bishop of Paris over the latter's rights in the fair of Lendit. *Actes* 3, no. 1298.

105. *Actes* 4, no. 1625. For the king's intervention between the water merchants and the count of Beaumont over tolls on commodities in 1210–1212), see *Registres* 510.

106. Lombard-Jourdan, *Aux origines* 119.

107. Le Roux de Lincy, "Recherches sur la grande confrèrie Notre-Dame" 273–74.

108. For a fuller account of the Romanists', canonists' and theologians' discussion of the functions of the merchant, see Baldwin, *Masters* 1, 261–69.

109. Chobham, *Summa confessorum* 301–02.

110. Baldwin, *Masters* 1, 267–96; Baldwin, *Medieval Theories of the Just Price* 21–31, 42–57, 68–71.

111. Chobham, *Summa confessorum* 302, 514.

112. Baldwin, *Medieval Theories of the Just Price* 71, n. 136.

113. Pierre de Poitiers, *Sententiarum libri quatuor,* PL 211: 1152. On the definition of usury, see Baldwin, *Masters* 1, 270–73.

114. Chanter, *Summa de sacramentis* 3(2a), 222; Chobham *confessorum* 513; Courson, *Summa* ed. Lefèvre 59. Baldwin, *Masters* 1, 274–75.

115. X: 5.19.6 *In civitate*; Chanter, *Summa* in Baldwin, *Masters* 2, 194, n. 52; Courson, *Summa* ed. Lefèvre 61; Chobham, *Summa confessorum* 512.

116. *Actes* 3, no. 1108; Bove, *Dominer la ville 241.*

117. Chanter, *Summa de sacramentis* 3 (2a), 184–85; Courson, *Summa* ed. Lefèvre, 71, 73; Chobham, *Summa confessorum* 516. Baldwin, *Masters* 1, 286–90.

118. Françoise Dumas, "La monnaie dans le royaume au temps de Philippe Auguste," *La France de Philippe Auguste* 541–72.

119. *Cartulaire de Notre-Dame* 2, 429.

120. Langton, *Questiones,* text in Baldwin, *Masters* 2, 202, nn. 161, 162, 1, 291–95.

121. Flamborough, ed. Firth, 192.

122. Courson, *Summa* ed. Lefèvre 65; Chobham *Summa* confessorum 513.

123. Rigord 132. Baldwin, *Masters* 1, 296–307.

124. Chanter, *Summa de sacramentis* 3 (2a), 175, Chobham, *Summa confessorum* 148–49; Baldwin, *Masters* 1, 135–36.

125. Chanter, *Summa de sacramentis* text in Baldwin, *Masters* 2, 210, n. 87 and Caesar of Heisterbach, *Dialogus* ed. Strange, 1, 107. Baldwin, *Masters* 1, 307–11.

126. Courson, *Summa* ed. Lefèvre, 25–37; Langton *Questiones* in Baldwin, *Masters* 2, 211, n. 94; Mansi 22, 851.

127. Innocent III, *Regesta* PL 217: 229, 230; Robert d'Auxerre, *Chronicon* 280.

128. *Obituaires de Sens* 1 (1), 176, 179.

129. This is the explanation of Henry Kraus, *Gold Was Their Mortar: The Economics of Cathedral Building* (London, Boston, 1979), 19–38, esp. 24, 25.

130. The explanation of Gaëtan Demarais, *La morphogenèse de Paris; Des origines à la Révolution* (Paris, 1990), 208–209, is based on no documentary evidence and purely deductive reasoning.

131. Rigord 24, 25.

132. Rigord 24–31; Baldwin, *Government* 51–52; Jordan, *French Monarchy and the Jews* 23–37.

133. Diceto, *Ymagines* 2, 4.

134. *Actes* 1, nos. 90, 95, 96; for the disposal of other confiscated properties, *Actes* 1, nos. 166, 263, 2, no. 627.

135. Rigord 141, echoed by Robert d'Auxerre, *Chronicon* RHF 18, 262–63.

136. *Actes* 2, 582, 583; *Budget* 13,58.

137. On display at the Musée de l'art et d'histoire du Judaisme, Hôtel de Saint-Aignan, 71 rue du Temple.

138. *Actes* 2, no. 955; Baldwin, *Government* 160–61, 230–33; Jordan, *French Monarchy and the Jews* 38–90.

139. *Registres* 240, 570, 571. Baldwin, *Government* 230–32; Jordan, *French Monarchy and the Jews* 66–70 argues that this may represent still another *captio* by Philip inspired by a contemporary despoiling the English Jews by King John.

140. *Registres* 239; *Actes* 3, nos. 1013, 1236; *Actes* 3, no. 1091; A. Dutilleux, "Abbaye de Joyenval au diocèse de Chartres," *Mémoires de la Société historique, archéologique de Pontoise et du Vexin* 13 (1890), nos. 4, 8. See page 41.

141. Chanter, *Verbum abbreviatum* PL 158BC; Courson, *Summa* text in Baldwin, *Masters* 2, 204, nn. 18, 19; Chobham, *Summa confessorum* 510; Baldwin, *Masters* 1, 298–300.

142. *Actes* 4, no. 1554. For an undated and enigmatic charter (*Actes* 4, no. 1555), see the discussion of Jordan, *French Monarchy and the Jews* 71–89, who situates it before 1219 and further develops the provisions of the ordinance of 1219.

143. Teulet 2, no. 1610. For the later situation, see Jordan, *French Monarchy and the Jews* 93–104, 128–54.

144. Teulet 1, no. 1439; *Registres* 163; *Actes* 4, no. 1805. See the discussion in Lombard-Jourdan, *Aux origines* 103–110, 115–119, 127, 128.

Notes to Chapter Two

1. Gerald of Wales, *De rebus a se gestis Opera* 1, composed around 1208 and after. The account of Philip's birth was inserted into his *De principis instructione, Opera* 8, 292–93. On Gerald, see Robert Bartlett, *Gerald of Wales, 1146–1223* (Oxford, 1982).

2. Mortet, "Maurice de Sully."

3. J. Warichez, *Étienne de Tournai et son temps (1128–1203)* (Paris and Tournai, 1936).

4. The following is drawn from F. S. Gutjahr, *Petrus Cantor Parisiensis: Sein Leben und seine Schriften* (Graz, 1899) and Baldwin, *Masters* I, 3–16.

5. The fullest treatment of this problem is found in Anthime Fourrier, "Raoul de Hodenc: est-ce lui?" *Mélanges de linguistique romane et de philologie médiévale offerts à M. Maurice Delbouille* (Gembloux, 1964), 2, 165–93.

6. The charter evidence for his public activities has been collected in Baldwin, *Masters* 2, 235–40.

7. *CUP* I, 46.

8. Coggeshall 79.

9. For a summation of his theological production, see Baldwin, *Masters* I, 11–16, 88–116.

10. Otto of Saint-Blaise, *Chronicon*, MGH SS 20, 326.

11. *CUP* I, 46.

12. Chanter *Summa de sacramentis* 3(1), 311, 312, 326; Baldwin, *Masters* 2, 82, n. 27.

13. See below, pp. 162–63.

14. Baldwin, *Language* 44–47, 247–50.

15. Chanter, *Summa de sacramentis* 2 275; *Verbum abbreviatum* in Baldwin, *Masters* 2, 224, n. 170; Baldwin, *Aristocratic Life* 86–90.

16. Ms. London, British Library, Cod. Addit. 19767 (1228–1246). Paul Lehmann, "Mitteilung aus Handschriften 2," *Sitzungsberichte der Bayerischen Akademie der Wissenschaften* (Phil.-hist. Abteilung), 1930, Heft 2, 5, 6. The manuscript contains the *Ars predicandi,* sermons and letter to Guillaume de Montpellier by Alain de Lille and an abbreviated version of the *Verbum abbreviatum* by Pierre the Chanter. Picture reproduced in Baldwin, *Masters* 1, frontispiece.

17. For recent attempts to assess Philip's personality, see Robert-Henri Bautier, "Philippe Auguste: La personnalité du roi," Raymonde Foreville, "L'image de Philippe Auguste dans les sources contemporaines," and Jacques LeGoff, "Philippe Auguste et les 'exempla'," in *La France de Philippe Auguste* 33–57, 115–130, 145–54; Baldwin, *Government* 356–62; Jim Bradbury, *Philip Augustus: King of France, 1180–1223* (London, 1998), 43–45, 333; Gérard Sivéry, *Philippe Auguste* (Paris, 1993), 384–86.

18. *Chronicon Sancti Martini Turonensis* in RHF 18, 304.

19. For a recent summary, see Baldwin, "La vie sexuelle de Philippe Auguste."

20. First version in Benedict of Peterborough, *Gesta Regis Henrici secundi,* 2, 7; abbreviated version, Roger de Hoveden, *Chronica* 2, 318.

21. See Stephen Jaeger, *Ennobling Love: In Search of a Lost Sensibility* (Philadelphia, 1999), 11–26.

22. Rigord 120, 121; Guillaume le Breton, *Gesta* 1, 194, 195; *Gesta Francorum* in RHF 18, 426.

23. Walter Map, *De nugis curialium* 5, 5, ed. Thomas Wright (London, 1850), 216; Gerald of Wales, *De principis instructione Opera* 8, 276–82.

24. Baldwin, "Tibi et regno tuo"; Rigord 134.

25. See below, p. 277.

26. Rigord 125.

27. Text in Léopold Delisle, "Étienne de Gallardon, clerc de la chancellerie de Philippe Auguste, chanoine de Bourges," *BEC* 60 (1898), 23, 24; historical and codicological context in Baldwin, "Philippe Auguste, Pierre le Chantre et Étienne de Gallardon;" and Baldwin, "Étienne de Gallardon and the Making of the Cartulary of Bourges."

28. Chanter, *Summa de* sacramentis 3(2a), 101; Baldwin, "Philippe Auguste, Pierre le Chantre et Étienne de Gallardon," 442, n. 17; Baldwin, *Masters* 1, 172–73; see especially Philippe Buc, *L'ambiguïté du livre* 314–28.

29. See below, pp. 132–33.

30. Wright, *Music and Ceremony* 198–206.

31. *Statuts synodaux,* ed. Pontal, 1, 96, 97 (Ms. Paris BnF lat. 14443).

32. *Notre-Dame,* Anderson, ed. 6, l (music 48).

33. *Notre-Dame,* Anderson, ed. 6, lxvii (music 72–74). It would be difficult to know how the audience would understand the reference to baldness, but the author was perhaps alluding to Jeremiah 47:5: "Baldness comes over Gaza."

34. Innocent III, *Regista* PL 215:87; *Budget* CLVII(1) 127; Florens Deuchler, *Der Ingeborgpsalter* (Berlin, 1967).

35. Paul and Marie-Louise Biver, *Abbayes, monastères, couvents de femmes. À Paris des origines à la fin du XVIIIe siècle* (Paris, 1975), 4, 92, 139, 478.

36. A photographic collection of sculpture can be found in Erlande-Branden-burg, *Notre-Dame de Paris*.

37. For an accessible facsimile, see *Bible moralisée*, Codex Vindobonensis 2554, Vienna, Oesterreichische Nationalbibliothek, commentary and translation of Biblical texts by Gerald B. Guest (London, 1995). For a recent study, see John Lowden, *The Making of the Bibles Moralisées*. Vol. 1. The Manuscripts. Vol. 2. The Book of Ruth (University Park, Pa., 2000). Each page consists of eight medallions arranged in two vertical columns of four each. Reading horizontally, the first, second, fifth and sixth medallions illustrate the Biblical text. Under each, the third, fourth, seventh and eighth illustrate the moral interpretation. To the left and right of the vertical columns are placed texts in French that the medallions illustrate. The medallions are numbered by folio (recto and verso, indicated by r and v), by ABCD for the Biblical texts and abcd for the corresponding moralizations.

38. Under chastity (third figure from the left), *luxuria* is wrongly portrayed as a woman with scales. Adolf Katzenellenbogen, *Allegories of the Virtues and Vices in Medieval Art* (New York, 1964), 75, 76.

Notes to Chapter Three

1. This chapter is based on Baldwin, *Government*, the first section on 28–58.
2. *Actes* 1, no. 168.
3. Statistics in Baldwin, *Government* 66.
4. *Actes* 1, no. 345; Baldwin, *Government* 40, 77–80, 102–04, 137–40.
5. Baldwin, *Government* 402–12.
6. Edited in *Budget*; Baldwin, *Government* 405–07.
7. Baldwin, *Government* 125–36.
8. *Budget* CLXXXII (1), CLXXXIII (2), CXLIX (2), CC (2), CXLIII (2), CLXXI (1), CXCII (2).
9. Baldwin, *Government* 163.
10. *Actes* 2, no. 727; Baldwin, *Government* 143.
11. *Budget* CLII (1), 64.
12. For royal revenues see Baldwin, *Government* 144–64.
13. Baldwin, *Government* 154.
14. Baldwin, *Government* 155–64.
15. This also contains a small number of farm accounts from the march chapters.
16. Baldwin, *Government* 164–66.
17. Baldwin, *Government* 166.
18. Baldwin, *Government* 351, 352.
19. *The Course of the Exchequer by Richard son of Nigel*, ed. Charles Johnson (London, 1950); Baldwin, *Government* 151, 152.
20. *Budget* CXLVI (1), CLXXIV (1), CLXXXIX (1).
21. *Budget* CLV (2), CLXXXII (1), CCI (1).
22. Baldwin, *Government* 104–06.
23. *Histoire des ducs de Normandie* 120; *Chronique des rois de France* 764.
24. *Actes* 2, no. 688; Baldwin, *Government* 115–18.

25. Guillaume le Breton, *Gesta* I, 256.

26. Baldwin, *Government* 118–22.

27. Françoise Gasparri, *L'Écriture des actes de Louis VI, Louis VII, et Philippe Auguste* (Paris and Geneva, 1973), 25, 26, 52, 73–78. Baldwin, *Government* 403–05.

28. Edited in *Registres*. See the discussion in Baldwin, *Government* 412–18.

29. Chanter, *Summa de sacramentis* 3(2a) 34 and (2b) 658; Baldwin, *Masters* 1, 180–182, 2, 120, n. 35.

30. *Actes* 1, p. 468; *Foedera* (London, 1816), 1, 75, 76; see Sidney Painter, *The Reign of King John* (Baltimore, 1944), 94, 95.

31. Chanter, *Summa de sacramentis* 3(2a) 36 and (2b) 655; Courson (*Summa* fol. 45vb) copied this passage verbatim with the addition *ut dicebat cantor*; Mansi, 22, 1007.

32. Chanter, *Summa de sacramentis* 3(2a), 401.

33. Baldwin, *Government* 109–14.

34. Baldwin, *Government* 34, 35, 107, 108.

35. *Recueil des monuments inédits de l'histoire du tiers état*, ed. Augustin Thierry (Paris, 1850), 1, 118.

36. *Actes* 2, no. 633.

37. Coggeshall 135, 136.

38. *Budget* CLVII (2), CLXXXIV (1), CCIV (2); Baldwin, *Government* 166–75.

39. Audouin, *Essai sur l'armée* 98–118; Baldwin, *Government* 168–70.

40. *Registres* 254–57.

41. *Budget* CXLVIII (1).

42. Baldwin, *Government* 191–96.

43. Baldwin, *Government* 207–19.

44. Nortier and Baldwin, "Contributions" 5–30; Baldwin, *Government* 239–48, 352–53.

45. Edited in *Registres*. Baldwin, *Government* 289–94, 412–18.

46. Edited in *Recueil des jugements*; Baldwin, *Government* 225–27, 418–20.

47. Statistics in Baldwin, *Government* 40.

Notes to Chapter Four

1. Pierre de Roissy made a special note that the bells of churches are silent during an interdict because the mouth of preaching has been stopped. *Manuale*, ed. D'Alverny, 1100.

2. The text of the interdict is in PL 214: xcvii n. 60. The exceptions are in *Recueil de Saint-Germain-des-Prés*, 2, no. 290; and Germaine Lebel, *Catalogue des actes de l'abbaye de Saint-Denis* (Paris, 1935), no. 131. See Edward Krehbiel, *The Interdict: Its History and Operation with Special Attention to the Time of Innocent III* (Washington D.C, 1909), 114–22. The Chanter discussed the practices of applying an interdict on a people for the fault of their lord *Summa de sacramentis* 3 (2a), 282 and 3 (2b) 735.

3. *Gesta Innocentii* in PL 214: xvii. Innocent III, *Regesta*, PL 214:1–3.

4. Innocent III, *Regesta* PL 214: 148; Baldwin, "Tibi et Regno Tuo" 985–1007.

5. Innocent III, *Regesta*, PL 214: 1191–94 (1202); PL 214: 1130; (1202), *Novit* (1204).

6. Rigord 137.

7. Mortet, "Maurice de Sully," 105–318.

8. Jacques de Vitry, *Die Exempla aus den Sermones feriales et commune* ed. Joseph Greven, *Sammlung mittellateinischer Texte* 9 (1914), 10–11. For the rival story, see Caesar of Heisterback, *Dialogus* ed. Strange 1, 371, which portrays Maurice as choosing himself to be bishop.

9. Mortet, "Maurice de Sully" 273; Baldwin, *Masters* 1, 157.

10. Coggeshall, 79; Adam de Perseigne, *Epistole*, in PL 211; 598CD.

11. *CUP* 1, 35–37.

12. Baldwin, *Government* 177 and 554 no. 19.

13. *Actes* 2, no. 650; Baldwin, *Government* 178–79.

14. Rigord 102; Baldwin, *Government* 64–68.

15. Léopold Delisle, "Étienne de Gallardon, clerc de la chancellerie de Philippe Auguste, chanoine de Bourges," *Bibliothèque de l'École des Chartes* 60 (1988), 23. Baldwin, "Philippe Auguste, Pierre le Chantre et Étienne de Gallardon," 433–48.

16. *Analecta Bollandiana* 3 (1884), 275–80.

17. *Cartulaire de Notre-Dame* 1, 5–11.

18. Mortet, "Maurice de Sully," 201–03.

19. Friedmann, *Paris, ses rues* 118–19.

20. Chanter, *Summa de sacramentis* 3 (2a), 33, 37; 3 (2b), 654–56, 658–59; Courson in Baldwin, *Masters* 2, 121, n.46; for Master Arnulph's debts, see Hillary Jenkinson, "William Cade, a Financier of the Twelfth Century," *English Historical Review* 28 (1913), 226; Baldwin, *Masters* 1, 181–83.

21. Chanter, *Summa de sacramentis* 3 (2a) and (2b), 658; Courson in Baldwin *Masters* 2, 122, n. 57, 58.

22. Michael Tangl, *Die päpstlichen Kanzleiordnungen* (Innsbruck, 1894), 53–55, 59–61; *Cartulaire de Notre-Dame* 1, 355–57.

23. Paul Fournier, *Les officialités au moyen âge* (Paris, 1880), 1–12, 311; Baldwin, "Pénétration," 212.

24. *Cartulaire de Notre-Dame* 1, i–v; Jean-Loup Lemaître, *Repertoire des documents nécrologiques français*, RHF, Obituaires 7 (Paris, 1980), 555, 556.

25. *Cartulaire de Notre-Dame* 1, 5–19; *Pouillés de la province de Sens* ed. Auguste Longnon, RHF, Pouillés 4 (Paris, 1904), 349–59.

26. The most comprehensive study of the chapter is Guérard in *Cartulaire de Notre-Dame* 1, lxvii–lxix, c–clxvii.

27. *Actes* 2, no. 649.

28. *Cartulaire de Notre-Dame* 1, 270–71.

29. Chanter, *Summa de sacramentis* 3 (1), 311, 326 and below, pp. 229–30.

30. *Cartulaire de Notre-Dame* 1, 390; 3, 365.

31. Lasteyrie nos. 204, 208; Fourier Bonnard, *Histoire de l'abbaye royal de Saint-Victor de Paris* (Paris, 1907), 1, 32, 34, 251, 252.

32. *Cartulaire de Notre-Dame* 1, 227–28.

33. *Cartulaire de Notre-Dame* 1, 355.

34. This section on worship is drawn from the comprehensive treatment in Wright, *Music and Ceremony.*

35. Wright, *Music and Ceremony* 69–70.

36. *Obituaires de Sens* 1(1), 153 and Wright, *Music and Ceremony* 68–71.

37. Rigord III, 134, 165.

38. Rigord 162; Cartulaire blanc de Saint-Denis, AN LL 1157, 63–63v; Blaise de Montesquiou-Ferensac, Danielle Gaborit-Chopin, *Le Trésor de Saint-Denis. Inventaire de 1534* (Paris, 1973–1976) 2, 9; 2, 10, 355–57, 367, 372–73. There was also competition over who possessed the true head of St. Denis.

39. Doubts about the use of relics appeared early in the twelfth century. Reinhold Kaiser, "Quêtes itinérantes avec des reliques pour financier la construction des églises (XIe–XIIe siècles)," *Le Moyen Âge* 101 (1995), 205–25. Chanter, *Summa de sacramentis* 3 (2b), 770; Courson, *Summa* ed. Kennedy, 333; C. 62, Mansi 22, 1049, 1050; Baldwin, *Masters* 1, 109.

40. *Actes* 1, no.324, 325; 5, no. 1831; *Obituaires de Sens* 1(1), 153; Chanter, *Summa de sacramentis 3* (2a), 62, 63; Baldwin, *Aristocratic Life* 87–88.

41. Mortet, "Maurice de Sully," 276; Erlande-Brandenburg, *Notre-Dame* 63.

42. See the diagram and discussion in Wright, *Music and Ceremony* 98–101.

43. Pierre de Roissy, *Manuale* ed. D'Alverny, 1097, 1103–1104. These passages were inspired by Jean Beleth, *Summa de ecclesiasticis officiis* c. 115, ed. Heribert Douteil, Corpus christianorum; Continuatio medievalis 41a, (Turnholt, 1976), 215, 216. Manhes-Dremble, *Vitraux narratifs . . . de Chartres* 23, 24.

44. Pierre de Roissy, *Manuale* ed. D'Alverny, 1097.

45. Achille Luchaire, *La société française au temps de Philippe Auguste* (Paris, 1909), 118–22.

46. Wright, *Music and Ceremony* 101–104.

47. Wright, *Music and Ceremony* 70–75.

48. St. Bernard: *Cartulaire de Notre-Dame* 1, 430 (semiduplex, which the calendar does not mention). As for St. Thomas Becket, the canons made use of responses first devised at Canterbury and perhaps transmitted to Paris by Stephen Langton. Wright, *Music and Ceremony* 72, 9. In 1228 the canons of Paris created a feast (7 July) of the Translation of the relics of St. Thomas at Canterbury (1220) that was doubtlessly sponsored by Stephen Langton and his brother Simon, canon of Paris. *Cartulaire de Notre-Dame* 4, 105; at semiduplex rank it contained an organum. Wright, *Music and Ceremony* 72, 265, 370.

49. Pierre de Roissy, *Manuale* ed. D'Alverny, 1104.

50. Pierre de Roissy, *Manuale* ed. D'Alverny, 1100.

51. Wright, *Music and Ceremony* 81–89.

52. Wright, *Music and Ceremony* 274–78.

53. Wright, *Music and Ceremony* 31, 278–81.

54. Text in Wright, *Music and Ceremony* 237.

55. It survives in three manuscripts: Ms F: Florence, Biblioteca Laurenziana, Pluteus 29.1; mss. W1 and W2: Wolfenbüttel 628 and 1099; Wright, *Music and Ceremony* 243–58, 281–94.

56. Baldwin, *Masters* 2, 142, n. 218; "Jongleur" 645.

57. Wright, *Music and Ceremony* 317–45 for the principal discussion of performance.

58. *Cartulaire de Notre-Dame* 1, 439.

59. *Obituaires de Sens* 1 (1), 169; *Notre-Dame* ed. Anderson, 4, viii, (music) 13–15; 6, xx–xxi (music for one voice) 22–23.

60. Pierre de Roissy, *Manuale* ed. D'Alverny, 1096–97.

61. Wright, *Music and Ceremony* 107, 267, 339–41.

62. *Cartulaire de Notre-Dame* 1, 88–89. Wright, *Music and Ceremony* 132.

63. Pierre de Roissy, *Manuale* ed. D'Alverny, 1097.

64. *Statuts synodaux* ed. Pontal, 1, 82. Chanter, *Summa de sacramentis* 1, 150–53. Pierre de Roissy, *Manuale* fol. 38v and 29r. For a collection of texts on the debate see V. L. Kennedy, "The Moment of Consecration and the Elevation of the Host," *Mediaeval Studies* 6 (1944), 121–50.

65. Pierre de Roissy, *Manuale* ed. D'Alverny, 1094, 1095, 1102. Mahnes-Deremble, *Vitraux narratifs . . . de Chartres* 24.

66. Roland Recht, *Le croire et le voir: l'art des cathédrales (XIIe–Xve siècle)* (Paris, 1999), 162–77.

67. Marcel Aubert, Louis Grodecki, Jean Lafond, Jean Verrier, *Les vitraux de Notre-Dame et de la Sainte-Chapelle* Corpus Vitrearum Medii Aevi, France 1, (Paris, 1959), 23–34; further examples in Erlande-Brandenburg, *Notre-Dame* 64, 100, 101.

68. Chanter, *De oratione*. See Baldwin, *Masters* 2, 253–55 and the introduction to the edition by Richard Trexler 66–121. The treatise *De penitentia et partibus eius*, in which the *De oratione* is found, has two versions, long and short.

69. Chanter, *De oratione* 171.

70. Chanter, *De oratione* 183, 213, 195, 199, 194, 218–19.

71. Ms. Leipzig, University Library 432, fol. 9r–127v.

72. Chanter, *De oratione* 182–91.

73. Chanter, *De oratione* 182, 185, 195, 208.

74. Chanter, *De oratione* 226–30.

75. Chanter, *De oratione* 185.

76. Chanter, *De oratione* 196, 227–33.

77. Kathryn Horst, " 'A Child Is Born': The Iconography of the Portail Ste.-Anne at Paris," *Art Bulletin* 69 (1987), 187–210; Erlande-Brandenburg, *Notre-Dame* 24–36; Anne Lombard-Jourdan, "L'invention du roi fondateur à Paris au XIIe siècle. De l'obligation morale au thème sculptural," *Bibliothèque de l'École des Chartes*, 155 (1997), 510–42.

78. William M. Hinkle, "The King and the Pope on the Virgin Portal of Notre-Dame," *Art Bulletin* 48 (1966), 1–13; Erlande-Brandenburg, *Notre-Dame* 113, 124–37.

79. Erlande-Brandenburg, *Notre-Dame* 108–113, 114–24, 144–45.

80. Erlande-Brandenburg, *Notre-Dame* 113, 137. Dany Sandron, "Observations sur la structure et la sculpture des portails de la façade," in "Dossier Notre-Dame de Paris," *Monumental* 2000, 10–19; "La galerie des rois de Notre-Dame de Paris," *Commission du vieux Paris*, Procès-verbal (2002, no. 5), 10–15.

81. Adam of Eynsham, *Magna Vita Sancti Hugonis*, ed. D. L. Douie and Hugh Farmer, Oxford Medieval Texts (Oxford, 1985), 2, 140–41.

82. Mortet, "Maurice de Sully," 178–85.

83. Chanter, *Verbum abbreviatum* PL 136–40, ed. Boutry 278.

84. C. 60, Mansi, 22, 1047.

85. The authoritative study of parishes is Adrien Friedmann, *Paris, ses rues.*

86. *Pouilliés de la province de Sens* RHF, ed. Auguste Longnon (Paris, 1904), 4, 358–59.

87. Friedmann, *Paris, ses rues* 117–20, 190–97.

88. Chanter, *Verbum abbreviatum* PL 107AB, ed. Boutry 278. The long version has the title "Contra multiplicationem ecclesiarum et altarum."

89. Chanter, *Summa de sacramentis* 2, 323, 430; *Verbum abbreviatum* PL 116A. Friedmann, *Paris, ses rues* 277–93.

90. Friedmann, *Paris, ses rues* 277–93.

91. Friedmann, *Paris, ses rues* 232–60.

92. Friedmann, *Paris, ses rues* 295.

93. Mortet, "Maurice de Sully," 172–75.

94. *Statuts synodaux* ed. Pontal, I, and c.6 Mansi 22, 991, 992.

95. Both versions of Maurice's sermon are edited by Robson, *Maurice de Sully* 55–58, 79–82. *Statuts synodaux,* ed. Pontal, 1, 52–54.

96. *Statuts synodaux,* ed. Pontal, 1, 74.

97. *Statuts synodaux,* ed. Pontal, 1, 98.

98. Baldwin, *Masters,* 1, 230–32, nn. 214, 218, 219.

99. C. 14, Mansi 22, 1003; Baldwin, *Masters* 1, 237–41.

100. Baldwin, *Masters,* 2, 96, n. 161.

101. *Statuts synodaux,* ed. Pontal, 1, 70, 74, 84.

102. Robson, *Maurice de Sully* 18–21, 82–87.

103. *Statuts synodaux,* ed. Pontal, 1 84.

104. *Statuts synodaux,* ed. Pontal, 1, 54; Chanter, *Summa de sacramentis* 1, 84–93.

105. *Statuts synodaux,* ed. Pontal, 1, 56, 68, 72.

106. *Statuts synodaux,* ed. Pontal, 1, 82.

107. Robson, *Maurice de Sully* 98.

108. *Statuts synodaux,* ed. Pontal, 1, 64, 66.

109. Baldwin, *Masters* 1, 50–55.

110. Chanter, *Summa de sacramentis* 2, 3, 323–24, 430.

111. Chobham, *Summa confessorum* 251; Pierre de Poitiers in Baldwin, *Masters* 2, 42, n. 73.

112. C. 21, Mansi 22, 1007–10.

113. Nicole Bériou, *L'avènement* 1, 21–29; Michel Zink, *La prédication* 32–36, 173–80, 221–26; *Statuts synodaux,* ed. Pontal, 1, 84.

114. Baldwin, *Masters* 1, 107–11; Bériou, *L'avènement* 1, 30–48.

115. Jacques de Vitry, *Historia occidentalis* 90–103. Baldwin, *Masters* 1, 36–39; C. 10, Mansi 22, 998.

116. Zink, *La prédication* 173–80.

117. Baldwin, *Aristocratic Life.*

Notes to Chapter Five

1. Alexander Neckham, *De naturis rerum* and *De laudibus*, ed. Thomas Wright (London, 1863), 308–11, 414; Chanter in Baldwin, *Masters* 2, 31, n. 55; Chrétien de Troyes, *Cligès* vv. 28–33, ed. Alexandre Micha (Paris, 1982), 2.

2. *Cartulaire de Notre-Dame* 1, 339; *CUP* 1, 56.

3. Mansi 22, 227–28; Gaines Post, "Alexander III, the *licentia docendi*, and the Rise of Universities," *Anniversary Essays in Medieval History by Students of Charles Homer Haskins* (Boston, 1929), 255–77; Gaines Post, Kimon Giocarinis and Richard Kay, "The Medieval Heritage of an Humanistic Ideal: 'Scientia donum dei est, unde vendi non potest'," *Traditio* 11 (1955), 195–234.

4. *CUP* 1, 56.

5. Text in Baldwin, *Masters* 2, 51, 52, n. 59. *CUP* 1, 79.

6. *CUP* 1, 5, 6. Chanter, *Summa de sacramentis*, 2, 440.

7. Chanter, *Summa Abel* text in Baldwin, *Masters* 2, 51, n. 57; *Summa de sacramentis* 3 (2a), 256.

8. Jacques de Vitry, *Historia occidentalis* 92.

9. Baldwin, "Masters at Paris," 149–50.

10. Chanter, *Summa de sacramentis* 2, 323, 432; for more discussion, see Baldwin, *Masters* 1, 139–40.

11. *Statuts synodaux*, ed. Pontal, 1, 99; *CUP.* 1, 74.

12. Robert Génestal, *Le privilegium fori en France*, Bibliothèque de l'École des Hautes Etudes, Sciences religieuses 35, 1921, 1, ii–iv; Baldwin, *Masters* 1, 141–45.

13. Courson, *Summa*, text in Baldwin, *Masters* 2, 99, n.188.

14. Chanter, *Verbum abbreviatum* PL 188D.

15. *CUP* 1, 78, 79; Chanter, *Verbum abbreviatum* PL 32B, 188D, that was based on Jerome.

16. Génestal, *Privilegium fori*; Baldwin, *Masters* 1, 145–48.

17. *CUP* 1, 47.

18. M. M. Davy, *Les sermons universitaires Parisiens de 1230–31*, Études de philosophie médiévale 15, (1937), 337, 338; Baldwin, *Masters* 2, 51, n. 55.

19. Diceto, *Ymagines* 1, 337; *CUP* 1, 21–23; Beryl Smalley, *The Becket Conflict and the Schools* (Totowa, N.J., 1973), 201–08.

20. Chanter, *Summa de sacramentis* 3(2a), 388; *Verbum abbreviatum* PL 231A, 547B, ed. Boutry 508.

21. *Actes* 2, no. 644; 3, no. 1125.

22. Post, "Alexander III," 276; Baldwin, *Masters* 1, 118–21.

23. Courson, *Summa*; texts in Baldwin, *Masters* 2, 80, nn. 15, 16; C. 29, Mansi 22, 1015, 1018.

24. *CUP* 1, 91.

25. Pierre Abélard, *Historia calamitatum*, ed. Jacques Monfrin (Paris, 1959), 94.

26. *CUP* 1, 8, 73–77.

27. For more on the complicated discussion, see Baldwin, *Masters* 1, 123–27.

28. Courson, *Summa*; text in Baldwin, *Masters* 2, 86, n.68.

29. Courson, *Summa*; text in Baldwin, *Masters* 2, 87, n.74.

30. *CUP* I, 15, 16, 49.

31. Chanter, *Summa de sacramentis* 2, 440; *CUP* I, 79.

32. *CUP* I, 56; Guillaume le Breton, *Gesta* I, 230; *CUP* I, 75, 76.

33. Charles H. Haskins, *Studies in the History of Medieval Science* (Cambridge, Mass., 1926), 372–76; *CUP* I, 78–79.

34. See Baldwin, "Masters at Paris," 138–72 for an introduction to this approach.

35. R. W. Southern has attempted to estimate the number of masters at Paris around 1200. "The Schools of Paris and the School of Chartres," in Benson and Constable, *Renaissance and Renewal* 128, n.44.

36. Baldwin, "Masters at Paris," 145–46, 165–66.

37. *CUP* I, 70. See later in this chapter for full documentation.

38. Texts in Baldwin, *Masters* 2, 53–55, nn. 90, 93.

39. Seneca, *Epistolae morales* 49 (R. M. Gummere ed., Loeb Classical Library) I, 326; Martin Grabmann, *Geschichte der scholastischen Methode* (Feiburg im Br., 1909), 2, 112–17.

40. Chanter, *Verbum abbreviatum* PL 30B.

41. Jacques de Vitry, *Sermo XVI ad scholares,* in J. B. Pitra, *Analecta novissima* (Paris, 1888), 2, 368.

42. C. Vieillard, *Gilles de Corbeil: Essai sur la société médicale et religieuse au XIIIe siècle* (Paris, 1909); Baldwin, *Masters* I, 41.

43. Gerald of Wales, *De rebus a se gestis, Opera* I, 45–48.

44. For the recently discovered work of Pierre le Breton, see Anne Lefèbvre-Teillard, "Petrus Brito legit . . . Sur quelques aspects de l'enseignement du droit canonique à Paris au début du XIIIe siècle," *Revue historique de droit français et étranger* 79 (2001), 153–77. Pierre taught between 1205 and 1210 and was acquainted with the Chanter's work.

45. Alexander Neckham, *De naturis* 331; Geoffroy de Vinsauf in Edmond Faral, *Les arts poétiques* 228.

46. Otto of Saint-Blaise, *Chronicon*, MGH SS, 20, 326.

47. *CUP* I, 65, 85.

48. Chanter, *Verbum abbreviatum* PL 160C; *Summa de sacramentis* 2, 202.

49. *Bible moralisée* Ms. Vienna, Nationalbibliothek 2554, fol. 37rb.

50. Texts in Baldwin, *Masters* 2, 58, 59 nn. 142, 143.

51. Mansi 21, 459, 528, 1179; 22, 845.

52. *CUP* I, 90–93.

53. Chanter, *Verbum abbreviatum* PL 25AB, ed. Boutry 9.

54. A recent study that analyzes the sophistication of the Chanter's Biblical exegesis is Buc, *L'ambiguïté du livre*.

55. Chanter, *Verbum abbreviatum* PL 23A.

56. Chanter, *Verbum abbreviatum* PL 25D, 26D, 27CD.

57. Chanter, *Verbum abbreviatum* PL 553BC, ed. Boutry 537.

58. Chanter, *Verbum abbreviatum* PL 32B, 188D.

59. Chanter, *Verbum abbreviatum* PL 27D, 28A; Baldwin, *Masters* I, 94, 95.

60. Chanter, *Verbum abbreviatum* ed. Boutry 9.

61. Chanter, *Verbum abbreviatum* ed. Boutry 15, 16.

62. *CUP* 1, 47, 48.

63. Chanter, *Verbum abbreviatum* PL 31D, 33D, 34A, ed. Boutry 23–25.

64. Chanter to Deut. 16:21, text in Baldwin, *Masters* 2, 71, n. 96.

65. Langton to Amos 2:1, text in Baldwin, *Masters* 2, 70, n.81.

66. Chanter, *Verbum abbreviatum* PL 34D–36B, ed. Boutry 30, 33, 34.

67. Guillaume le Breton, 1, *Gesta* 233; Baldwin, *Masters* 1, 104–07.

68. Phyllis Barzillay Roberts, *Studies in the Sermons of Stephen Langton*, Pontifical Institute of Medieval Studies, Studies and Texts 16 (Toronto, 1968). For a sample, see her edition of *Selected Sermons of Stephen Langton*, Medieval Latin Texts 10 (Toronto, 1980).

69. Thomas de Chobham, *Sermones*, ed. Franco Morenzoni, Corpus christianorum, Continuatio mediaevalis 82A (Turnhold, 1993).

70. Statistics in Baldwin, "Masters at Paris," 148–51.

71. Baldwin, "Masters at Paris," 151–53, 167–70.

72. Courson, *Summa*; text in Baldwin *Masters* 2, 59, n. 143.

73. Nigel Wireker, "*Speculum stultorum*," in *The Anglo-Latin Satirical Poets and Epigrammatists of the Twelfth Century*, ed. Thomas Wright (London, 1872), 1, 53.

74. For example, of twenty-six occurrences found for Master Roger the Norman, only two omit his degree. John W. Baldwin, "A Debate at Paris over Thomas Becket Between Master Roger and Master Peter the Chanter," *Studia Gratiani* 12 (1967), 124–25.

75. Baldwin, *Gouvernement* 163–68.

76. C. Warren Hollister and John W. Baldwin, "The Rise of Administrative Kingship: Henry I and Philip Augustus," *American Historical Review* 83 (1987), 867–905.

77. Chanter, *Verbum abbreviatum* PL 233, 235, ed. Boutry 520, 521. On this Ivo, see Beryl Smalley, "Master Ivo of Chartres," *English Historical Review* 50 (1935), 684.

78. G. Morin, "Le discours d'ouverture du concile général de Latran (1179) de Maître Rufin, évêque d'Assise," *Pontificia academia di archelogia memorie* 2 (1928), 116–20.

79. For preliminary studies, see Baldwin, "Paris et Rome," *Masters* 1, 315–43.

80. Chanter, *Verbum abbreviatum*, ed. Boutry 522.

81. Chanter, *Verbum abbreviatum*, ed. Boutry 229; Langton, *Super historias scholasticas*, Paris BnF 14414, fol. 131ra; Courson, *Summa* fol. 109rb; texts in Baldwin, *Masters* 2, 224–26, nn. 169, 182.

82. C. 50, Mansi 22, 1035, 1038; Chanter, *Summa de sacramentis* Ms. W, fol. 136ra; text in Baldwin, *Masters* 2, 227, n. 191.

83. Chanter, *Summa de sacramentis* 3 (2a), 387.

84. Chanter, *Summa de sacramentis* 3 (2a), 162, 163, 382, ms W. fol. 132ra, rb; Courson, *Summa*, texts in Baldwin, *Masters* 2, 213, nn. 32, 34; Chobham, *Summa confessorum* 494.

85. Chanter, *Summa de sacramentis* 3 (2a) 162.

86. Chobham, *Summa confessorum* 433.

87. A fuller discussion of ordeals may be found in Baldwin, "Ordeals," 613–36, and *Masters* I, 323–332.

88. J. Warichez, *Étienne de Tournai et son temps* (Paris, Tournai, 1936), 53–55.

89. Chanter, *Verbum abbreviatum* PL 226–33.

90. Chanter, *Summa de sacramentis* ms. B, fol. 154rb, va; text in Baldwin, *Masters* II, 219, n. 107; *Verbum abbreviatum* PL 230D, 231A, 547A, ed. Boutry 507.

91. Chanter, *Verbum abbreviatum* PL 543A, ed. Boutry 495.

92. Baldwin, *Masters* I, 330–31; C. 18, Mansi 22, 1007.

93. Mathew Paris, *Chronica maiora* 5, 192.

94. Guillaume le Breton, *Gesta* I, 230, 231.

95. Gaines Post, *Studies in Medieval Legal Thought: Public Law and the State* (Princeton, 1964), 27–60.

96. *CUP* I, 67–68, 82–83.

97. *CUP* I, 73–76.

98. *CUP* I, 99.

99. *CUP* I, 89; Pearl Kibre, *The Nations in the Medieval Universities* (Cambridge, Mass., 1948), 65.

100. *CUP* I, 136–39.

Notes to Chapter Six

1. Rigord 150; Robert d'Auxerre, *Chronicon* 260; *Chronique des rois de France* 760.

2. Rigord 7; Gerald of Wales, *De principis instructione*, 292–93.

3. Rigord 81, 82.

4. Rigord 21–22.

5. Guillaume le Breton, *Gesta* I, 226.

6. *Chronique des rois de France* 763; Roger of Wendover, in Mathew of Paris, *Chronica majora* 2, 524; *Budget* CCI (I).

7. Guillaume le Breton, *Gesta* I, 296, 297.

8. *Registres* 502.

9. Gislebert de Mons, *Chronique* 127.

10. Gislebert de Mons, *Chronique* 95–160; For a summary of the tournaments in the *Histoire de Guillaume le Maréchal*, see Georges Duby, *Guillaume le Maréchal* (Paris, 1984), 11, 12.

11. Benedict of Peterborough, *Gesta regis*, 1, 350; Roger de Hoveden, *Chronica* 2, 309; Guillaume le Breton, *Philippidos* 2, 59.

12. *Actes* I, no. 325, 5, no. 1831; *Obituaires de Sens* 1(1) 153, 169; Chanter, *Summa de sacramentis* 12, 446, 3 (2a), 276; Chobham, *Summa confessorum* 261. More discussion in Baldwin, *Aristocratic Life* 86–90.

13. Gerald of Wales, *De principis instructione*, 176; Rigord 68–69.

14. Baldwin, *Aristocratic Life* 70–86; and "Jean Renart et le tournoi de Saint-Trond: Une conjonction de l'histoire et de la littérature," *Annales, Économies, Sociétés, Civilisations* 45 (1990), 656–88.

15. Jean Renart, *Roman de la rose* vv. 1530–35; for clothing see Baldwin, *Aristocratic Life* 183–91.

16. Robson, *Maurice de Sully* 117; Zink, *La prédication* 365–67.

17. (1225) *Cartulaire de Notre-Dame* 2, 525–26; Lombard-Jourdan, *Aux origines* 99. For a fuller discussion of jongleurs see Baldwin, "Jongleur," 635–663; *Aristocratic Life* 21–30.

18. Chanter, *Verbum abbreviatum* PL 153C; Rufinus, *Summa decretorum*, ed. H. Singer (Paderborn, 1902), 176.

19. Chanter, *Verbum abbreviatum* PL 155B–D; Chobham, *Summa confessorum* 293.

20. Rigord 72–73; *Budget* CC(1)–CCI(2) records only the robes given to new knights at Pentecost, but no accounting is found for robes to the poor either.

21. Chanter, *Verbum abbreviatum* PL 155D; *Summa de sacramentis* 3 (2a), 239, 241; Mansi 22, 840, 919, C. 16, 1003–6.

22. Chanter, *Summa de sacramentis* 3 (2a), 176–77; *Verbum abbreviatum* PL 101AB; Chobham, *Summa confessorum* 291, 292.

23. Zink, *La prédication* 370–75; texts published by Tony Hunt, "De la chanson au sermon: *Bele Aalis* et *Sur la rive de la mer*," *Romania* 104 (1983), 433–56.

24. Each lyric is set off with a decorated capital, and often the verses are not copied out in separate lines like the text of the romance but are run on like prose, the scribal practice of the later *chansonniers*.

25. The texts and music of the complete corpus have been edited in *The Lyrics and Melodies of Gace Brulé*, ed. S. N. Rosenberg, S. Danon and H. van der Werf, Garland Library of Medieval Literature A39 (New York, 1985). The text of *Quant flors et glaiz et verdure s'eloinge* is at 142–46, the music at 384.

26. *Registres* 201–03.

27. Conon de Béthune, *Chansons*, ed. A. Wallensköld III, 1–2 (Hellsingfors, 1891), 223.

28. Chanter, *Verbum abbreviatum* PL 322, 323, ed. Boutry 740.

29. Courson, text in Baldwin, *Aristocratic Life* 327, n. 21; Chobham, *Summa confessorum* 549.

30. For these endemic difficulties see Corinne Leveleux, *La parole interdite. Le blasphème dans la France médiévale (XIIe–XVIe siècles): Du peché au crime, Romanité et modernité du droit* (Paris, 2001).

31. Chobham, *Summa confessorum* 551; Courson, text in Baldwin, *Aristocratic Life* 327, 328 n. 23.

32. Gerald of Wales, *Gemma ecclesiastica Opera* 2, 161; *De principis instructione Opera* 8, 318, 319. See p. 79.

33. Chanter, *Verbum abbreviatum* PL 322D, ed. Boutry 742; Rigord 14; Guillaume le Breton, *Gesta* 1, 181; Leveleux, *La parole interdite* 293–99.

34. Innocent III, *Regesta* PL 216: 786–87.

35. See the fundamental study of Craig Wright, *Music and Ceremony* 237–43.

36. Parisian sacramentary, Paris BnF lat. 1112, fols. 6v, 1r.

37. Jean Beleth, *Summa de ecclesiasticis officiis* ed. Herbert Douteil, Corpus chris-

tianorum, Continuatio medievalis 41a (Turnhout, 1976), 1, 130–34, repeated in Pierre de Roissy, *Manuale*, fol. 61r–62r.

38. *Notre-Dame* ed Anderson, 1, xxix (text), 54–60 (music).

39. *Notre-Dame* ed, Anderson, 5, xxxvii (text); 82 (music).

40. *Notre-Dame* ed, Anderson, 9, ii–iii (text); 2–3 (music).

41. Pierre de Roissy, *Manuale* fol. 76r.

42. *Cartulaire de Notre-Dame* 1, 73–75.

43. Texts in Baldwin, "Jongleur," 647, n. 43, n. 45.

44. Mansi 22, 842, 920.

45. For a fuller treatment of this section see Baldwin *Language.*

46. Baldwin, *Language* 10–16.

47. *The Prose Salernitan Questions* ed. Brian Lawn, Auctores Britannici Medii Aevi 5 (Oxford, 1979), 7.

48. Texts in Baldwin, *Language* 294, n. 32; 311, n. 4.

49. Text in Baldwin, *Language* 314, n. 47.

50. Baldwin, *Language* 198–200.

51. David de Dinant, *Quaternuli*, 23, 24, 31.

52. Baldwin, *Language* 230–34.

53. For fuller discussion see Baldwin, *Language* 16–25.

54. Charles H. Haskins, *Studies in the History of Medieval Science* (Cambridge, Mass., 1924), 372.

55. Text in Baldwin, *Language* 251.

56. André le Chapelain, *Traité de l'amour courtois* ed. Claude Buridant (Paris, 1974), 45, 127, 142, 185. Most recently, see Donald A. Monson, *Andreas Capellanus, Scholasticism and the Courtly Tradition* (Washington, 2005).

57. Innocent III, *Regesta* PL 214: 9, 319.

58. Chanter, *Summa de sacramentis* 2, 219, 3 (2a) 195, 196, 204, 3 (2b), 502–05, 753.

59. Chanter, *Verbum abbreviatum* ed. Boutry 758.

60. Geoffroy de Villehardouin, *La conquête de Constantinople*, ed. Edmond Faral (Paris, 1938) 1, 1–15; Coggeshall 130.

61. Courson, *Summa* 22, 7, 8, fol. 83 r–v. An exception in which the context of the crusade is explicitly mentioned is found in Chanter, *Summa* 3 (2a) 293. Most of the Chanter's discussion is framed in terms of the pilgrimage vow, such as to Santiago or to Jerusalem. This was the prevailing approach of the decretists and early decretalists. See my review (*Speculum* 46, 1971, 131–33) of James A. Brundage, *Medieval Canon Law and the Crusader* (Madison, 1969). Jessalyn Bird, "Innocent III, Peter the Chanter's Circle, and the Crusade Indulgence: Theory, Implementation, and Aftermath," in *Innocenzo III. Urbs et Orbis*, Atti del Congresso Internazionale, Roma 9–15 settembre 1998 ed. Andrea Sommerlechner (Rome, 2003), 1, 501–25, esp. 514, 515, presents an opposing interpretation.

62. Innocent III, *Regesta*, PL 215: 636–38 (25 May 1205).

63. Roger de Hoveden, *Chronica* 4, 121.

64. *Annales Aquicinctensis monasterii,* MGH, SS, 6, 421; André de Marchiennes, *De gestis* MGH, SS, 26, 210.

65. Mansi, 21, 532; 22, 232.

66. Chanter, *Verbum abbreviatum* PL 231B–D; Scriptural commentaries in Baldwin, *Masters* II, 215–16, n.56.

67. Chanter, *Verbum abbreviatum* PL 229D, 545A, ed. Boutry 502, 503.

68. Chanter, *Verbum abbreviatum* PL 231B, ed. Boutry 508; Chobham, *Summa confessorum* 433–35.

69. Chanter, *Verbum abbreviatum* PL 230B, 545C; Coggeshall 122–24; Chanter, *Summa de sacramentis* Ms B, fol. 150va.

70. X: 5.7.9 *Ad abolendam*; X: 5.7.10 *Vergentis.*

71. Robert d'Auxerre, *Chronicon,* 260; *De gestis episcoporum Autissiodorensium* PL 138: 318; Pierre des Vaux de Cernay, *Historia albigensis,* ed. Pascal Guébin and Ernest Lyon (Paris, 1926), 1, 25, 26.

72. Texts in Baldwin, *Masters* 2, 128, n. 105, 216, n. 61.

73. The chief sources for the Amauricians consist of three fragments of official documents edited in *CUP* 1, 70–71; Marie-Thérèse d'Alverny, "Un fragment du procès des amauriciens," *Archives d'histoire doctrinale et littéraire du moyen âge* 18 (1950–1951), 331–33; and four chronicles, Guillaume le Breton, *Gesta* I, 23–33; Caesar of Heisterbach, *Dialogus,* ed. Strange I, 304–07; Robert d'Auxerre, *Chronicon,* 275–76; *Ex chronica anonymi Laudunensis canonici,* RHF 18, 714–15. Additionally, G. C. Capelle, *Autour du décret de 1210: Amaury de Bène. Étude sur son panthéisme formel* (Paris, 1932) is a collection of the major sources. Among the major studies see Gary Dickson, "The Burning of the Amalricians," *Journal of Ecclesiastical History* 40 (1989), 347–69 and J.M.M.H. Thijssen, "Master Amalric and the Amalricians: Inquisitorial Procedure and the Suppression of Heresy at the University of Paris," *Speculum* 71 (1996), 43–65.

74. Text in Buc, *L'ambiguïté du livre* 164 n. 96.

75. Text in Thijssen, "Master Almaric" 64, 65.

76. C.1, Mansi 22, 986.

77. Text in Baldwin, *Masters* 2, 216, n. 60.

78. *Statuts synodaux* ed. Pontal, 1, 88, 94.

Index